DEATH AND THE AFTERLIFE IN PRE-COLUMBIAN AMERICA

DEATH AND THE AFTERLIFE IN PRE-COLUMBIAN AMERICA

A Conference at Dumbarton Oaks

OCTOBER 27TH, 1973

Elizabeth P. Benson, *Editor*

Dumbarton Oaks Research Library and Collections

TRUSTEES FOR HARVARD UNIVERSITY

Washington, DC

ISBN-13: 978-0-88402-062-2 [hardcover]
ISBN-13: 978-0-88402-456-9 [paperback]
Library of Congress catalog number 74-22694
LCCN permalink: https://lccn.loc.gov/74022694

Manufactured in the United States of America by
Sheridan Books, Inc., 450 Fame Avenue, Hanover, PA 17331 | (717) 632-3535

EU GPSR Authorised Representative
LOGOS EUROPE, 9 rue Nicolas Poussin, 17000, La Rochelle, France
E-mail: Contact@logoseurope.eu

To the memory of

Dee Furst

Preface

MANY of the finest artifacts of Pre-Columbian civilizations have been found in tombs. It is possible that most of the handsomest objects may have been made only as grave goods for use in an afterlife; if some were also used as ceremonial or prestige objects in the world of the living, they still ended up in burials that were often of great opulence. The knowledge that death and the belief in an afterlife were immensely important to Pre-Columbian peoples is part of the background that those who work with Pre-Columbian studies must always consider.

At the time that this fifth conference in Pre-Columbian studies at Dumbarton Oaks was planned, Michael Coe was making a study of Maya painted pots; he began to realize that most, if not all, of the scenes depicted thereon take place in the underworld. Elizabeth Benson was working with the iconography of Mochica pottery; she became aware that a large number of depictions on this pottery relate to sacrifice, death, burial, and the afterlife. In some of the conferences at Dumbarton Oaks, we attempt to deal with themes that are vital to art and cosmology throughout Pre-Columbian Latin America, as, for example, in the conference on The Cult of the Feline. The subject of death and the afterlife, an important theme over a wide span of space and time, seemed particularly appropriate as a subject for a cross-cultural conference. Besides the papers based on the archaeology of North America, Mesoamerica, and the Central Andes, we concluded this conference with a paper by an ethnographer on the present-day death-related beliefs of Warao cosmology, which reflect a number of the pervasive ancient elements. The paper by Peter Furst was given as a public lecture the day before the conference.

In the past, we have sometimes published the discussion after each paper. Because the papers presented at this conference were long, there was so little discussion that we have decided not to publish it.

We wish to express our thanks for the interest and cooperation of the Dumbarton Oaks staff who worked to make this conference a success, particularly to William R. Tyler, the Director of Dumbarton Oaks, to Michael Dziedzic, Alexis DeBoeck, Richard Amt, and, most especially, to Anne-Louise Schaffer, the Assistant for the Pre-Columbian Collection.

ELIZABETH P. BENSON
MICHAEL D. COE

THE PANEL

Michael D. Coe, *Chairman*

Elizabeth P. Benson
James A. Brown
Edward B. Dwyer
Jane Powell Dwyer
Cecelia F. Klein
Johannes Wilbert

THE PARTICIPANTS

Carlos B. Arostegui
Mino Badner
María Antonieta Cervantes
Frederick J. Dockstader
Gordon F. Ekholm
Marguerite Ekholm
Clifford Evans
Kent V. Flannery
Dee Furst
Peter T. Furst
Gillett G. Griffin
Julie Jones
David Joralemon
M. E. Kampen
S. H. Koenig
George Kubler
Floyd G. Lounsbury
Masako Lounsbury
Joyce Marcus
Betty J. Meggers
Jeffrey H. Miller
Marta F. de Molina
Juan Munizaga
Esther Pasztory
Andrea K. Scott
John F. Scott
Marion Stirling
S. Jeffrey K. Wilkerson
Gordon R. Willey
Stephen Williams

Contents

Spiro Art and Its Mortuary Contexts

JAMES A. BROWN

NORTHWESTERN UNIVERSITY

INTRODUCTION

EASTERN North America contains few sites of the Mississippian Period that have evoked as much interest and as widespread attention as Spiro has. Some sites are known for their size and complexity of layout, others for their contribution to regional historical synthesis. Spiro is neither large nor complex by comparison with other Mississippian Period sites; it is known almost entirely for the extraordinarily rich inventory of unusual and well-preserved artifacts associated with the dead.

There is something about the discovery of such a considerable cache of art and artifacts that inspires its own interpretation. Unfortunately, this interpretation is often divorced from archaeological context. It is almost inevitable that students of Spiro should seek all or part of its origins elsewhere because the material antecedents of this art are so poorly known. Archaeologists have looked to the Southeast, Mesoamerica, and even to the Southwest for the stylistic and iconographic sources of Spiro art. Of these, Mesoamerica stands out as the principal primary source, although there are alternative preferences as to the routes and times of diffusion (Griffin 1952; Krieger 1945; Waring and Holder 1945).

I will depart from custom and not offer any notions as to the sources of the art styles and their iconography, but instead I will offer a model of Spiro mortuary-house organization that will make Spiro less mysterious without detracting from its remarkable record.

THE SOUTHERN CULT

The distinctiveness of the Spiro materials has constantly attracted attention. From the time of their initial discovery in a mound in eastern Oklahoma, they were recognized as constituting an unusual find that replicated on a grander scale the older discoveries

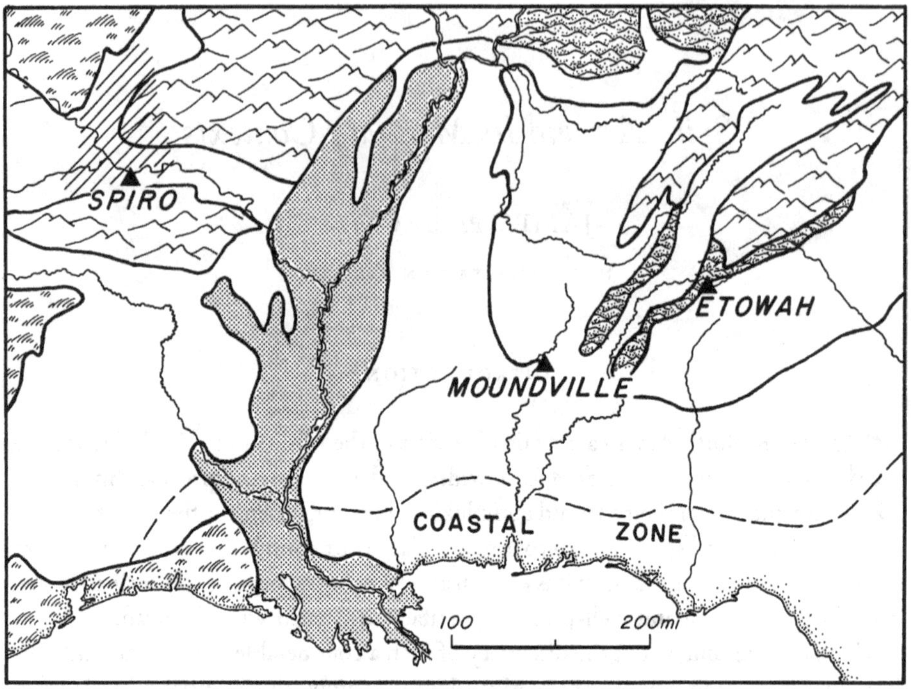

Fig. 1 *Locations of the big three Southern Cult sites in the southeastern United States. Map shows major physiographic zones and the Coastal and Prairie vegetational zones.*

from the Deep South at Moundville, Alabama, and Etowah, Georgia. The artwork in stone, copper, and marine shell from the three major locales—Spiro, Moundville, and Etowah—now constitutes what archaeologists of eastern North America have come to call the "Southern Cult." In this group Spiro stands out as having what has been called a "gaudy" assemblage (Willey and Phillips 1958: 166), due to the relative "freedom, abandon, and completely heterodox manner" of Southern Cult motifs at Spiro as compared with those at the other centers (Waring 1968a: 68). It has even been proposed that Spiro is sufficiently different to warrant consideration as a special Spiro complex of the Southern Cult (Krieger 1945). Baerreis (1957) followed this line of thought one step further in advancing the notion of an antecedent "Spiro Ceremonial Cult."[1] Nevertheless, the Spiro finds are so identified with the Southern Cult as to be virtually inseparable from it in the minds of most archaeologists (Fig. 1).

1. Griffin (1961) ably argued against this notion.

There is by no means unanimity about what and how much the term "Southern Cult" is meant to include. It is one of those terms on which everyone seems to have reached consensus, although the emphases of individual scholars are sufficient to create real differences in definition. The reason for this ambiguity is that the Southern Cult is a conceptual aggregate, defined originally from the specialized artifacts, iconographic themes, and basic motifs found in greatest frequency in the big three centers (Waring and Holder 1945). In other words, it is defined by a list of specialized traits selected for their common distribution, not because of an underlying formal definition or because they are the product of a coherent underlying social, political, economic, or artistic organization. Depending on the point of view and interest, one could single out from the Southern Cult laundry list a symbolic system, the trappings and accoutrements of status, a cosmology, trade networks, ritual life, art style, and even a technology. Obviously there is plenty of room for misunderstanding when discussion extends beyond traits, particularly today when everyone concedes that there is more information to be extracted from such a list than cultural traits. The percolation of Southern Cult artifacts from the regional centers to the primary village level is so attenuated that many archaeologists do not believe that the Cult is a cultural horizon.[2] With the relation of the Cult to either horizon or tradition left in doubt, it remains to be discovered precisely what the specialized artifacts and associated symbols pertain to at Spiro and other sites. I will continue to refer to the Southern Cult by name, even though the use of the term "cult" to cover this list of traits conveys an artificial sense of unity.

The distributional pattern of a specific set of specialized artifacts and symbols among sites of different cultural traditions should be familiar to us from the similar cases of the Chavín, Olmec, and Hopewell cultures that have already been described as instances of cultural interaction (Caldwell 1964; Flannery 1968). Key features of similarity are the specific contexts in which the specialized mortuary goods are found, the similarity of those contexts among distinct traditions, and the transfer of some of the symbolism found in the grave goods to artifacts produced locally. These common patterns have customarily called forth in the minds of archaeologists invasions of peoples, colonizations by elites, and missionizing by cult-bearers, in the case of the Olmec as well as the Southern Cult. Unfortunately for these kinds of explanations, detailed scrutiny has failed to identify the foreign peoples, and such explanations have not been easily reconciled with the archaeological evidence of cultural continuity in place. Migrations and diffusions continue to be advanced, but fortunately there are some alternative ex-

2. But see Willey and Phillips (1958: 33, 166) for a contrary position.

planations. Specifically, in the case of the Southern Cult, the similarities among sites can be more effectively explained by adopting a model of social interaction among the cultural traditions of diverse regions, such as that ably advanced by Flannery (1968) in his paper "The Olmec and the Valley of Oaxaca: A Model of Inter-regional Interaction in Formative Times," and by Caldwell (1964) and Struever (1964) for the Hopewell.

SPIRO AND ITS REGIONAL TRADITION

Some of the mystery surrounding Spiro can be dispelled by providing an archaeological context. The Spiro site lies on the first terrace and surrounding upland along the Arkansas River in extreme eastern Oklahoma where the eastern temperate forest begins to share the rolling landscape with outliers of western prairie. This transitional zone is the habitat of the Caddoan archaeological tradition of the Arkansas Valley. In this zone we find highly dispersed farmsteads and only a few documented nucleations of any size that can be called villages. At strategic locations there are mound centers, of which the largest and principal center is Spiro. The location of Spiro is strategic in that it lies near the eastern limits of the Spiroan cultural tradition in the Arkansas Valley, which is one of the major east-west corridors of travel between the Mississippi Embayment province and the Great Plains. In effect, Spiro lies athwart a riverine gateway in a habitat divide separating the rich waterways and woodlands of the Southeast from the grasslands of the interior plains.

The subsistence base of the tradition is mixed hunting-gathering and agriculture in which the principal cultivated plants are corn and squash. The location of known occupation sites is on the alluvial bottomlands and adjacent bluff crests where all major environmental zones necessary for subsistence are within easy reach. Despite the optimal strategic location of these primary base occupation habitations with respect to local resources, there is no evidence of village concentrations greater than ten acres, and the largest known villages are actually in the environs of Spiro itself. The picture that emerges from our present knowledge is that of a dispersed agricultural population aggregated in locations of greatest subsistence security, principally at the eastern edges where Southeastern vegetational zones occur.

The Spiro site is spread over an area of about eighty acres as a result of shifting occupation over the five hundred years or more of its history. The earliest substantial occupation was about A.D. 900, but the period of interest here is in the later Spiro phase of about A.D. 1200–1350, when the site was devoted to ceremonial functions and no longer contained domestic houses.

The site is the most complex of the sites of its tradition. Nine mounds of different types are present. Six are low dome-shaped mounds that cover the floors and foundations of dismantled structures. Two others are platform mounds. The remaining mound, which is the famous location of the majority of the Spiro grave goods, is composed of four linearly conjoined conical forms hiding a platform mound within.

DISPOSAL OF THE DEAD

Although systematic modern archaeology is just beginning in the Arkansas Valley, there is a substantial amount of information on social and political organization of the Spiro phase that can be derived from existing sources. The most important source is the study of Spiro disposal-of-the-dead patterns (Brown 1971).

The only known disposal mode in the Arkansas Valley prior to the Spiro phase was that of storing the dead as cremations or partially articulated bodies in a charnel house. The major elements in this mode of treatment of the dead are given in Bell's (1972) analysis of the Harlan site located upstream from Spiro. This site consists of a ring of mounds without any evidence of a surrounding village midden. The ring was composed of several low, mound-covered structure floors, a large burial mound, and a pyramidal mound. The first two forms are significant for understanding the disposal-of-the-dead patterns. Although the burial mound is obviously a final interment location, Bell was able to show that the structures beneath the other mounds were probably mortuaries housing the dead before final disposal. There are several reasons for linking the two features together as a sequence of phases in a single disposal pattern. Chief among these is the fact that the number of layers in the mound, which contains only secondary interments, corresponds to the number of buried structures. These buried structures were not true habitations since they were equipped with doorway closures in the form of either clay walls or post molds. Some such device to restrict entry into the charnel house is entirely consistent with the mortuary-house function.

The details of treatment are obscure, since none of the early-period mortuaries have been discovered with the burials in place, and since burials from recently excavated mounds have not been intensively investigated by an osteologist. But preliminary analysis indicates that all individuals attaining the age of twelve were qualified for care in a local mortuary house that serviced a definable community (Brues n.d.). All charnel houses were presumably on an equivalent footing, although some may have been larger or richer due to their geographical location and inclusion within a ceremonial center.

Of all the remains of mortuary treatment of the dead at Spiro, the most celebrated is the Great Mortuary, which was exceptional both in size and the fact that the remains were not disposed of in a mortuary dump. Its remains were left in place and covered with a mound that was the base for what is presumed to be a successor mortuary (Fig. 2). The closing of the Great Mortuary marks a departure in procedures for treating a charnel house. The fact that its contents were not discarded and that its location was covered with a platform mound rather than a low dome-shaped pile was a happy event for archaeology, since the resulting entombment beneath a large earthen platform sealed the contents of the Great Mortuary. Even perishables were preserved, presumably accidentally and due to the sheer quantity of bulky items. It can be supposed that, if the mound were packed over piles of marine shell cups, stacks of fabrics, and rows of litter burials that were resting on the mortuary floor, a sufficient amount of air could be trapped in and around this accumulation to make a much more bulky deposit than is actually represented by the items themselves. Once the artifacts settled, a "hollowed cavity" could be produced upon the separation of the artifacts from the shell of gumbo clay. This thick shell then later could grow with successive additions to provide platforms for the series of structures above until it was abandoned as a large mound.

All of the mortuaries were essentially alike up to the close of the Great Mortuary. From the admittedly incomplete information at hand, it appears that they differed mainly in their size and probably also in the richness and diversity of their burial offerings. The erection of a mortuary platform mound built over the Great Mortuary signaled an important transition in the evolution of Spiro society by increasing the complexity of its disposal practices. At the same time, the elevation of the mortuary can be regarded as symbolizing the increased social distance between the Spiro elite, the regional high-status families, and the population at large (Brown n.d.). This change in location can be interpreted as a sign of increased social and political complexity and possibly as an enlargement of the political sphere, if not an increase in the territorial population.

THE CONTENTS OF THE GREAT MORTUARY

The contents of the Great Mortuary have given us not only an extraordinary artifactual record but also an important cultural document. Its importance rests in the evidence of social stratification in the disposal of the dead at Spiro and in the evident managerial importance of the Spiro elite in organizing inter-group exchange on all social levels from the inter-village to the inter-polity.

The floor of the Great Mortuary was filled in a very special way that illustrates the

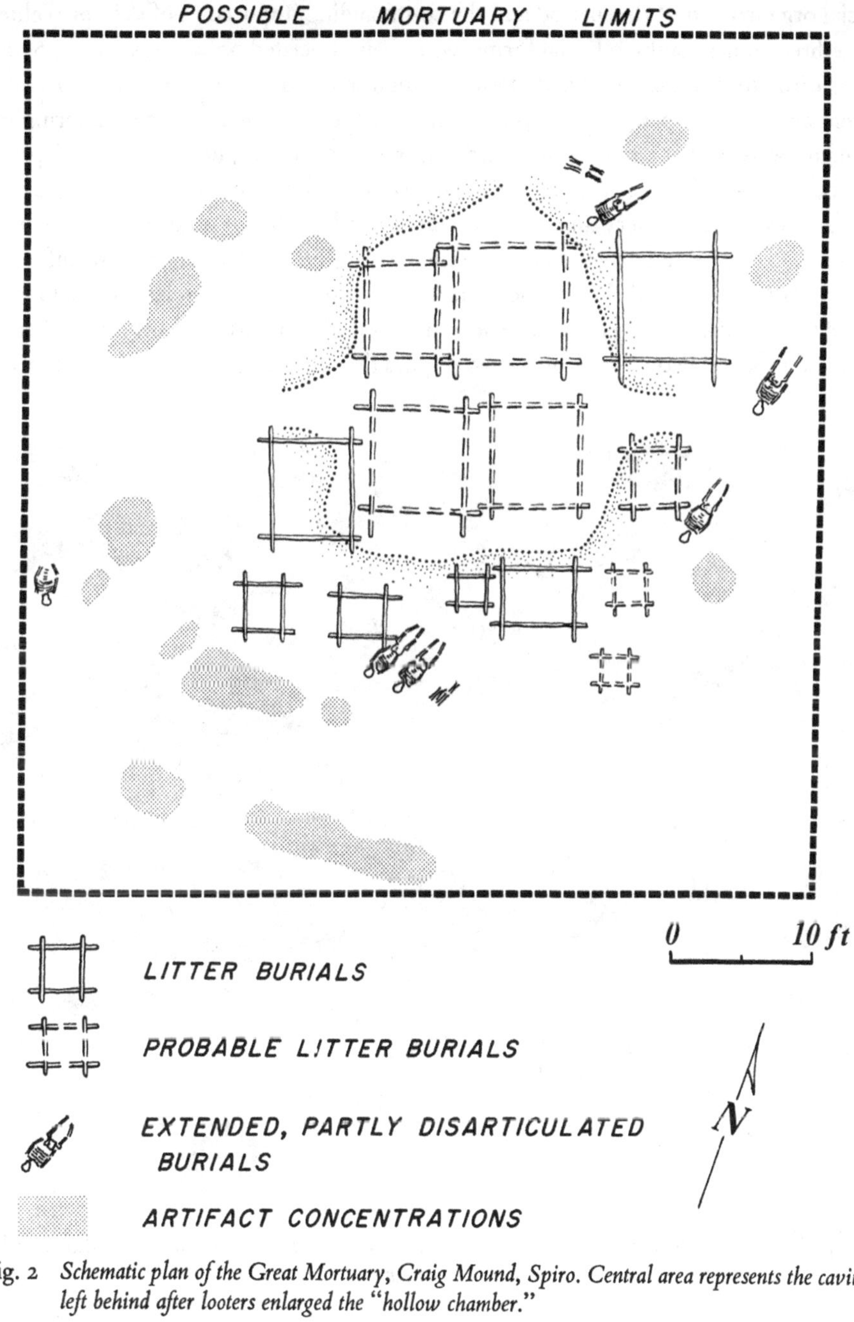

Fig. 2 *Schematic plan of the Great Mortuary, Craig Mound, Spiro. Central area represents the cavity left behind after looters enlarged the "hollow chamber."*

social organization of that period and the commanding importance of the Spiro elite. The three highest-ranking burial forms, with their associated prestigious grave goods, were carefully laid on top of a scattering of disarticulated remains that probably represent an entirely separate social stratum of the population. Among this scattering of remains were piles of fabric capes and kiltlike skirts, large piles of shell and pearl beads, conch-shell cups, shell gorgets, chipped stone knife and club forms, ground stone clubs, beads, pottery and stone vessels, and a long list of unique items, such as human effigy pipes and fragile copper-bitted axes (Fig. 2). A complete list unfortunately cannot be compiled since the center of this mortuary accumulation was looted prior to scientific investigation. The accumulation of so many artifacts made of raw material procurable only far from Spiro implies that the Great Mortuary served more

Fig. 3 *The highest-ranking Spiro burial type, the litter burial (B62).* Photo courtesy of the Stovall Museum, University of Oklahoma, Norman.

Fig. 4 *The second-ranking Spiro burial type, the partly disarticulated extended burial (at right).* Photo courtesy of the Stovall Museum, University of Oklahoma, Norman. (Note: correct field number on slate should be Lf Br3 B3.)

functions than merely that of a repository for the high-ranking dead and their grave goods.

Of the three highest-ranking burial forms, the most spectacular is the litter burial, upon which lay the condensed skeletal remains of the honored dead within a large pile of conch-shell cup pieces and other contributed grave goods (Fig. 3). The litters tended to be square in shape, ranging in size from small litters that could easily be carried by two persons to very large litters that had to be carried by a minimum of four individuals and that had ten times the capacity in grave goods. The fact that the very form of the burial facility was a litter implies that the rank of an office of political leadership in Spiro society was being conferred on the deceased. Gradations in the size of the litters likewise imply gradations in rank; this is further communicated by the gradation in size from the north end of the Great Mortuary to the south end. Although the individual burials so ranked may represent succeeding paramount rulers, it is even more likely that both paramount and intermediately subordinate chiefs are represented, considering the number of litter burials and the magnitude of litter-size difference. If there is any doubt as to the ranking principles underlying the disposition of the Great Mortuary dead, one need only reflect on the fact that the litters were much larger than necessary to enclose the paltry remains of an individual burial that usually consisted of skull fragments and teeth. The other two ranking forms of burial contrast with the excessive size and bulkiness of the litter burials. The most specialized is a partially disarticulated skeleton reserved for a limited number of adults (probably female) that had not undergone any special treatment, and took no more room than

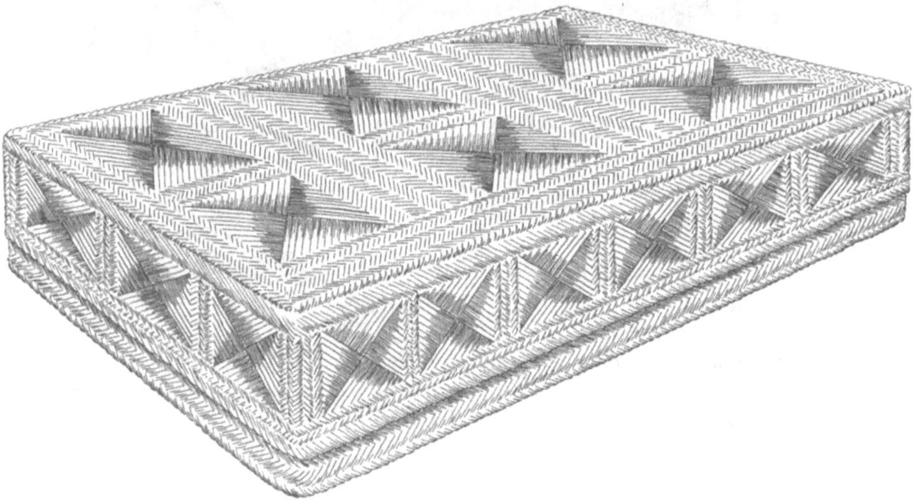

Fig. 5 *The third-ranking Spiro burial type, a box burial of cane twillwork basketry, 48×24×10 cm.* Restoration of the basket in the University Museum, University of Arkansas, Fayetteville. Drawing by Louis Gregoire.

was necessary to accommodate the skeleton and grave goods heaped on top of it (Fig. 4). The third form is the box burial in conveniently sized facilities large enough to accommodate the disarticulated elements of adults and children and the copper plates and other artifacts included as grave goods (Fig. 5).

The three burial forms found so well preserved in the Great Mortuary are unusual, but there is ample evidence that they were standard for the Spiro mortuaries in Spiro-phase times. Although the elevated mortuary structure that followed the Great Mortuary involved further elaboration of the mortuary treatment, the three forms reappear in the grave pit disposals; furthermore, the symbolic superposition of the litter form over the odd, disarticulated skeletal elements of a subordinate portion of the population is likewise found in some of the large grave pits.

Contemporary burials in another regional center, the Norman site, are confined to the traditional burial treatments that included cremation. The significance of this record of proliferation of burial practices is that it records the growth of hierarchical grading of status in the Spiro culture, in which the apex of the social pyramid is occupied by a few individuals with exclusive rights to burial in the Spiro mortuaries. The remainder of the population was graded in rank down to individuals in the primary production units of the scattered villages and farmsteads.

Spiro society of the period 1200 to 1350 was graded in rank, if not divided into social classes. The information from the Spiro burials is particularly clear when compared with that from the remainder of the population. The economic basis for ranking has not been documented thoroughly from subsistence data, but presumably rank and prestige were based on control over the distribution of agricultural products and other resources.

THE MORTUARY TEMPLE COMPLEX MODEL

One of the leading students of the Southern Cult, Antonio J. Waring, Jr. (1968a: 58–62), in a paper entitled "The Southern Cult and Muskhogean Ceremonial," concluded that the Cult was associated with a "mortuary temple complex."[3] The association had the advantage of explaining the archaeological context of the Southern Cult material and the appearance of stone mortuary figures, an additional element that is found in some sites. Moreover, the mortuary temple model provided a convincing bridge between the ethnological descriptions of the Natchez mortuary houses with their celebrated death rites and the prehistoric archaeological context of the Southern Cult. His argument ran as follows: at several key sites, including not only the type Cult sites of Etowah and Moundville but also the historic Natchez site of Fatherland, "the most spectacular ceremonial material belonging to the Complex [Cult] has been found with burials intrusive into the floors of ceremonial structures on platform mounds. The presence of these burials, moreover, does not seem a fortuitous, but rather an integral part of the structure, despite the fact that they are intrusive" (Waring 1968a: 58–9). A short reference to exhumed shell beads in the de Soto narratives of the famous Talimeco mortuary in Georgia convinced Waring that temporary inhumation in a mor-

3. Waring's position is actually an updating of the same position by Willoughby (1932).

tuary floor was a valid historic form of burial treatment. The connection between the archaeological inhumations in the tops of platform mounds and mortuary houses was thus made. Subsequent research on the important Fatherland site of the Grand Village of the Natchez by Neitzel (1965) has convincingly strengthened Waring's original argument. For Waring the important elements of the mortuary temple complex were the presence of burials cared for in the mortuary temple and the presence of mortuary-cult figurines. The temple function was a contribution of the Natchez analogy, since we know that the all-important tribal cult figure was housed in the temple mortuary.

However, to Waring the existence of mortuary temples was something of a contradiction to his notion concerning the organizing principles of Muskhogean tribal ceremony. His resolution was simply to advance a theory of atavistic survival of the mortuary in Mississippian society. It had to be a Hopewellian survival in which the old "preoccupations with the burial of the dead"—in addition to other themes basically relating to a hunting-gathering subsistence—had not been quite supplanted by a more adaptive sun and fertility symbolism (Waring 1968a: 65–6). The retention of "obsolete customs" exclusively among the Mississippian elite has been hypothesized as due to their natural self-interest in maintaining power.

> In the Natchezean oligarchy a sort of ceremonial despotism had developed, and the entire ceremonial life of the group was dominated by a handful of individuals headed by a human god. Naturally, the various institutions and rites were subject to the caprice of individuals, and one would expect that such customs and practices as would enhance authority would remain and be reinforced. (Waring 1968a: 67)

In a later paper Waring came to see the faults of a model based essentially on cultural trait distributions. When fresh excavations were made into Mound C at Etowah, Waring (1968b) then began to see that there were more subtle connections between aspects of the Southern Cult and mortuary-house organization.

> At the first this writer opposed the notion of a "Southern Death Cult," but this stand must be modified. Mound C, Etowah reflects about as complicated a series of mortuary rituals as could be conceived, complete with individuals dressed in the paraphernalia of the "eagle warrior being" [sic] and armed with ceremonial weapons whose very fragility must have endowed them with a sort of magical power. There was a special temple, special rites, and special handling of the special dead.

Since then archaeologists have simply added more detail to this picture of special disposal of the dead around Mound C at Etowah (Larson 1971). Recent advances in the analysis and explanation of burial practices render particularistic explanations unnecessary (Brown 1971, n.d.; Saxe n.d.; Binford 1971).

Waring was not alone in his preference for explaining the mortuary temple complex and other evidence of what is so frequently and ambiguously referred to as "preoccupation with the dead" as a survival from the Middle Woodland Period that is "out-of-place" with the Mississippian Period. Spiro was thought of as an example of such a survival since the main mound from which most of the material came appeared to be simply a burial mound rather than a platform mound (Orr 1946; Waring 1968a: 68). To many the hint of Hopewell survival and the marginal location of Spiro were sufficient to explain the cultural unorthodoxy of Spiro in eastern North American archaeology. But, like most facile and neat conceptions, this one was based not only on false premises but was drawn from a superficial understanding of the organizational complexities of Spiro and the other centers. In retrospect, we can see that we have here a classic case in which the grip of rigid typologies, based on what was thought to be a progression (or evolution) of culture traits, impeded understanding of the underlying cultural organization of these elements. Until we discover these organizations and advance theories to explain them, our archaeological patterns will remain largely ciphers that will defy explanation in their own terms.

THE MORTUARY AS AN ANCESTRAL CULT HOUSE

Although Waring was content to consider the mortuary temple complex as a trait complex, the potential of his construct for building a useful model makes it worthwhile to strengthen it in order to explain both the kinds and frequencies of exotic and costly grave goods as well as aspects of Spiro iconography.

Since Waring completed his research, a number of critical features of Spiro's social and political organization have been established from the analysis of Spiro burial forms and from a consideration of the grave goods associated with them and their archaeological contexts. The first point is that the Spiro mortuaries were probably the repository of the principal family from which the rulers of the Arkansas River Valley territory were drawn. Of all the mortuaries known in the region, only the Spiro ones in the Craig mound were constructed sequentially in phases of a single mound. The superimposed mortuaries which were built on top of each other were the exclusive location of the three burial types in the Spiro disposal-of-the-dead domain that rank over other burial forms found in the region (Brown 1971, n.d.).

Second, the elite burial forms at Spiro record a comparatively high amount of labor expended in the processing of the corpses and the curation of the selected remains of the dead. At the same time the construction and maintenance of the elaborate facilities for enclosing the dead required additional quantities of labor. The amount of energy implied in the labor commitments is comparatively large for Spiro society and amounts

Fig. 6 *Representations in Spiro engraved shell art of the human skull, long bone, and severed head* (after Hamilton 1952: Pls. 113A, 121B, 120A).

to a strong symbolic subscription to ranking principles in this society. At the same time, the relatively large number of separate burial forms given specific symbolic expression is indicative of social complexity and stratification.

Third, the mortuaries represent considerable accumulation of wealth in valuables. All of the items were procured from long distances, and considerable energy was expended in manufacturing them. The Great Mortuary contained the remains of well over one thousand different engraved shell cups among a series of two to three times that number of plain cups. The number of copper plates is placed conservatively at 258 (Hamilton, Hamilton, and Chapman 1974). The number of shell and pearl beads is enormous. Hamilton (1952: 30) has estimated eight hundred pounds of shell and one gallon of pearl beads from the looted excavations alone.

With these points in mind, the observation of Waring and others (Willoughby 1932; MacLeod 1928) that the Natchez mortuary is really a cult house dedicated to the honoring of ancestors of the premier family takes on additional significance. We can augment the mortuary-temple-complex notion with propositions concerning the role of wealth and energy accumulations in a central place to construct a model of the mortuary as an ancestral cult house that is instrumental in the management of flows of exchange through ranks of hierarchically organized status. The premier mortuary is simultaneously a treasury for the managers of exchange and a repository for the remains of the individuals important in acquiring the critical managerial status. The mortuary amounts to a cult headquarters from which the politically significant descendants of the honored dead draw their ideological power. This power is principally manifest in their capacity to mount successful war parties and in their authority to manage the distribution of food and other critical resources.

The symbolism in some of the art plays on the importance of the mortuaries as ancestral cult houses. Skull, long-bone, and detached-hand devices that are common motifs at Spiro (and elsewhere) are obvious references to mortuary handling of the dead (Fig. 6). To this group can be added the many masks and maskettes without eye slits and their manifold representation in wood and shell.[4] The use of skulls and other body parts to represent the ancestors is quite consistent with the Spiro mortuary practice of according the greatest curatorial care and energy to the highest-ranking and most prestigious dead. Skulls, teeth, long bones, and hands are parts that are cared for separately at Spiro. Sometimes this care is exhibited in unusual ways: for instance, the cache of hands found in a jar and the occurrence of spheres ground from the tough

4. None of the masks could have been easily used in impersonation since none have eye holes. The mortuary reference of these masks and maskettes is suggested by the open, drawn mouths that resemble the appearance of mummies and dried corpses. This very similarity has been noted by Willoughby (1932), following an even earlier reference by C. C. Jones. Waring (1968a: 60) objected to what he called the Jones-Willoughby representation without mentioning an additional attribute—the drawn facial appearance. Admittedly, the portrayal of protruding tongues in the effigies is not sufficiently distinctive since it is also a common convention in the portrayal of very lively warriors in Southern Cult art. But the remainder of Waring's argument does not hold, since desiccated corpses can easily be placed in sitting position or any other position. Lest the use of dried corpses as mortuary figures seem too bizarre for eastern North America, one need only read the explicit account of an eighteenth-century Biloxi mortuary to learn otherwise (Swanton 1912: 7).

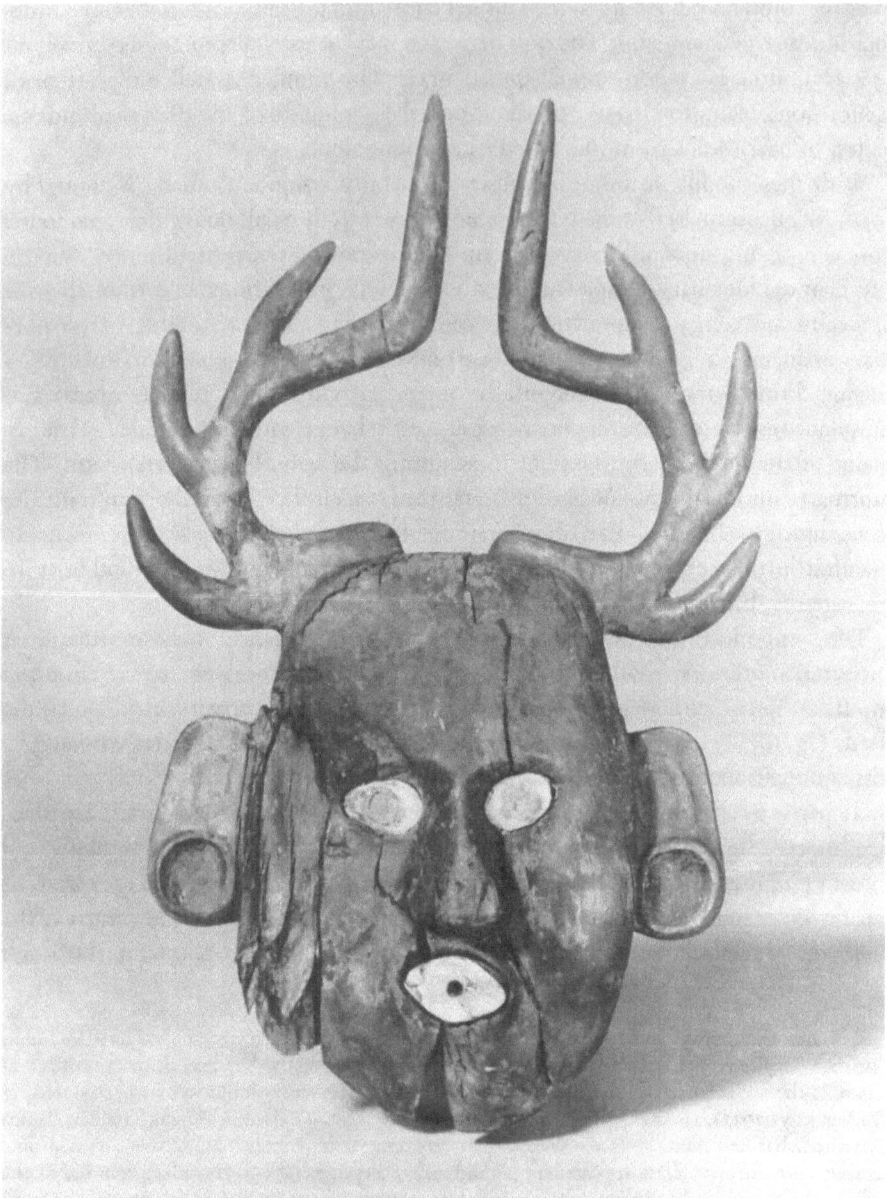

Fig. 7 *Spiro mortuary mask. Wood with marine shell inlays. Height, 28.9 cm.* Photo courtesy of the Museum of the American Indian, Heye Foundation, New York.

petrous portion of the skull after a long period of attrition. Mortuary symbolism has worked its way into conch-shell cup decoration and probably into the use of shell masks and maskettes that are known to have been worn in warrior headdresses. The employment of such masks in headgear could be readily interpreted as directly invoking the power of the ancestors (Fig. 7).

It has been common practice to refer to the skeletal elements associated with the Southern Cult as a "preoccupation with the dead" (see, for example, Jennings 1968: 222–3). The overtone implicit in some of the statements is one of brutality and human sacrifice, complete with trophy heads. Although brutality as an inevitable outcome of warfare may be represented in Spiro art, skulls do not occur in art themes that are convincingly warlike. For instance, heads are found in the hands of the dancing falcon-warrior. However, an explicit example of combat is represented on pipe sculpture wherein the head of the enemy is being crushed by a club.[5] But, considering the central role of the principal mortuary at Spiro at least, a less lurid explanation would see these motifs and art themes as portraying aspects of mortuary ritual life. And, contrary to the impression that terms such as "trophy heads" convey, skulls, masks, hands, and other skeletal elements are even more likely to symbolize the elite, most prestigious, and honored dead. I would suggest that repeated iconographic reference to the ancestors is not a morbid fascination but is more credible as a means of asserting the legitimacy of the rulers and revalidating their social control over such important resources as agricultural land. It is significant that in the De Soto accounts, which are our best historical documents relevant to the prehistoric Southeast, the mortuary that housed the bones of the honored ancestors was considered the ideological heart of the town or community. Military defeat was truly complete once the mortuary was breached, the structure burned, and the bones defiled and scattered.

True to their mortuary function, the Spiro mortuaries contained items that are manifest references to the dead. There are wooden mortuary figures (Fig. 8), wooden face masks (Fig. 7), and scaled-down versions of masks in the many maskettes that are known. In almost all cases the eyes are filled with lustrous shell, and in a few other cases teeth and earspools are likewise emphasized. In this light, the report of a find by the original looters of a miniature wooden box makes more sense. This box held four shell maskettes, face up, under a cover of mica. If we do not believe that the Spiroans went in for trivial representations, a mortuary representation is implied.

5. After the conference session, Flannery reminded me that a trophy head would scarcely survive such clubbing. Even the head in the dancing falcon-warrior's hand is ambiguous, since it could represent the magical power of the ancestors just as easily as a trophy head.

Fig. 8 *Spiro mortuary figurine. Wood with painted face. Height, 32.5 cm.* Photo courtesy of the Smithsonian Institution, Washington.

WARFARE REPRESENTATIONS

The items that found their way into the Spiro mortuaries are related to much more than mortuary symbolism. Good preservation has provided us with abundant evidence of ritual paraphernalia in the costumery. This is one of the major classes of artifacts from Spiro mortuary contexts. It runs over a wide spectrum of perishables such as capes, cloaks, dresses, sashes, headbands, and caps to more durable items such as bone and horn parts, complex headdresses, stone earspools, shell beads, and columella-core pendants. From this array of dress and ornament one can single out actual outfits identifiable on engraved shell objects. Chief among these is the costumery of the falcon-impersonator. The very items of costume that shell engravings and copper work would lead us to expect are represented in burials—if we allow for the ambiguity resulting from the different styles of depicting the falcon-impersonator and the various degrees of subordination of the human elements to the bird. The more realistic ones show the impersonator with shell-bead necklace and columella-core pendant. Burials have yielded the headdress plates, shell beads, columella-core pendants, and polychrome cloth mantles with embroidered hawk-wing feather-markings of the characteristic barred form (Fig. 9). There are several such assemblages known, including one from one of the second-ranking burial types. In the latter case, the headdress plates consist of copper plates cut in the outline of a falcon. Beads, pendants, and fragments of polychrome cloth carrying only an unidentifiable element of a key-type design constitute the remaining parts of the falcon outfit in this burial (Brown 1966). Only the square-shaped plaque headdress and heart-shaped apron have not been convincingly identified. The wings of the falcon-impersonator figures are usually displayed so prominently and conventionally that it is difficult to identify them physically. In fact, the famous plates from Etowah show unrealistic angel wings. However, the mantle from Spiro strongly suggests that the impersonator wore his wings on a mantle attached to his arms in the manner actually suggested in one shell engraving from Spiro (Fig. 10). There are sufficient clues to suggest other impersonator roles, but none as clear-cut as these at Spiro. For example, a case can be made for the presence of a costume consisting of wooden deer antlers and polychrome cloth with a design similar to that reserved for snakes on engraved shell objects.

The use of birds, snakes, spiders, cats, raccoons, and occasionally other animals is so pervasive in Spiro art of the period as to require more space than this brief paper can devote to the subject. But I would like to observe that some of the obvious symbolism is associated with warfare, in contrast to the various kinds of associations with fertility in all its different aspects. The most frequently depicted bird is the falcon or duck hawk, which in various guises invests itself in many facets of Spiro iconography. The

Fig. 9 (above) *Polychrome cloth mantle pieces, Spiro. The design is composed of wing feathers in black and red. The longest piece is 31.7 cm.* Photo courtesy of the Museum of the American Indian, Heye Foundation, New York.

Fig. 10 (right, above) *Shell cup engraving of the falcon-impersonator in the style of the Craig school* (after Burnett 1945: Pl. xxx).

Fig. 11 (right, below) *Side view of a male peregrine falcon or duck hawk* (Falco peregrinus). *Provenience is the southeastern United States.* Mount from the collection of the University Museum, Michigan State University, East Lansing.

role of the falcon-impersonator has already been suggested as an important status in Spiro social organization. We find the tail element worked into ornaments in its own right. But the essential element of the falcon is represented by the forked-eye motif, which is one of the more distinctive and widespread motifs in Late Prehistoric North America. Its connection with falcon symbolism is assured by the characteristic moustachal stripe below the falcon eye. The forked property is even more striking when a yellow stripe above the eye is present to set off the black circumocular marking (Fig. 11). There should be little surprise in finding the falcon occupying such an important role in Spiro symbolism, since the falcon is famous for its spectacular aerial attacks that literally knock ducks and smaller birds out of the air. Its aggressive hunting behavior is quite in contrast to the more passive feeding habits of the eagle, which is mainly a carrion eater. In any case, it is all of the attributes of the hawk that are represented on copper work and engraved shell objects, rather than those of the eagle, whose attributes have been too readily read into Spiro and Southern Cult art. The falcon emerges as a major symbol of aggressive warfare, and is indeed appropriate to employ as a symbol of fierceness and boldness. The stance of the falcon-impersonator is correspondingly aggressive, since he is often shown brandishing a macelike club in one hand and a human head, or a head-rattle substitute, in the other (Figs. 12, 13).

The reference to warfare does not restrict itself to the falcon symbolism. Weapons themselves find depiction on engraved shell objects, and the essential elements occur in headdress ornamentation. One of the more common symbols is the mace form of club, but equally common are axes and a knife or stick form that is analogous to the Old English falchion. The spud form, which takes its name from the English agricultural tool of similar shape, is actually an elaborate ax head that is clearly non-functional in the utilitarian sense of performing work. All of the weapon-derived forms are non-utilitarian in this sense and are made out of exotic stone, shell, and copper. In their non-utilitarian form they more properly represent symbols of rank derived from war rather than weapons from a functional arsenal.

Another component of the grave goods pertains to the control of the supernatural. Crystals, fossils, and deformed objects are grave goods that could only have importance to shamanism. There are other less obvious items—among them the effigy and T-shaped pipes—that have a potentially less restricted context of utilization.

Largely in the same vein, but at a different level of abstraction, is the diverse and easily confounded symbolism associated with the sun, fire, wind, and the four directions that has occupied most of the scholarly interest in Southern Cult symbolism (Howard 1968; Waring 1968a).

Although the dead and the supernatural find substantial representation in the Spiro mortuaries, two other dominating aspects actually constitute key parts of the cult-house model. One is the excessive wealth represented in precious objects. The other is the degree to which objects developed from weapons of war dominate symbols of prestige and authority, as well as the pervasiveness of war-related symbolism in decoration and costumery. A conclusion justified by the Spiro mortuaries is that a substantial component of political power vested in the elite is due to, and maintained by, military prowess or, at least, managerial effectiveness in warfare.

GRAVE GOODS SOURCES

A large accumulation of valuables is represented by the grave goods in the Great Mortuary at Spiro. The marine-shell cups, shell beads, copper plates, and many other items represent a form of wealth. Of these, the cups and plates are associated with the elite burials to such an extent that we could regard them as exclusively under the control of the elite. Shell cups and copper plates are quite uncommon outside the major centers. In the Spiro hinterland only one engraved shell fragment is known (Finklestein 1940: 9) and only fourteen copper plates (cf. Bell 1972: 241–3). Shell beads are a different matter. They commonly occur in all Mississippi Period sites and are frequently used as grave goods. Not only is such an excessive number of beads represented in the Great Mortuary of Spiro that a great hoard is suggested, but also beads occur in seventeen different forms, one of which is the representation of a human phalange.

A reasonable conclusion that could be drawn from the Spiro accumulation is that it represents a form of economic power of the elite through their control of internal exchange as well as long-distance exchange.

SOURCES OF GRAVE GOODS AND ART STYLE

One of the puzzling aspects of Spiro art is its amazing diversity: it does not resemble the work of a single workshop, school, or tradition. The natural inclination is to assign all Spiro artifacts to local artisans. But what if these artifacts are derived from far-flung sources? There is some confirmation of this thesis in the stylistic diversity of engraved shell and embossed copper objects. In a study in progress on the engraved shell art by Philip Phillips, two basic schools of engraving can be demonstrated, one of which (the Craig) can certainly be tied to the Caddoan area. Unfortunately, a simple survey of stylistic distributions cannot tell us much because so little engraved shell art is found outside of Spiro.

One thing is certain: the source of the raw material for both the shell cups and the

Fig. 12 *Sprio warrior pipe in bauxite (B99-2). Height, 27.3 cm.* Photo courtesy of the Stovall Museum, University of Oklahoma, Norman.

Fig. 13 *Spiro warrior pipe. Height, 26 cm.* Photo courtesy of the Museum of the American Indian, Heye Foundation, New York.

copper work must lie elsewhere. For years the west Florida coast and adjacent waters have been suggested as the most likely source for the marine shell. However, there is a more extensive coastline along the South Atlantic and Gulf to which the species are native. T. E. Pulley, of the Houston Museum of Natural History, recently pointed out, following his inspection of the collection of Spiro shell art in his museum, that the Mexican coastal waters below the Rio Grande are not ruled out either. The main copper source is undoubtedly the large lode around Lake Superior. There may have been minor secondary sources, but it is unlikely that sufficiently plentiful large nuggets could have come from any other source, such as the southern Appalachians. Although marine shell and copper are difficult to trace to unique sources, this is not the case with the materials of some of the minor artifacts, including the large human effigy pipes. The "greenstone" schist, white marble, and mica came from the southern Appalachian area, and the quartz crystals and bauxite came from Arkansas. The flints came from sources in Arkansas and possibly as far away as southern Illinois and western Tennessee. What is remarkable is the large area from which the war materials were derived; the Florida shoals, the southern Appalachians, and the Lake Superior region are the principal probable source areas for the raw materials.

The important fact of Spiro's location is that it is not in the center of the distribution of its indigenous cultural tradition, but is upstream from all the lesser centers and most of the support villages. The implication of the location of the largest site of the tradition at the margin of the tradition's distribution is that it is related to a center of gravity outside the resident tradition. In this case, that center of gravity is in Arkansas and in the direction of Moundville, Etowah, and the southern Appalachians. It is evident that the location of Spiro owes its advantage to its strategic position in the control of intertribal exchange. The resident elite naturally emerges as controlling the traffic in the most valuable of the valuables, that is, the shell cups and copper plates.

The items from the mortuary deposits show that the mortuary was basically a cult house for the honoring of the ancestor spirits, and that an overriding concern with prowess in warfare is recorded in its artifacts. Secondarily, the Spiro mortuary functioned as a kind of treasury or "cult strong house" necessary to the political and economic organization of the Spiro chieftainship. Thirdly, the location of the Spiro mortuary within the range of supporting settlements indicates a locational strategy in controlling inter-regional exchange.

MISSISSIPPIAN ECONOMY AND INTER-REGIONAL INTERACTION

In my review of quantities and sources of Spiro grave goods, the geographical scope and economic control over these goods by the Spiro elite were emphasized. More reasons are implied here for the accumulation and burial of these goods than mere happenstance or sentiment.

The issues require some detailed exposition, but I would like to return to the archaeological consequences of prehistoric "inter-regional interaction," to use Flannery's (1968) term. Widespread cultural similarities among contemporary cultural traditions of distinct regions have come to be regarded as the product of cultural interaction rather than the effects of population displacements or the activities of an influential minority. Some of the aspects in which interaction manifests itself have been outlined in a recent collection of essays edited by Wilmsen (1972). However, with regard to the Olmec, Kent Flannery (1968: 105) clearly outlined the conditions sufficient for inter-regional interaction and their probable cultural effects in differing traditions. In the model that Flannery proposed, interaction between regions is generated by what could be called a managerial solution to subsistence insecurity among a series of polities in similar environments or between two or more societies in different environments. The imbalances between subsistence requirements and actual productivity can be evened out by gift exchanges. The potential number and circumstances of such exchanges are very great. Although these exchanges take place under the guise of meeting obligations or of maintaining prestige, they invariably have the long-term effect of maintaining a flow of food in a population larger than the basic productive unit (Dalton 1965). But, interestingly enough, the exchange involves the circulation of durable valuables, often of many different types that are scaled in value or dedicated to specific types of transactions (*ibid.*). Not only are such durable exchange items standardized to symbolize common transactions much like money, but valuables of unique and exotic source become incorporated into the exchange to symbolize specially important transactions (Vayda 1967; Chagnon 1970). Significantly for us, the circulation of valuables as records of exchange is susceptible to inflation if the valuable continues to accumulate. But this inflation by proliferation can be quite easily solved by the periodic destruction of a portion of the stock of valuables. Such items as feathers can be expected to lose their value in time, but marine shell and stone artifacts are much more durable. One of the historic solutions has been to bury the durables, and one of the more convenient occasions for doing this is the death of an individual who was important in maintaining the exchange. The result is recorded archaeologically in the appearance of artifacts of exotic material and manufacture as grave goods or as ritually destroyed caches. The mechanics of exchange have been ably analyzed by Vayda

(1967) and Chagnon (1970) for the Pomo and other California tribes. The interaction model gives us still other expectations. Flannery has pointed out that living societies participating in exchanges "adopt the behavior, status trappings, religion, symbolism, or even language" of a particular dominating group (Flannery 1968: 105). Thus, participants in an exchange system not only have objects in common that can find their way into middens and burials, but they also tend to establish common contexts of utilization and disposal of these objects.

The archaeological effects of interaction are twofold: in facilitating burial of exotic artifacts, mainly in ceremonial precincts, and in the appearance of specific symbolism in the artifacts produced locally. Sufficient evidence is available in the extraordinary archaeological record to document the participation of Spiro in a sphere of interregional interaction. Artifacts of foreign design and exotic material appear in special mortuary contexts at Spiro. These valuables are treated in different ways roughly coincident with the distance it took to acquire them. All of the valuables were deliberately destroyed by their entombment on the floor of the Great Mortuary and in the graves used for disposal of items from the later Spiro mortuaries. Special pains were taken to destroy the chipped stone artifacts and the marine-shell cups by smashing them and subsequently distributing them among contemporary burials in the Great Mortuary. Beads and other artifacts were frequently fire-scorched, and the copper plates were folded and sometimes crumpled like tinfoil. Evidence for the transfer of the Southern Cult symbolism to locally produced artifacts is rare in the Arkansas Valley but less infrequent in the Mississippi Valley and points east. Sun-circles, birds, and animals associated with Cult symbols are found transferred to locally made pottery. One of the most common symbolic abstractions during this period in the Southeast was the forked-eye motif, which is a specific reference to the falcon and possibly to other hawks. It is the widespread currency of this symbol—undoubtedly standing for prowess in war—that constitutes one of the more distinctive pan-regional motifs of the period. It shares with sun and fire symbolism the honor of being the most widely diffused symbols in Mississippian art specific to the period. The equally pervasive scrolls and waves usually associated with water and fertility symbolism are not as specific to the period of the Southern Cult.

CONCLUSIONS

At one time it was accepted that the Southern Cult represented a material response to a social and religious revitalization movement analogous to the Ghost Dance. The late, nearly historic dating of the Cult seemed to favor this interpretation. However, even though current chronology has made the Cult older, archaeologists have been slow to replace the revitalization model with another.

Waring has been one of the few archaeological students of the Cult to see the connections between it and the organizations surrounding the care of the ritually important dead. But he concentrated attention on the brutal aspects rather than on the mortuary temple as a cult house important to the operation of Mississippian societies (Waring 1968b).

At Spiro the socially important dead were given special treatment in a charnel house, one example of which was the elaborate Great Mortuary that contained the remains of the burials intact. The specialized facilities that were present in the Spiro Great Mortuary graphically define the degree of symbolic distance between these burials and other interment types current at the time. The two most valuable commodities (as measured in terms of their distance from their source)— copper and marine shell—were the exclusive possession of the social segment that found its way into the three most prestigious burial types at Spiro. Most of the formal content of the art and symbolism pertained to warfare and its ritual observance. A major portion of the artifacts belonged to essentially similar contexts. Other components of the grave goods pertained to the outfitting of the mortuary itself and to the banking of standardized exchange artifacts such as shell beads. The symbolism of the falcon and the sun, which has been held to be fundamental to the Southern Cult, finds representation in simple motifs that are repeated innumerably in the most extensive range of artifacts.

Spiro shows that the Southern Cult is not a cult in the conventional meaning of the term. The archaeological record is the result of a network of participation in interregional interaction. Its documents are specific accumulations of exotic and costly artifacts. In the case of Spiro these accumulations reflect the social and political capacity of the premier lineage to funnel critical resources through its hands. If there is a cult involved at Spiro, it is an elaborate ancestor cult, which has as one of its pan-regional aspects the honoring of falcon war ceremonialism. The Great Mortuary represents the cult of the strongest lineage that acquired rank over all the others. Symbolizing this strength is the large accumulation of exchangeable items which were presumably validated through the ritual and social control of military organization.

BIBLIOGRAPHY

Baerreis, David A.

1957 The Southern Cult and the Spiro Ceremonial Complex. *Bulletin of the Oklahoma Anthropological Society*, vol. v, pp. 23–38. Oklahoma City.

Bell, Robert E.

1947 Trade Materials at Spiro Mound as Indicated by Artifacts. *American Antiquity*, vol. xii, no. 3, pp. 181–184. Society for American Archaeology, Menasha.

1972 The Harlan Site, Ck-6, A Prehistoric Mound Center in Cherokee County, Eastern Oklahoma. *Memòir, Oklahoma Anthropological Society*, no. 2. Norman.

Binford, Lewis R.

1971 Mortuary Practices: Their Study and Their Potential. *In* Approaches to the Social Dimensions of Mortuary Practices (James A. Brown, ed.). *Memoirs of the Society for American Archaeology*, no. 25, pp. 6–29. Washington.

Brown, James A.

1966 Spiro Studies, vol. 2: The Graves and Their Contents. Second Part of the Second Annual Report of Caddoan Archaeology – Spiro Focus Research. University of Oklahoma Research Institute, Norman.

1971 The Dimensions of Status in the Burials at Spiro. *In* Approaches to the Social Dimensions of Mortuary Practices (James A. Brown, ed.). *Memoirs of the Society for American Archaeology*, no. 25, pp. 92–112. Washington.

n.d. Cultural Evolution and the Rise and Fall of Spiro. Paper given at the Southeastern Archaeological Conference, Memphis, Tennessee, 1973.

Brues, Alice M.

n.d. Spiro Studies, vol. 5: Analysis of the Spiro Skeletal Material. Annual Report of Caddoan Archaeology – Spiro Focus Research. University of Oklahoma Research Institute, Norman. (In press.)

Burnett, E. K.

1945 The Spiro Mound Collection in the Museum. *Contributions from the Museum of the American Indian, Heye Foundation*, vol. xiv, pp. 9–47. New York.

Caldwell, Joseph R.

1964 Interaction Spheres in Prehistory. *In* Hopewellian Studies (Joseph R. Caldwell and Robert L. Hall, eds.). *Illinois State Museum, Scientific Papers*, vol. xii, pp. 133–143. Springfield.

Chagnon, Napoleon A.

1970 Ecological and Adaptive Aspects of California Shell Money. *Archaeological Survey, Annual Report*, vol. 12, pp. 1–25. Department of Anthropology, University of California, Los Angeles.

Dalton, George

1965 Primitive Money. *American Anthropologist*, vol. 67, no. 1, pp. 44–65. American Anthropological Association, Menasha.

Finklestein, J. Joe

1940 The Norman Site Excavations near Wagoner, Oklahoma. *The Oklahoma Prehistorian*, vol. iii, no. 3, pp. 2–15. Oklahoma State Archaeological Society, Tulsa.

FLANNERY, KENT V.

1968 The Olmec and the Valley of Oaxaca: A Model for Inter-regional Interaction in Formative Times. *In* Dumbarton Oaks Conference on the Olmec (Elizabeth P. Benson, ed.), pp. 79–110. Dumbarton Oaks Research Library and Collection, Washington.

GRIFFIN, JAMES B.

1952 An Interpretation of the Place of Spiro in Southeastern Archaeology. *The Missouri Archaeologist*, vol. 14, pp. 89–106. Missouri Archaeological Society, Columbia.

1961 Relationships between the Caddoan Area and the Mississippi Valley. *Bulletin of the Texas Archeological Society*, vol. 31, pp. 27–37. Austin.

HAMILTON, HENRY W.

1952 The Spiro Mound. *The Missouri Archaeologist*, vol. 14, pp. 17–88. Missouri Archaeological Society, Columbia.

HAMILTON, HENRY W., JEAN T. HAMILTON, and ELEANOR F. CHAPMAN

1974 Spiro Mound Copper. *Memoir, Missouri Archaeological Society*, no. 11. Columbia.

HOWARD, JAMES H.

1968 The Southeastern Ceremonial Complex and Its Interpretation. *Memoir, Missouri Archaeological Society*, no. 6. Columbia.

JENNINGS, JESSE D.

1968 Prehistory of North America. McGraw-Hill Book Company, New York.

KRIEGER, ALEX D.

1945 An Inquiry into Supposed Mexican Influence on a Prehistoric "Cult" in the Southern United States. *American Anthropologist*, vol. 47, no. 4, pp. 483–515. American Anthropological Association, Menasha.

LARSON, LEWIS H., JR.

1971 Archaeological Implications of Social Stratification at the Etowah Site, Georgia. *In* Approaches to the Social Dimensions of Mortuary Practices (James A. Brown, ed.). *Memoirs of the Society for American Archaeology*, no. 25, pp. 58–67. Washington.

MACLEOD, WILLIAM CHRISTIE

1928 Priests, temples, and the practice of mummification in southeastern North America. *Atti del XXII Congresso Internazionale degli Americanisti, Roma, Settembre 1926*, vol. II, pp. 207–230. Roma.

NEITZEL, ROBERT S.

1965 Archeology of the Fatherland Site: The Grand Village of Natchez. *Anthropological Papers of the American Museum of Natural History*, vol. 51, part 1. New York.

ORR, KENNETH GORDON

1946 The Archaeological Situation at Spiro, Oklahoma; A Preliminary Report. *American Antiquity*, vol. XI, no. 4, pp. 228–256. Society for American Archaeology, Menasha.

PHILLIPS, PHILIP, and JAMES A. BROWN

n.d. Pre-Columbian Shell Engravings from the Craig Mound at Spiro, Oklahoma. Peabody Museum of Archaeology and Ethnology, Harvard University, Cambridge. (In press.)

SAXE, ARTHUR A.

n.d. Social Dimensions of Mortuary Practices. Unpublished doctoral dissertation, University of Michigan. Ann Arbor, 1970.

STRUEVER, STUART

1964 The Hopewell Interaction Sphere in Riverine–Western Great Lakes Culture History. *In* Hopewellian Studies (Joseph R. Caldwell and Robert L. Hall, eds.). *Illinois State Museum, Scientific Papers*, vol. XII, pp. 85–106. Springfield.

SWANTON, JOHN R.

1912 Historical Sketches of the Biloxi and Ofo. *In* A Dictionary of the Biloxi and Ofo Languages (James Owen Dorsey and John R. Swanton), pp. 5–12. *Smithsonian Institution, Bureau of American Ethnology, Bulletin* 47. U. S. Government Printing Office, Washington.

VAYDA, ANDREW P.

1967 Les fêtes commerciales des Indiens Pomo. *Économies et Sociétés*, Cahiers de l'Institut de Science Économique Appliquée, Serie V (Humanités, Économie, Ethnologie, Sociologie), 10, pp. 237–244. Presses Universitaires de France, Paris.

WARING, ANTONIO J., JR.

1968a The Southern Cult and Muskhogean Ceremonial. *In* The Waring Papers: The Collected Works of Antonio J. Waring, Jr. (Stephen Williams, ed.), pp. 30–69. *Papers of the Peabody Museum of Archaeology and Ethnology, Harvard University*, vol. LVIII. Cambridge.

1968b The Southern Cult Revisited. *In* The Waring Papers: The Collected Works of Antonio J. Waring, Jr. (Stephen Williams, ed.), p. 93. *Papers of the Peabody Museum of Archaeology and Ethnology, Harvard University*, vol. LVIII. Cambridge.

WARING, A. J., JR., and PRESTON HOLDER

1945 A Prehistoric Ceremonial Complex in the Southeastern United States. *American Anthropologist*, vol. 47, no. 1, pp. 1–34. American Anthropological Association, Menasha.

WILLEY, GORDON R., and PHILIP PHILLIPS

1958 Method and Theory in American Archaeology. The University of Chicago Press, Chicago & London.

WILLOUGHBY, CHARLES C.

1932 Notes on the History and Symbolism of the Muskhogeans and the People of Etowah. *In* Etowah Papers (Warren King Moorehead, ed.), pp. 7–67. Department of Archaeology, Phillips Academy, Andover.

WILMSEN, EDWIN N. (ed.)

1972 Social Exchange and Interaction. *Anthropological Papers, Museum of Anthropology, University of Michigan*, no. 46. Ann Arbor.

House of Darkness and House of Light: Sacred Functions of West Mexican Funerary Art

PETER T. FURST

STATE UNIVERSITY OF NEW YORK AT ALBANY

INTRODUCTION

EVER since the art of ancient West Mexico first caught the eye of collectors, it has become virtual dogma that here is one Mesoamerican art tradition that presents no great esoteric mystery, that can be understood and appreciated as secular and anecdotal, that is, focused on what was "real" in life instead of on the supernatural. The literature on Pre-Columbian art is filled with arguments that the peoples of prehistoric Colima, Jalisco, and Nayarit, unlike their contemporaries, were somehow unconcerned with gods and priests—"free," to quote one writer, "from religious ties and the constraining bonds of tradition" (Linné 1960: 26). Accordingly, we are often told there are no deities—indeed, no sacred subject matter as such—in West Coast art, or, if there are, we cannot recognize them because they lack the criteria by which we distinguish them in Central Mexico (von Winning 1972: 29).

As to this last argument, it has long been recognized that, whatever the reason, western Mexico, at least on the time level that concerns us here, did not participate in, and, judging from the evidence available to us, was barely touched by, the great Early Classic civilization then emerging in Central Mexico. From this it would logically follow that to look for identifying characteristics of the gods or priests of Teotihuacan or its successors in early shaft-tomb art is an exercise in futility. Under such circumstances, we would obviously have to look elsewhere and for different kinds of clues by which to tell the gods from men.

"Non-ordinary" subject matter—effigies whose iconography does not lend itself to naturalistic, literal, or, if you will, "anecdotal" interpretation—is actually by no means uncommon in West Mexican art. One thinks here of such immediately apparent manifestations of the supernatural or magical as duck-persons, dog-women, dogs with human masks, bird-men and other manifestations of transformation, various kinds of vessels with animal or human characteristics, double-headed serpents, horned and armed men that remind one of the Hopi Kwanitaka (the One-Horn Society of shamanistic warrior-guardians of initiates and souls of the dead) or of one-horned kachinas and deities in Pueblo myth and ritual, big-horn sheep carrying tiny human beings on their backs, hunchbacked dwarfs either lacking external genitalia or else with giant erect phalluses, fish and crabs with human extremities, anthropomorphized sharks swallowing or disgorging small human beings (Fig. 1), armed men with trees or hu-

Fig. 1 *Polished red-slipped brownware effigy of an anthropomorphic shark monster swallowing a small human being. Colima, ca. 100 B.C.–A.D. 200. Length, ca. 33 cm. The symbolism of this and related effigies from Colima and elsewhere in prehispanic Mesoamerica conforms closely to characteristically shamanistic initiatory, funerary, and death-and-rebirth beliefs and rituals in both the Old and New Worlds. That the shark, or possibly killer whale, might have played such a role in Colima suggests a strong maritime orientation.* Private collection. Photo by the author.

mans growing from their backs, serpents that with their feather ruffs closely resemble the Great Kolowisi serpent of the Zuni, and other themes that have their closest analogies in the rich traditional religious lore of the Pueblos and the Cora-Huichol of Jalisco and Nayarit (cf. Furst 1973).

Space and time do not permit a recapitulation of these analogies and their cultural historical implications, except to say that, in light of recent archaeological, linguistic, folkloristic, and other research, in the Pueblo country as well as in western Mexico, it appears more and more that the "Greater Southwest," which Ralph Beals (1943) long ago postulated as a single culture area extending in historic times from the Gila in the north to the Santiago in the south, can be pushed back deeply into prehistory, at least to the time of the shaft-and-chamber-tomb cultures, if not centuries earlier.

This is not to divorce West Mexico completely from the rest of Mesoamerica prior to the onset of the Post-Classic, when numerous Mixteca-Puebla and other manifestly Central Mexican traits made their appearance in this region. As Isabel Kelly's recent studies demonstrate, at least in Colima there existed an Early to Middle Formative ceramic horizon with unmistakable ties to the Valley of Mexico and to Morelos (Kelly 1974). Further, there are certain stylistic and some iconographic relationships between shaft-tomb art, dating between 200–100 B.C. and the first two or three centuries A.D., and Late Formative ceramics from Central Mexico and Guanajuato, not to mention some evidence of far-flung trade, especially in the form of conch-shell trumpets of Caribbean origin in many western shaft-and-chamber burials. We should also not overlook the fact that the numerous analogies to be drawn between shaft-tomb art and Cora-Huichol and Pueblo myth and ritual may be giving us too narrowly conceived a rendition of the actual historical situation. While suggesting direct genetic relationships across time and space, they could be in part a function of demonstrably greater preservation, among these particular contemporary groups, of aboriginal traditions that in former times were the common property not just of speakers of Greater Nahua (Uto-Aztecan) languages but of linguistically diverse populations as well, that have long since disappeared except in refuge areas where special conditions favored survival. None of this, of course, negates the probability of common historical origins and sustained contacts over a long period of time as the most economical explanation for the many parallels between the archaeological and ethnographic cultures of western Mexico and the Southwest; rather, it reminds us that our information and understanding of the prehistoric and even the historic situation are very limited, and that future research can be counted on to lead to different, or at least greatly expanded, explanations.

To return to meaning in West Mexican art, however "non-ordinary" we may admit the above-mentioned non-naturalistic effigies to be, this would not necessarily

Fig. 2 *"Mother Goddess" or "Great Mother" effigy figure from Colima of unslipped solid reddish-brown clay,* ca. *100 B.C.–A.D. 200. A number of iconographically similar figurines in various sizes and styles have been found in southern Jalisco and Colima; that illustrated here is one of the largest and most complete, measuring 30.5 cm. in height. Arms, shoulders, and front and back of the upper body are covered with numerous small children, of which some are nude while others wear loincloths, suggesting sexual differentiation. As in other effigies of this type, two of the children are suckling from the Mother's breasts. A larger male figure wearing a frontal horn on a rayed headdress sits astride her shoulders and embraces her head; three others, all with frontal horns and two with rayed headdresses, are seated on her lap. The closed eyes of the Mother are curiously asymmetrical, as are those of certain other Colima figures. On other similar "Great Mother" figurines some or all of the heads of the children have been removed, evidently deliberately and hence for some ritual purpose (see Fig. 4), suggesting beliefs about the head as repository of the essential life force similar to those held by the contemporary Huichol Indians.* Private collection. Photo by the author.

Fig. 3 (left) *Rear view of "Great Mother."* Photo by the author.

Fig. 4 (right) *"Great Mother" effigy of reddish-brown clay, essentially similar to that in Figures 2 and 3, but with the heads of some of the twenty-eight children missing. Height, 20.5 cm. Again, some of the children are nude while others wear loincloths; those clinging to the back are arranged in alternating clothed and unclothed rows. It may be that figurines of this type played a role in shamanistic curing of barrenness, in which case a woman desirous of children might be given the head of one of the small effigy children as a symbol of the unborn child's life force, or soul. If so, this might explain why some of these effigies are found with some or even all of the children's heads missing. In this example, the figure on the shoulders and those on the lap lack the elaborate headdresses and frontal horns found in Figure 2.* Private collection. Photo by the author.

make them gods *per se* in a prehistoric pantheon. There is, however, one type of figure (Figs. 2–4), from Colima and adjacent southern Jalisco, that by itself so unmistakably contradicts the alleged absence of clearly recognizable deities in West Mexican art that one can only marvel at the stubborn persistence of this allegation in the literature. Apparently "obvious" or overt characteristics have led us astray in the past, but the attributes of this class of figurines would seem to point unmistakably in the direction of a Mother Goddess or Earth Mother. If so, she might be equated with Xochiquetzal, or, in the pantheon of the Huichol Indians, Our Mother Niwetúkame, the Earth Mother Goddess as divine mother of children.

In any event, we would have to agree that such effigies hardly support the popular view of "people without gods." Nevertheless, I would not insist on separating even such recognizable deities or supernaturals from "daily life." For if we are ever to achieve a measure of understanding of content and function in West Mexican art, we will have to put aside the separation we usually make between daily life and religion, recognizing it as a Western construct that is fundamentally incompatible with the ideational universe of traditional cultures, past and present. With this we come to the main theme of this discussion—the *function* of funerary art. For in all the arguments over external vs. intrinsic characteristics, or secular vs. sacred subject matter, the crucial question—why daily life in effigy should have been buried with the deceased in the first place—has received little attention. I hope to demonstrate in the following pages that it is not really important to this question—in fact, it is irrelevant—whether, as some prefer, the various kinds of mortuary sculpture are literal representations of everyday life, or whether, as I have argued (Furst 1965; 1974), the great legacy of West Coast art includes themes from the metaphysical as well as the physical environment of its creators. Whatever the subject matter, as in the tomb art of ancient China and the mortuary art of other traditional cultures, it is the phenomenon of its interment with the deceased that by definition puts it firmly in the realm of the mystical, the cosmological, the sacred. What we need to seek, then, is a key to underlying motivations, i.e., an appreciation of the ideology that dictated this particular form of artistic endeavor. Two models are used here to help us do so, however imperfectly. The first is traditional China, the second the Huichol Indians.

FUNERARY ART IN CHINA

About twelve years ago, when he was nearly eighty, the late Professor Carl Hentze published as one of his last major works a comparative study entitled, in translation from the German, *The House as Locus Mundi of the Soul* (1961).[1] Professor Hentze was one of the leading and most prolific European Sinologists, but his interests carried him far beyond the boundaries of China and traditional Chinese thought and symbolism. He was also concerned with ideological and artistic analogies from other cultures, including the New World, that might help illuminate the esoteric pictorial language into which the Chinese rendered their *Weltanschauung*, and the natural, cosmological, and mystical phenomena that populated their natural, social, and metaphysical environment.

As Professor Hentze develops it, the Chinese model is very much to the point in our consideration of West Mexican funerary art. However, it is not directly related to the question of trans-Pacific culture contacts, and I should not wish to be misunderstood on that score, whatever the degree of real or fancied resemblances between Nayarit house and village models and those of the Han or Dongson peoples of ancient China and Southeast Asia. We will have occasion to consider the diffusionist argument again later on.

Hentze sounds somewhat the same warning with respect to traditional Chinese symbolism that Carl Lumholtz (1900; 1903), the Norwegian pioneer of West Mexican ethnology, voiced at the turn of the century with respect to Huichol art: each line, each symbol has its meaning, but so long as we persist in trying to explain and replace what is essentially mystical with our characteristically Western system of logic and rationality, the fundamental content, the true meaning and function, of the symbolic arts of traditional societies will elude us.

As Hentze develops the argument, the linear-historical view of time that dominates the thinking of Western man is fundamentally opposed to traditional Chinese thought, as also to that of the American Indian. Our concept of the inexorable passage of time—of time that once passed is lost forever, never to return—is inseparable from the dichotomy we make between a here and now and a radically different beyond. In contrast, where we perceive time as a fleeting and destructible commodity (e.g., time "lost," "gained," "spent," etc.), the Chinese, like the American Indian, constantly extrapolated from that which was to that which is, and vice versa. Accordingly, the ancient Chinese calendar, like that of Mesoamerica, was one of cyclical repetition, not linear, historical passage. For the Chinese, as for the native American, there was simply no

1. I would like here to express my appreciation to Prof. Richard C. Rudolph of the University of California at Los Angeles, who first introduced me to Hentze's work and who, over many years, has never failed to share his time, his erudition, and his library to assist the writer in avoiding at least some of the errors which ignorance of the complexities of Chinese culture, history, language, and symbolism would otherwise have made inevitable.

such concept as time irreversible, and therefore no death as the finite condition of man.

These primary postulates of Hentze's traditional Chinese model are of decisive importance to the interpretation of funerary objects and the world of the dead. In traditional society, to be sure, the world of the deceased is another world from that of the living. But it is never separate. It is not, therefore, a "beyond" as we use that term—that is, another world in the sense of being distinct. Such rigid division can exist only where time is considered to be unrestorable, and where the past is, as the saying goes, "dead and gone forever." For the European, the conceptualization of two separate and qualitatively different worlds implies complete and finite separation, predetermined by a historical, linear course of events. It is interesting that the ancient Chinese language does not even have terminology that would equate with our "here and now" and "hereafter." Instead, it stresses polarity and interdependence, as between two halves of a single whole, between light and dark, positive and negative, the yin and the yang, forever shading into one another without any clear-cut break between them. For the Chinese, a time that for us constitutes the "dead" past can constantly be conjured up to merge with the "living" present. In traditional China, then, as in Indian America, these two qualitatively equivalent states stand in a wholly interdependent, complementary, and interchangeable relationship to one another.

This philosophical given had its expression in funerary ceremonialism. As we know, during the Han Dynasty, which dates from *ca.* 206 B.C. to A.D. 220 (and is thus roughly equivalent to the shaft-and-chamber-tomb phase in western Mexico and to the transition from the Late Formative to the Early Classic elsewhere in Mesoamerica), and during subsequent dynasties as well, a man who had died was customarily interred with the effigies of his daily existence: his houses, his wives, his servants, his horses and camels, his cows and pigs, his oxcart and draft animals, his dog, even his wells, granaries, and hearths. Now, Hentze asks, is this ceramic world in miniature effigy a special, separate world of the dead, one with which he alone is capable of coping, one that belongs exclusively to him? That is certainly how it is often interpreted in the West. Not so, he writes, because such an interpretation again presupposes a distinction between the living and the dead, which would have been alien to Chinese thought. Instead, for the living as for the dead, the figurines and artifacts, the houses and domestic animals replicate that which was and continues to be. From the point of view of the Chinese, and of other traditional societies that buried effigies of life with the deceased, the reasoning would have been rather like this: "We give our dead their familiar things to take along with them, so as to help us keep in touch with them whenever we wish. This we can do more easily if our dead have exactly that which we also possess. And by seeing to it that they do so, we restore that essential equilibrium between ourselves and them, after it was temporarily disrupted by the fact of their death."

This then, is the key: the restoration of an absolutely essential equilibrium. Temporarily shaken by so terrible a fact as death, balance must be restored, the social universe put back in order. The world of the living does not stand alone but has its spatial-temporal analogy in the world of the dead. Only they together, in equilibrium, make up a total world, a total universe. Neither can exist by itself, because alone each represents but a part of the essential whole. At the same time, the totality of the two halves, the house of the ancestors below and the house of the living above, is reversible and interchangeable. Seen in this light, the effigies in the womb-house of the dead represent but a modus of reactivation or rebirth, the revivification of the past. This mode of experiencing the natural world, or "reality," is clearly of a different order than that following from the Judeo-Christian tradition and, even more, Western "rational" thought. But these are relatively recent developments. The farther one moves back in time, the less distinct become the boundaries, and the more alike the basic philosophical themes. In the end, after all, the base religion of Europeans and Asians alike was the shamanism of our common Paleolithic past, modified, to be sure, by local environments, but—judging from its scattered survivals in the New World and the Old—essentially alike in its fundamental assumptions.

CONTEMPORARY INDIAN MEXICO

Let us see now whether and to what degree the Chinese model might correspond to contemporary Mexico. Ideally, of course, the society selected for analogical data should be one that has retained a high degree of traditionalism—i.e., one whose fundamental world view, religion, and ritual have been relatively little modified by European Christian elements. This is certainly true of the Huichol, whose territory in the rugged Sierra Madre Occidental adjoins part of the area in which shaft-and-chamber tombs are found. While some of their ancestors may have migrated into the Sierra relatively recently—perhaps in the sixteenth century to escape the consequences of the Conquest—the ten thousand or so Huichol-speakers have strong cultural and linguistic affinities to the neighboring Cora, who appear to represent a much more ancient locally resident population, and whose own forebears may, as Konrad Theodor Preuss (1912) suggested, have been among the ancient shaft-tomb builders of Nayarit.

First, and by necessity very briefly, the ethnographic context: like some of the Pueblos and many Mesoamerican Indians, the Huichol belong to the Greater Nahua, or Uto-Aztecan, language family. Their relative geographical isolation in difficult and, for the Spaniards, economically undesirable terrain helps explain the strong survival of their aboriginal religious system; they and the Cora were not even brought under Colonial Spanish control until 1722—two hundred years after the Conquest—and even then Spanish and, later, Mexican influence was to remain at a minimum.

Unlike most other Mesoamerican Indians and mestizo farmers, the Huichol do not reside in villages or pueblos but live in small, geographically rather isolated and, hence, somewhat independent kin groups. Typically, the residential unit consists of a man and his wife or wives, some married and unmarried offspring and their children, and, occasionally, more distant relatives as well. These extended family communities rarely exceed fifteen individuals, who occupy the several small, thatch-roofed huts that make up the typical *rancho*. The elder or headman of such a *rancho* is usually also a *mara'akáme*, or shaman, who conducts rituals and does the curing for his immediate kin, and, if he has sufficient prestige, for some of his neighbors as well.

The subsistence pattern is characteristically of the slash-and-burn and digging-stick type. Small plots are cleared of brush and planted with maize and, usually, some beans and squash. There is private land use but not private land ownership; fields left fallow for an extended time revert to the community as a whole for reassignment. Many families also own some livestock, but relatively large Huichol-owned herds are rare. In general, the society is egalitarian; even men of great prestige are more often than not quite poor.

The Huichol pantheon is a crowded one, too crowded and complex to enumerate here, except to say that the system is typically pantheistic and animistic, with the major deities personifying important natural phenomena, especially fire and sun ("Grandfather" and "Father") and the female earth in her numerous manifestations ("Grandmother," "Our Mothers," etc.). All the supernaturals are addressed by kinship terms. In myth and story-telling, as in ritual, the past and the present, the world of the ancestors and the world of the living typically merge and are interchangeable and interdependent.

There is no dividing line between sacred and mundane. Indeed, one would be hard put to differentiate *any* activity or thought whatever into sacred or secular categories; religion is life and life religion, and all things man does or contemplates have their sacred component. In a sense, *all* phenomena and actions are sacred because they represent and re-enact that which was anciently established by the divine ancestors. Some ceremonies really involve little more than the preparation and consumption, in a ritually prescribed manner and attended by ritual acts, of certain foods which elsewhere in rural Mexico have long since lost whatever sacred meanings they once had (e.g., tamales, deer meat, etc.). Under the circumstances, the uninitiated observer may be hard put to distinguish what is really a most profound ritual from an ordinary meal (a circumstance that suggests caution in assigning "ordinary" meanings to representations of cooking or eating in West Mexican art).

Any ceremonial is, of course, by definition sacred, having been first established by the gods and ancestors, and involving their continued participation. But actually even the most practical community deliberations presuppose decisive input from the supernatural sphere. Plants and at least all *indigenous* animals have souls like men; in fact, there is really no inanimate object at all in our sense. Even tools, such as axes and machetes used to clear small plots for subsistence maize cultivation with the traditional digging stick, are considered to be alive and to require food and ritual, as do their human owners. In addition, since their vital essences are considered to be "the same," the outer forms of certain phenomena are interchangeable. Likewise, the gods and other supernaturals may appear in a variety of forms, sometimes as animals, sometimes as men and women doing tasks within their province (such as grinding maize on the *metate*), and, in some instances, even as objects, whose true nature is, of course, well known from earliest childhood to all participants in the culture.

Like the Chinese of Hentze's model, the Huichol are much concerned with the maintenance of the proper equilibrium—between man and his social and natural environment, between the people and their ancestral deities, between the male and female principles that permeate the universe, and between the worlds of the living and the dead which together make up a "unity." Huichol mortuary beliefs and rituals—not only for human beings but also for those animals with whom people stand in a special relationship—are directed toward the re-establishment of the equilibrium that was temporarily upset by the fact of death. This is precisely why, when a deer has been slain on the ritual hunt, the dead animal, laid out on embroidered cloths belonging to the women, is supposed to be gently addressed by the hunter and his kin, who thank it for giving its life to its younger brothers (the deer is "Elder Brother"), and who rub its mouth and tongue with maize beer and the five kinds of grass that are believed to constitute its favorite foods in life. Since the sacred hallucinogenic peyote cactus is also Deer, the first such plant to be ritually hunted and "slain" on the peyote quest is likewise propitiated in order to restore the proper balance.

When a Huichol dies there are five days of mortuary ritual—five being the sacred number signifying the four world directions and the center (up and down). In the course of these rituals the soul, or, more correctly, the essential life force that resides in the anterior fontanelle, is guided on his or her journey through the underworld to the *rancho* of his deceased relatives in the west (the body itself was traditionally interred in a cave, a practice still observed wherever feasible).

The world of the dead is conceived on the order of the typical Huichol community. Life is thought to go on much as before, but without some of the more onerous aspects of earthly life. Since the mortality rate among children is high, such sexual intercourse as there may be in the otherworld is said not to lead to pregnancy. On the other hand, just as the special gifts and esoteric knowledge of the *mara'akáme* are essential to general well-being and equilibrium on earth, so they are also required in the world of the dead in order for "that other life" to be complete. It is important to note that "the other life" is definitely not thought of as a "next world" or "afterlife" in the Christian sense, but rather in terms of complementarity and continuum.

At death, a platform is erected on which the personal belongings of the deceased are laid out, surrounded by votive objects, such as prayer feathers, offering gourds, food, etc. His calves or pigs and other livestock are likewise brought to the platform, so that his soul may select what it wants in the other world. Through the *mara'akáme*'s magical powers, these objects travel in miniature effigy to the village of the dead. My Huichol informants were very clear about why this is done: not only to make the deceased comfortable in his new dwelling, so that he will not be tempted to return to his former home at inopportune times, but also so that the relatives can think of him in surroundings that are familiar to them.

When the shaman speeds the soul on its way, he instructs it to stamp its feet loudly on the Ringing Rocks at the entrance to the underworld, so that the relatives below will hear it coming and can make the proper preparations for its festive reception—with song and dance, much peyote, and much drinking of the ceremonial maize beer the Huichol call *nawá*. The dead are said to be so inordinately fond of *nawá* that they are forever trying to return to the *rancho* of their living relatives to partake of the intoxicating beverage. So eager are they for it that they often fall into the *nawá* pots, thereby spoiling the drink before it is even properly fermented. So the people protect their *nawá* from the dead with magical plants and spirit traps that look just like the familiar thread crosses made for the protection of children, but which are called *tüwe*, "jaguar," and have a different function. At the same time, to make certain that their dead relatives are not disappointed, they brew special *nawá* for them and set it aside for their pleasure.

The absolute interdependence between the living and the dead is also underscored by an interesting tradition about the journey of the soul to the underworld which several informants gave me in more or less similar versions. According to this myth—which, incidentally, is part of the shaman's chants that speed the soul on its way to the *ranchos* of the dead in the west—when setting out on the long and arduous road, the male soul carries on its back the vaginas of all the women with whom the deceased had intercourse during life. Correspondingly, the female soul is weighted down by all the penises "she enjoyed in that other life," as the Huichols say. At various points along the way the soul, increasingly tired and hungry and eager to reach its destination, attempts more or less surreptitiously to rid itself of the burden, but the ancestors and the owners of the underworld will not permit this: "You wanted to enjoy yourself in that other life," they call out to the relative, "now you must carry all of that on your back until you arrive here."

At first sight this may sound very much like a characteristically Huichol form of punishment for "sin" in the Christian sense, but its wholly traditional motivation quickly becomes apparent with the ultimate disposition of the physical evidence of sexuality. The dead await their relative on a dancing ground beneath a giant wild fig tree (clearly the Tree of Life at the center of the world), laden with ripe fruits that are required for the feast of greeting the new arrival. However, there is only one way in which the fruit can be harvested, and that is for the male and female soul, respectively, to fling their collections of sexual trophies high into the branches. This will knock down the fruit so that it can be collected and prepared. "Then," says the tradition, "all the people there are happy, for their relative has brought them life."

As for the concept of time reversed, nothing illustrates this better than the peyote pilgrimage, that extraordinary, emotion-charged event on which so much of Huichol religious thought and effort is concentrated. Each such quest is the re-enactment of the primordial peyote quest of the divine ancestors, so that the participants themselves "become" the gods. By ritual purification they are shed of their ordinary existence; as they embark on their sacred journey backward in time toward the peyote country, three hundred miles to the east, they are as embryos passing through the darkness of the symbolic womb of the Mother Earth, to emerge once more into the light in the sacred country of the Deer-Peyote. Here, too, the world of the living and that of the dead are fused: the exaltation of the successful *peyoteros* in their dances is matched by that of the dead, who are roused to joyful participation by the rhythmic slapping of sandals on the roof of their "house" in the underworld.

If an archaeologist of the future were to excavate a *tukí*, one of the circular temples that dot the Huichol country and serve as regional ceremonial centers, he would have little difficulty in distinguishing it from the much smaller, rectangular Huichol dwelling, and identifying its sacred purpose. But he would be hard put to do the same for the remains of a *xiriki*, one of the sacred structures that Lumholtz (1900: 9) called "god-houses." And yet the *xiriki* is the sacred center of the *rancho*, the special dwelling set aside as the residence of the soul of a deceased ancestral shaman who has returned in the form of a small rock crystal to dwell as guardian spirit among his relatives. He is the household god of the kin group, mentor of its shaman-elder, and guarantor of successful ceremonial deer hunts. The institutionalized ritual process of this transformation of the soul into quartz, and its retrieval and assimilation by the shaman on a celestial quest, is too complex a matter to do justice to in the space available here;

suffice it to say that it involves, among other ordeals, a perilous penetration by the shaman of a burning curtain of solar fire—the classic "dangerous passage" of so much shamanic, heroic, and funerary mythology (see Furst 1967).

Eventually the returning skeletal soul in its rock-crystal form is drawn into the *rancho* of its relatives by means of a proffered bowl of the intoxicating maize beer. Upon his magical arrival, he becomes *'urukáme*, from *'urú*, "arrow," so named because the little crystal—wrapped in a bit of cotton fluff and stuffed inside a small section of hollow cane[2]—is attached to the shaft of a composite, wooden-tipped arrow. This divine arrow is stuck into the wall or roof-thatch of the *xiriki*, which the shaman and his relatives previously erected to serve as an earthly dwelling for the soul. Upperworld and underworld, the world of the living and that of the dead, are thereby fused into a single whole, and equilibrium is assured.

A *xiriki* housing the guardian spirit, or household god, like those erected in front of the larger *tukí* as temporary dwellings of different principal male and female deities at times of communal ceremonials, looks very much like any common Huichol dwelling (Fig. 5). Indeed, one would expect this if the Chinese model has any validity here. Interestingly enough, according to native tradition, when the First Shaman, the old God of Fire, constructed such a sacred house in primordial times, it corresponded to the cosmological model with its five trees—four corner posts at the cardinal points and a fifth to support the sacred center at the apex of the roof. From the exterior the roof of this prototypical god-house looked like a four-sided pyramid, as, indeed, those of some god-houses still do today.

Within the god-house one is likely to note: the hearth, the manifestation of the First *Mara'akáme*, the old God of Fire; a *sipapu*-like symbolic emergence hole for the "Grandfathers" in the world below; some *ollas* for *nawá*-making; deer snares; agricultural and other tools; water gourds and bottles; peyote, strung necklacelike on cactus-fiber string, and other peyote plants stored in baskets and bags; a full-size *'uwéni*, or shaman's chair, belonging to the elder, and one or more miniature replicas of such seats of power for various gods (e.g., the Sun Father who was originally borne through

2. Since the rock crystal is conceived of as the consolidation of the skeletal remains of the deceased, the practice of placing it inside a hollow cane tube reminds one of the well-known practice by Australian aborigines and other hunting-and-gathering peoples of placing the defleshed bones of the dead inside hollow tree trunks. There are, in fact, suggestions in Huichol myth and ritual practices connected with birth that tree burial of some kind might have been practiced by their preagricultural ancestors. Nowadays, Huichol mothers still wrap the placenta in grass and place it in a tree. The umbilicus they bury with the seed of a fruit-bearing tree or cactus, whose subsequent growth and fate parallels that of the child, a practice which is analogous to the companion-animal concept of the Maya.

Fig. 5 *Typical Huichol house of mud-plastered stone walls and thatched roof, with a smoke hole at the end of the ridgepole. Materials used depend on the environment; other Huichol houses are constructed of wattle and daub or of closely set poles and thatch. Externally nothing distinguishes one of these domestic dwellings from the* xiriki, *the Huichol term for the house set aside as the residence of the ancestor spirit called* 'urukáme, *embodied in a divine rock crystal attached to a ceremonial arrow* ('urú). Photo by Ernesto Loera O.

the sky on such a chair by the first people); perhaps a small effigy of a god carved of wood or tufa; a bundle of dried grass tied to the ridge pole as the effigy of Opossum, mystic Fire-Bringer and one of the guardians of the underworld; bows and arrows; deer antlers; some tobacco gourds; thread crosses (Fig. 6) hung with tiny bows and arrows as prayers for boys, or with bits of embroidery for girls (hence, conceptually, though not structurally, quite distinct from the above-mentioned "jaguar" spirit traps in the form of the thread cross); perhaps a mask made of the facial skin of a deer representing Elder Brother *Kauyumarie*; snake effigies as the generic images of the divine Mothers, the female deities of water and fecundity; etc. Incidentally, the ancestral guardian himself can be variously depicted in ceremonial art as an arrow or as an ordinary-appearing person.

Since few of the contents of the god-house are imperishable, a future archaeologist would be left with little evidence for the true significance of the *xiriki*, which in his site report would most likely become one more ordinary dwelling. And what of the ancestor, the supernatural guardian whose mystical powers suffused the whole community of the living? Sad to say, as a tiny bit of unworked quartz, he wouldn't even make it into the category of artifact. So much for the limits of archaeology.

ANCIENT ART OF WEST MEXICO

The fundamental unity between the historical Chinese and the ethnographic Huichol models is unmistakable. With this in mind, let us now turn to the funerary art of western Mexico.

Apart from the already-mentioned non-naturalistic effigies whose inspiration lies in largely conjectural myth, if we examine West Mexican art as a whole, and especially the architectural models and figurine groups from Nayarit, what strikes us—indeed, what made this art especially attractive to Western collectors from the very beginning—is its high degree of realism, or naturalism. If we look to the Han Dynasty for analogy, it is immediately apparent that here, too, apart from chimeral or non-ordinary effigies with obviously supernatural meaning, funerary art consists of more or less faithful replications of living things and living beings, just as tools and other artifacts are, in form at least, analogous to those employed by the living.

As Hentze observes, it can hardly be otherwise. For that which is assigned to the dead belongs in a very real sense to the visible, not the invisible, world. There is no intrinsic difference between the representability of that world which serves the spirit of the deceased and that of daily intercourse among the living. In Hentze's view this phenomenon of representability constitutes an essential optical bridge, as it were, a

Fig. 6 *An old ritual yarn cross or* tsikúri *(erroneously rendered as "eye of god" by Lumholtz) in the* xiriki *on the* rancho *of Colás, the most prestigious* mara'akáme, *or shaman, of the territorial* comunidad *of San Andrés Cohamiata, Nayarit. The* tsikúri *is a multiple symbol embodying the conception of the four-directional universe and the sacred center; it is exclusively a magically-protective device for children, with the string referring to the "life thread" that holds the essential life force to the fontanelle. Structurally, however, it is indistinguishable from the* tüwe, *or "jaguar," which functions as a kind of spirit trap or barrier designed to keep the recent dead from re-entering the community of the living at inopportune times; when the dead are ritually invited, as in the case of certain ceremonies, no such barriers are placed in their path from the west, the direction of their chthonic "village."* Photo by the author.

bridge that connects the dead ancestors with their living kin. Without such an optical bridge a chasm would open up between them. And this must never be, for it would bar the essential continuity of all experiential phenomena and all ideas that arise therefrom. As in life, a man can cope properly only with the familiar, so in death can he deal only with that which he knows from daily use.

So, too, must it be with the houses of the dead—the dwellings of the soul. They may be literal replicas, or they may be symbolic combinations, or they may be reduced to elementary essentials, as in the Chinese ancestor tablets that ultimately derive from house models (significantly, the Chinese character *tsu*, with its primary meaning of ancestor, or forebear, consists of a simplified picture of a hut). Or their structural and symbolic elements may be differently ordered in space in accordance with symbolic rather than ordinary "reality." But they must always remain what they are—familiar houses.

The same applies to the gods. They may be chimeras, or they may appear as men or women; they may be composed of different phenomena selected from the natural environment, or they may combine the features of men and animals, real or mythic. But, however the different life forms are fused, these combinations must ultimately not diverge too far from optical perception or recognition. If there are spirits, writes Hentze, one must know how they appear and why they look just this way and no other. So the gods, like people, things, and events, are subject to certain laws: they cannot be different from the attributes ascribed to them by the living, with every element assigned its specific and familiar meaning, shared equally by the dead and their living kinfolk.

Now, rather than discuss individual figurines that might lend themselves to ethnographic analogy, or that might, by virtue of their more or less standardized replication over time and space, be better understood as generic effigies of particular gods or divine ancestors rather than as ordinary folk, I want to examine a few specific aspects of some architectural and group effigies, to see whether and how these relate to Mexican and Chinese funerary cosmology.

Anyone familiar with indigenous architecture in western Mexico, especially in regions less exposed than others to foreign styles and materials, will immediately recognize its basic similarity to the typical house model from ancient Nayarit, particularly that with a shed roof sloping downward at a relatively steep angle from a center ridgepole. A ceramic model of the Huichol or Cora house, for example, with its thatch roof and walls—depending on locally available materials—of wattle and daub, loosely laid stone, or, less commonly, sun-dried adobe brick, would not appear structurally very different from archaeological models of the four-walled, windowless, single door type. What would mainly differentiate it would be its lack of any painted or other external decoration of the kind that distinguishes the terra-cotta effigy dwellings. Unless we are to assume that the huts of prehispanic inhabitants were customarily covered from ridgepole to ground with painted symbols, the archaeological models seem unlikely to be completely literal transcriptions of their full-size prototypes.

Even the model houses with only one or two walls and/or free-standing poles have their counterparts in Huichol architecture—not, however, in the ordinary dwelling, but, rather, in temporary, ramada-type god-houses erected only for a specific ceremony, for which event they may serve the elder or shaman and his wife in their preparation of ritual foods and other ceremonial paraphernalia.

We may recall the earlier reference to a more traditional type of Huichol god-house,

Fig. 7 *Complex effigy sculpture in buff clay that could be interpreted as representing the great mythic world tree and below it the "village of the dead." Its precise origin is unknown; stylistically it is intermediate between Nayarit and the southern half of the shaft-and-chamber-tomb area of western Mexico (southern Jalisco and Nayarit). See the text for a discussion of the symbolism of this significant tomb sculpture. Height, 28 cm.* Photo courtesy of the American Museum of Natural History, New York.

with four corner posts and a pyramidal four-sided roof. These follow the pattern established in the mythic first times by the old God of Fire, "Grandfather," when he put the universe in order. They represent, in microcosm, the "world house" with its celestial vault in the form of a sacred mountain, held up by the trees of the cardinal points. Archaeological models resembling just this kind of sacred architecture of the Huichol do, in fact, exist, both as free-standing structures on slabs and as part of larger architectural assemblages of up to four houses, arranged in the form of a cross, the four-directional cosmic symbol. In the latter case they are sometimes differentiated from the more common shed-roof type also by different painted decoration, e.g., horizontal wavy lines in place of the series of rhomboid or upended squares that resemble the Huichol thread-cross motif.

It seems to me that we cannot ignore such deliberate differentiation. Clearly the perfectly square house with its pyramidal roof is of a different order than the house with horizontal ridgepole roof. The resemblance of the former to the cosmic model of the Huichol—itself reflecting the pan-Mesoamerican image of the celestial vault supported by the trees of the world directions—suggests that this type of hut may in fact be a god-house or temple; in other words, precisely the sacred architecture that supposedly cannot be recognized by us. With Lumholtz, I am convinced that there is no such thing as a meaningless design in "primitive art," so we may safely dismiss as unlikely any possibility that, in this case, the choice of roof type was accidental or arbitrary and thus has no particular significance. On the contrary, if nothing else, the symmetrical juxtaposition of the two kinds of roof and their different decoration in some of these house groups argues persuasively in favor of conformity to established norms.

The American Museum of Natural History has an interesting Nayarit village model (Fig. 7) that illustrates the symbolic aspects of this kind of conjunction particularly well. In this terra-cotta model four little houses, of which one facing pair has the pyramidal roof and the other the horizontal ridgepole-type roof, border a circular slab crowded with many little people engaged in apparently "everyday" activities, such as cooking and eating (which, as we have already noted, may not be such "ordinary" exercises after all). From the center of the slab rises a gigantic tree with two tiers of branches at the top that are arranged in the form of two superimposed crosses. Each arm of these crosses ends in a horizontal bar, so that it somewhat resembles the St. Anthony's or *tau* cross (so named because it resembles the Greek capital letter T). The crown of this curiously stylized tree is truly enormous, extending far beyond the little village below. The four arms of the upper cross are pointed more or less directly across the four huts, those of the lower approximately between them. At the apex of the crown sits a very large bird, perhaps an eagle, and numerous smaller birds and two unidentifiable animals are perched along its branches.[3] The four little huts and the people are of approximately equal height, with the exception of one very much larger male individual who wears a tall, pointed headdress and gestures toward the tree.

The iconography of the sculpture as a whole, the relative proportions of its different elements and, above all, the relationship between the two superimposed cruciforms that make up the crown and the four-directional arrangement of the houses below, all combine persuasively to suggest that this is something other than just a bucolic scene of village life. I would interpret it rather, in the light of what we know of pre-Hispanic and contemporary indigenous cosmology, as a representation of the great world tree, the *axis mundi*, standing at the center of the universe, its roots anchored in the underworld, its celestial branches covered with mantic birds and pointing in the cardinal and intercardinal directions. The four houses stand for the four quarters of the world, perhaps as dwellings of their ruling supernaturals. The symbolism is likely to be multi-referential, of course, so that the village with its feasting inhabitants can also be the chthonic counterpart of the *rancho* of the living. In that case, the largest figure might be that of a shaman, come to visit the deceased in their village at the very center of the underworld, perhaps in his role as psychopomp, or soul guide, escorting the spirit of the deceased, or seeking to retrieve and return it to the world of the living (as in the well-known and widely distributed American Indian Orpheus tradition, in which both the Cora and Huichol share in several known versions). It should be noted here that the American Museum's "world-tree" model is not the only one of its kind, though it may well be the most elaborate in public or private collections.

In the present context perhaps the most interesting type of Nayarit architectural effigy is the house of two levels (Figs. 8–10). Many of the single-house models are, in fact, of that type. On the face of it, two-story dwellings with only a single room above and one below would seem to make little sense, whether in terms of practicality, the

3. The symbolism of the great tree with birds perched on its spreading branches—repeated in several other examples from West Mexico—also reminds one of a rather widespread motif in archaic Siberian shamanism. Among others, the Goldi, Dolgan, and Tungus believe that, "before birth, the souls of children perch like little birds on the branches of the Cosmic Tree and the shamans go there to find them" (Eliade 1964: 272). This belief is closely related to the concept of the world tree, or *axis mundi*, rising as a kind of reservoir of souls from the navel of the earth mother (i.e., the underworld). Such beliefs would of course not conflict with the interpretation in these pages. In any event, the association of birds with a world tree, or trees, is well documented for pre-Hispanic Mesoamerica. The Huichol Indians also sometimes speak of the souls of unborn children as birds; likewise, children are magically transformed into birds in the shaman's chants during the Drum and Squash ceremonies held in the fall to introduce children to the tradition of the primordial peyote quest and its itinerary.

Fig. 8 *Polychrome Nayarit house model of the type generally described as a "two-story dwelling." Height, 47 cm. Four individuals are seated within the two-walled house, three others in front of it. Below, two individuals are seated inside a rectangular entrance to an enclosed chamber, flanked by a symmetrical five-stepped stairway, somewhat resembling the outlines of a five-level pyramidal temple platform. The roof of the house above and the facade below are covered with a repetitive design resembling the Huichol yarn cross, or* tsikúri *(see Fig. 6), which, in one form, functions as a protective symbol for children and, in another, as a spirit trap or barrier for the dead, in which case it is called* tüwe, *"jaguar," by some Huichol.* The Minneapolis Institute of Arts. Photo courtesy of Alfred Stendahl.

Fig. 9 *Nayarit house model of reddish clay, with white-on-red decoration. Height, 32 cm. Note the structural similarity to the "two-story house" in Figure 8, including the symmetrical five-stepped stairway flanking the rectangular entrance of the lower dwelling.* Collection of William P. Palmer, III, Portland, Maine. Photo by the author.

Fig. 10 *Ceramic model of a Nayarit house standing atop what is interpreted here not as the ground floor of a two-story village dwelling but rather as the symbolic chthonic dwelling of the dead, the essential counterpart of the house of the living above ground. Buff clay with red, black, and buff paint. Height, 33.5 cm. Figurine groups above and below include ten persons, as well as a parrot and a dog, the latter an important figure in funerary mythology and symbolism among most Mesoamerican peoples and other indigenous populations of the New World (as it was also in the Old World). Parrots or macaws were likewise of great ritual significance. At least one of the individuals on the stairway appears to be intoxicated and grieving; under aboriginal conditions drinking and intoxication were, and are today, always connected with ceremony. So, for example, heavy drinking is an essential element of funerals as well as other rituals among the contemporary Huichol populations in Nayarit.* Collection of Dr. and Mrs. Robert Kuhn, Los Angeles. Photo by the author.

need for shelter in a digging-stick type of subsistence economy, the settlement pattern that can be assumed for early western Mexico on the basis of the archaeological evidence, or the kinds of materials or customary architectural technology that are suggested by the majority of the house models themselves. Certainly, even today, two-story dwellings are hardly typical for indigenous communities, and free-standing two-story houses of the kind depicted in the models, constructed of wattle and daub or adobe bricks, would not only be completely impractical but would expose their owners to the twin risks of physical injury from collapse and the envy and numerous subtle and overt pressures that individual ostentation so often invites in traditional communities. Multi-story apartment houses of sun-dried and plastered bricks are characteristic, of course, of traditional Pueblo architecture, but these are to some degree environmentally determined and, in any event, conceived very differently from the type of two-level house here under consideration.

Apart from a few rare complex (and, like many of these rather fragile terra-cotta sculptures, often considerably repaired or reconstructed) models, the two-story or two-level effigy dwelling typically consists of but two chambers, one above the other. The lower chamber is enclosed by four walls, with a rectangular entrance at the front or back, and a ceiling that forms the living floor of the main dwelling above. Upper and lower rooms are generally occupied by individuals engaged in what appear to be "everyday" activities; sometimes one or more occupants of the lower level are curled up on their sides, as though resting or sleeping.

Usually, but not in every case, the two levels are connected by an exterior stairway, or, more rarely, two stairways that rise from either side of the entrance to the lower level. Although the number of steps seems to vary somewhat, five and seven predominate by far; in any event, I cannot agree with von Winning (1972: 19) that the number of steps is "irrelevant," even if the modeling is, as he says, often careless. I know of no traditional culture in which numbers are irrelevant, and especially not in a symbolic context, into which category funerary sculpture certainly fits. The Huichol carry this "numbers game" so far that, in ceremonial art, and sometimes even in its folk art derivations, as also in the oral literature, the natural order is often modified to conform to the sacred number five (e.g., "the five-pointed deer," five-ribbed peyote cactus, five colors of maize or of peyote, five corn maidens, five hundred as a metaphor for any large number, etc.).

The most common functional explanation in the literature for these anomalous two-story structures is that they are status dwellings for village chiefs (Meighan and Nicholson 1970: 30; von Winning 1972: 19). Lack of archaeological evidence for real houses of this type, or of any comparable type of aboriginal house in present-day Indian communities, does not, of course, constitute proof that no such two-story structures existed prehistorically. Likewise, there could have been social or ritual status differentiation of a kind that required such unusual houses. In the view of the same authors, small terra-cotta models of a personage seated, palanquinlike, in a covered chair, with or without bearers, indicate precisely "the deference awarded to high ranking persons" (von Winning 1972: 27).

Huichol iconography suggests at least one alternate explanation for the Colima "chiefs in palanquins," without necessarily disproving their existence. As mentioned, in Huichol cosmology the gods are provided with seats that are identical in all respects, excepting size, to the shaman's *'uwéni*. In ritual processions their images are carried about in these chairs, just as, in mythic "first times," a special chair was made for the newborn Sun Father, so that he might be lifted into the sky by the people to take his proper course at the proper distance from the earth (and just as, for that matter, the saints are still carried about in solemn religious pageantry). Might the "palanquins" or litters be archaeological prototypes for the "god chairs" of today?

A curious votive terra-cotta of Huichol origin suggests something on that order (Fig. 11). It depicts two men, wearing the characteristic Huichol hats and holding their hands stretched out in front of them, seated on a raised, four-legged platform under a rounded canopy. Although the style is different, the whole effect is strikingly like the so-called "chieftain on palanquin" terra-cottas from Colima, especially those lacking bearers. The men's faces are decorated with the yellow *uxa* paint that belongs to the peyote tradition, and tiny, colored beads adhere to bits of beeswax in the palms of their hands. There is yellow vegetable paint also on the canopy. The effigy was said to have been found in a sacred cave in the Sierra; it reached me by way of a Mexican doctor, who, in turn, received it from a Huichol in payment for medicine. There is no doubt of its Huichol manufacture, nor of its connection with the peyote tradition. My Huichol informants thought that it represented either a prayer offering for a safe peyote quest by two individuals, or else the Fire God, as leader of the peyote hunt, and his first assistant, seated in an unfamiliar type of *'uwéni*.

In any event, the fact that the Huichol place their gods on special chairs has its counterpart in the social universe *only* in relation to shamanism and the "non-ordinary" power that adheres to the shaman. Such "chiefs" as there are (elders, headmen of *ranchos*, governors of *comunidades*) are certainly respected, but their authority depends on their proven wisdom and on consensus. Furthermore, they are often just as poor as, and sometimes poorer than, their fellows; they live in the same kinds of thatched huts as everyone else; and such chairs as are theirs—mainly by virtue of their status as shamans—are the somewhat flimsy *'uwéni* they fashion themselves from materials prescribed in mythic times by the first shaman, the God of Fire. Certainly they would never dream of being carried about or even treated with particular deference,

Fig. 11 *Huichol votive offering of buff clay depicting two individuals within an* 'uwéni *(ceremonial chair of shamans and supernaturals), represented in the form of a sacred cave. A Huichol informant interpreted the figures as peyote pilgrims, as indicated by yellow* uxa *paint decoration on their faces; most likely, he thought, they were the leader of a peyote pilgrimage in his identity as* Tatewarí, *"Our Grandfather," the Fire God and First Shaman who originated the peyote rites, accompanied by his principal assistant. Height, 11.5 cm. The egalitarian Huichol Indians lack status roles requiring chiefly litters, but the* 'uwéni *as the seat of sacred power is an essential element of shamanistic beliefs, practices, and cosmology. So, for example, at the First Shaman's direction the newborn Sun (Our Father) is carried across the sky on an* 'uwéni *after he first emerges from the earth's womb in a great volcanic eruption.* Collection of the author, Delmar, New York. Photo by the author.

whatever their authority. I might add that while Zuni mythology tells of a litter in which the blind Kiaklo, the myth-bearer, was borne to the Lake of the Underworld on his quest to receive the great store of tales for the people in the Upperworld, Zuni social structure is wholly lacking in the kind of status roles that would require chiefly palanquins or litters.

Admittedly, none of this rules out exalted chieftainship in the shaft-tomb cultures. It is even conceivable that chieftainship developed to the point where, as in Polynesia, chiefs could have been imbued with so much *mana* that they had to be carried, lest their very footsteps contaminate the ground. Given what we know of Mesoamerica, and especially village culture, however, that seems doubtful at best. In any event, I am convinced that the standard interpretation of apparently two-storied house models in terms of social differentiation is much too literal and one-dimensional.

Instead, I would suggest that they can be understood, by analogy to ancient China and the contemporary but strongly traditional Huichol, as cosmic models that translate into three-dimensional, architectural form the essential unity between the house of the living above, and the house of the dead below, as two complementary halves of the total universe.

The steps that connect upper and lower house also cannot be taken literally. Whatever the number of steps, I suggest that they have their analogy in the symbolic "soul ladder" the Hopi place into, or beside, the grave of deceased kin[4] to enable them to climb out whenever the living require assistance (such as rain for their maize crop) or, on a different level of complexity, in the well-known "soul duct" that connects the Temple of the Inscriptions at Palenque with the magnificent subterranean crypt below. Indeed, at least some shaft-and-chamber tombs in Nayarit have ducts leading to the surface from the roof of the burial chamber which the local people call *claraboyas*, "portholes," and which I suggested some years ago might have been soul ducts connecting the living with their dead (Furst n.d.: 269ff.).

Needless to say, the concept of an interdependent house of light and house of darkness constituting the essential unity and interchangeability between the living and the dead, or past and present, does not presuppose superimposition of these two "houses" in a literal sense. However, burial directly in the living floor was commonly practiced in many parts of Mesoamerica, presumably precisely for the reasons outlined by Hentze. Whether many shaft-and-chamber tombs had houses over them is not known. Tomb

4. It is noteworthy that traditional Hopi burials, as described, for example, by Don C. Talayesva in *Sun Chief: The Autobiography of a Hopi* (1942), bear a marked resemblance to shaft-and-chamber tombs, although on a considerably reduced scale.

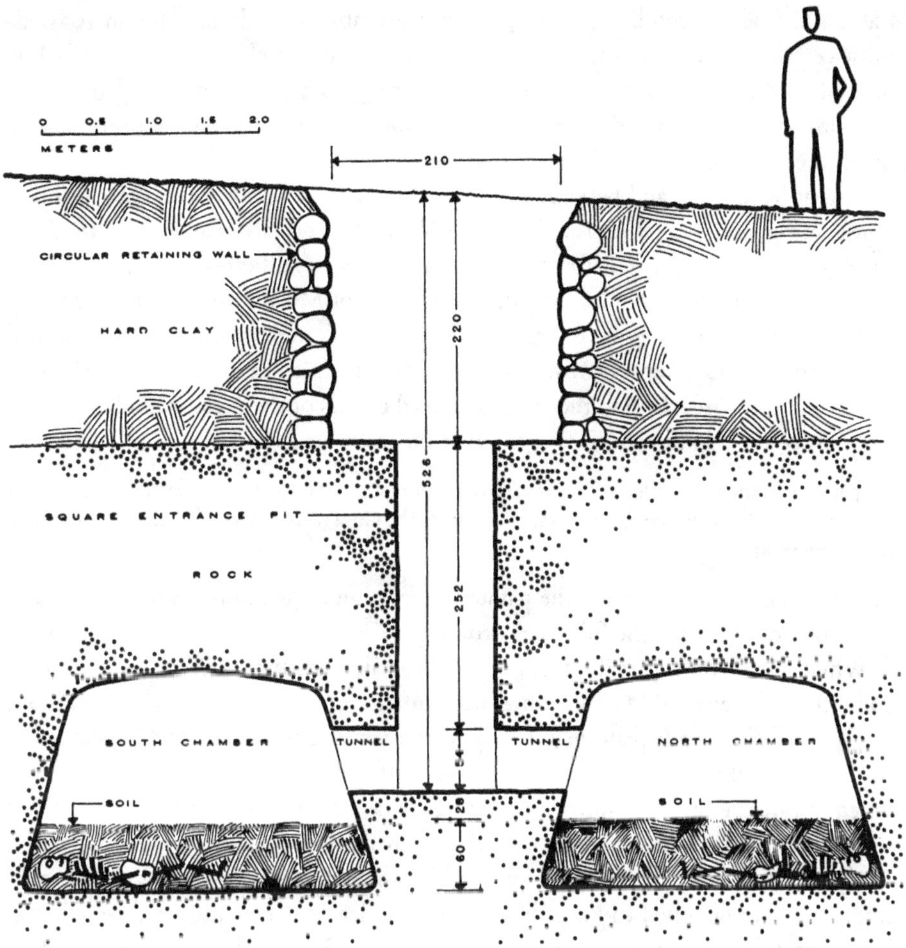

Fig. 12 *Diagram of Tomb I, Las Cebollas, near Tequilita, Nayarit, a two-chambered shaft tomb similar to many others found in western Mexico. The retaining wall of unworked stone above the vertical entrance shaft leading to the subterranean chambers may have been part of, or supported, a dwelling or other structure.* Drawing by Diego Delgado (after Furst n.d.: Fig. 1a).

I at Las Cebollas, Tequilita, Nayarit, which I was able to study in detail in 1965, almost certainly had some structure above its entrance, which was located in a low mound with remains of crude stone walls that suggested an ancient foundation (Fig. 12). However, in general, the evidence that people lived directly over or near many of these tombs is slight.

That at least some, and perhaps all, Nayarit terra-cotta house models are meant as houses of the dead—the *locus mundi* of the soul—and as such are analogous to the miniature houses the Maya Indians of Yucatán and Chiapas still erect on graves in their cemeteries (and also, I would suggest, to the reliefs of Maya dwellings depicted over many of the doorways in the so-called Nunnery Quadrangle at Uxmal), is suggested also by the rhomboid crosses with which some of them are decorated. Von Winning (1972: 17) compares these to the magical thread crosses of the Huichol and Cora. On the basis of their similarity he suggests that the rhomboid cross,

> . . . painted on the walls and roof of Nayarit house models, served as a magical symbol to protect the dwellings and their occupants from harm, since the Cora formerly lived in the region where the house models now occur.

In von Winning's view, then, the painted decoration on the house models replicates protective designs on their full-sized prototypes.

While the analogy may be valid as to external form and, if Preuss was right in connecting the ancestral Cora with shaft-tomb art, also as to historical connections, it is nevertheless inadequate in relation to the actual complexity of Cora-Huichol thread-cross symbolism and, by extension, to this motif in funerary art. It is only when we recall the two different, but nevertheless complementary, functions of thread crosses among the Huichol—on the one hand the protective *tsikúri* used exclusively for children up to the age of five, and, on the other, the *tüwe*, or jaguar, as spirit trap or barrier designed to keep dead souls from leaving their proper dwelling and bothering the living at inopportune times—that the rhomboid decorations on effigy houses take on meaning.[5]

A two-story model in the Milwaukee Public Museum is of special interest in this connection (Fig. 13). Here a single large rhomboid symbol (instead of the more com-

5. Provided, of course, that thread crosses have more or less retained their basic functions since prehistoric times. Interestingly enough, Professor Stephan Beyer recently informed me that thread crosses have a similar dual and complementary function also in Tibetan mortuary ritual. The wide distribution in time and space of extraordinarily similar thread crosses with—insofar as these are known—basically similar meanings in the Old World and the New suggests, at the very least, great antiquity. Even the Australian aborigines, who have no spinning or weaving, fashion magical objects of basically similar form with thread made of human hair and other materials.

Fig. 13 *Ceramic house model from Nayarit, buff clay with black-on-white decoration. Height, 18 cm. Note the* tsikúri-*like decoration above the rectangular lower chamber entrance, in which a dog—the classic chthonic guardian—is resting. Flanking the doorway are symmetrical pyramidal stairways of seven steps each; the facade is decorated with vertical wavy lines that might symbolize rain (among the Huichol, rain is a function of the Earth Mothers who are symbolized by snakes; among the Hopi and other Southwestern Pueblos, the dead function as bringers of life-giving rain). In connection with the stairways, it should be noted that not all upper and lower dwellings in the so-called "two-story models" are in fact so connected; see, for example, Figures 21 and 25 in the catalogue of the "Anecdotal Sculpture of Ancient West Mexico" exhibition sponsored by the Ethnic Arts Council of Los Angeles at the Los Angeles County Museum of Natural History (1972).* Photo courtesy of the Milwaukee Public Museum.

mon multiple rows) is located directly over the entrance to the lower floor. In the middle of the passage lies a dog—the chthonic guardian of the entrance to the underworld in Huichol and Cora, as well as in Aztec and innumerable other, funerary mythologies. On either side of the lower entrance are rows of vertical wavy lines, resembling the well-known Huichol (and Pueblo) lightning-rain snake. The upper house, which has solid walls only at either end but none in front or back, contains five seated individuals with food dishes in front of them. As a whole, this effigy house differs from other two-story examples in that, with its sloping sides, the lower half resembles less a lower floor than it does a platform mound with steps leading to the top at either side.

To recapitulate, the thread cross, erroneously called "eye of god," is far more complex than it would appear to be from the literature. On the one hand, it functions as *tsikúri*, the protective device or visual prayer meant exclusively for young children, who are thereby symbolically placed in the vortex of the universe, where the gods of the four directions may focus on it with their combined protective powers. In this case, the colored thread wound from the center outward on a pair of crossed sticks symbolizes the life thread by which the soul is attached to the crown of its head. On the other hand, the thread cross can be *tüwe*, jaguar, whose function it is to act as spirit trap or barrier, to keep the dead from upsetting the re-established equilibrium until such time as their actual presence among the living is desired. As in all such instances, these functions are not mutually exclusive but are complementary.

It is the *context*, then, in which we encounter the thread-cross symbol that can suggest its essential function. Its presence on funerary-house models indicates that it is here employed not so much in imitation of magical decorations that might or might not have been painted on the houses of the living, but rather to keep, and at the same time also to protect, the souls of the dead in their proper dwelling. That dwelling is the subterranean house of darkness, the *locus mundi* of the soul.

But, whether in effigy as the lower floor of a terra-cotta model or as the womblike chamber at the bottom of a shaft in the maternal earth herself, the house of darkness is not separate from the house of light, but rather it constitutes only the complementary lower half of that essential unity and harmony between past and present, light and dark, the living and their antecedents, that we, with our culture-bound tunnel vision, so often naively reduce to the level of a "cult of the dead."

DIFFUSION VS. INDEPENDENT ORIGINS

The analogies outlined in the preceding pages between funerary ideology in ancient China, on the one hand, and prehistoric and recent Indian Mexico, on the other, obviously bear on the question of Chinese origins or inspiration for the terra-cotta house and village scenes from Nayarit. Most recently this issue was raised in print by von Winning (1969; 1972: 28).

To the best of my knowledge, the problem was first publicly discussed by Gordon Ekholm of the American Museum of Natural History, who over the years has amassed a considerable body of data to support his case for trans-Pacific relationships and diffusion at various times before the Conquest. Ekholm (personal communication) was struck, as was I, by the parallels, first of all, between the basic concept of modeling house effigies of clay and interring them with the dead in China and Nayarit, and, secondly, by the similarities between at least some of the terra-cotta house or village effigy sculptures of the Han Dynasty and those of western Mexico. In 1963 the case appeared considerably strengthened with the publication in mainland China of new archaeological discoveries from Yunnan province, especially Dongson-style bronze vessel covers with lively three-dimensional scenes of ceremonial life that were somewhat reminiscent of the more complex and crowded multi-house terra-cotta models from Nayarit. Neither Ekholm nor I published our theories, limiting ourselves to raising the issue in lectures and informal discussion, in the hope that other data might come to light to support a case for diffusion.

Ten years later the similarities are still striking, but I have nevertheless come to doubt increasingly that the Nayarit effigy houses really derive from Asian prototypes —not only because it seems unlikely that, had there been an early Chinese landfall in Nayarit, only this one trait should have been locally adopted, and in only one restricted inland area at that, but because the replication in funerary art of daily life and architecture, domestic or otherwise, is as consistent with indigenous Mesoamerican cosmology as it is with its Chinese equivalent.

Needless to say, this does not rule out trans-Pacific contacts, for which not only Ekholm but several other serious scholars have established what must be regarded as an increasingly sophisticated and less and less easily refuted case. Nor does it answer why effigies of group activity, which are common to all western Mexico, should have evolved into such elaborate forms only in Nayarit. On the other hand, we should not overlook the fact that, notwithstanding the basic similarities that allow us to speak loosely of a pan-West-Mexican shaft-and-chamber-tomb culture, there are, nevertheless, within this generalized complex not only a number of distinct art styles, but also localized motifs that seem to reflect, if not a different basic ideology, at least different emphases and different lineage, clan, or tribal traditions.

Also, the archaeological evidence available to us is obviously incomplete. It is not at all impossible that replicas of houses and group activities were made, outside what is now Nayarit, with perishable materials, notwithstanding the high development of the potter's art in these areas. In Melanesia, for example, the house models that serve as repositories for ancestor skulls are constructed of the same perishable materials as their large-size prototypes in domestic architecture, even though ceramics are regularly made and used. No trace of perishable objects has been reported from West Mexican tombs, but that is hardly surprising in view of weather and soil conditions and the scandalously unscientific circumstances under which most funerary art has been excavated. The Huichol and other peoples fashion ephemeral effigies of the living world not only of straw or wood but of dough; and, at least in Michoacán, an apparently old tradition of making complex straw images of people, animals, houses, and even group scenes has survived, not just as folk art for sale to tourists but as religious artifacts.

New data supporting diffusion may, of course, turn up in western Mexico, but, in its absence, it is probably best to ascribe the admittedly striking conceptual parallels to basically similar beliefs about the interdependence and complementarity of the living and their ancestral dead, and, above all, about the house as *locus mundi* of the soul.

POSTSCRIPT

After the present paper was completed, I came across the following quotation from a Hopi informant in Alexander M. Stephen's *Hopi Journal* (1936, 1: 150–1) which, it seems to me, virtually clinches my interpretation of two-story house models from Nayarit and the relationship of house models to beliefs about the underworld in general:

> Masau wûh [the dualistic Hopi god of death, Upper- and Underworld, fire, etc.] has a two story house underground. . . . Masau' is death. The graveyard is Masau's kiva, Maski. The surface we see is the roof of the second [lower] story, we will not see the interior till we die. . . . The grave is the entrance to Maski, the dead go to the lower stage or story where the houses are as those we live in. The plan of the house was brought from the interior (underworld) and what is called dying is a return to the early house; men and women follow their usual avocations there.

Finally, while in Mexico in the summer of 1974, my wife, Dee, and I learned of the death of an old and respected friend, Colás, the charismatic senior *mara'akáme* of San Andrés Cohamiáta. One night in 1967, Colás had taken me into his *xiriki*, where he removed from an arrow stuck into the roof thatch the reconstituted skeletal soul of his own shaman-father and placed it, in its material manifestation as a small rock crystal, into my hands, to hold for a few moments. It was his way of teaching.

Though a traditionalist to the core, Colás was buried not in a cave, as used to be

Huichol custom. Instead, as he had requested a few days before his death, his relatives dug a nine-foot shaft into the dirt floor of his house and placed him at the bottom. They filled the shaft and sealed it, and then, with cement purchased for the purpose in Tepic, Nayarit, they reinforced the walls of the little hut, so that, as one of them told me later, "Colás will always live there in his house, below and above. So that his *kupúri* will have its place." His people, too, now have their house of two levels.

Since then, my wife herself has died in an auto accident. She always preferred the Huichol way of dealing with death to our own, and her contribution to this study, as to all our work in Mesoamerica, is considerable. It is to her memory that this paper is dedicated.

BIBLIOGRAPHY

Beals, Ralph L.

1943 Northern Mexico and the Southwest. *In* El Norte de México y el Sur de Estados Unidos: Tercera Reunión de Mesa Redonda sobre Problemas Antropológicos de México y Centro América, pp. 191–199. Sociedad Mexicana de Antropología, Mexico.

Eliade, Mircea

1964 Shamanism: Archaic Techniques of Ecstasy. (Trans. by Willard R. Trask.) *Bollingen Series LXXVI.* Pantheon Books, New York.

Furst, Peter T.

1965 West Mexican Tomb Sculpture as Evidence for Shamanism in Prehispanic Mesoamerica. *Antropológica,* no. 15, pp. 29–80. Instituto Caribe de Antropología y Sociología, Fundación La Salle de Ciencias Naturales, Caracas.

1967 Huichol Conceptions of the Soul. *Folklore Americas,* vol. xxvii, no. 2, pp. 39–106. Center for the Study of Comparative Folklore and Mythology, University of California, Los Angeles.

1973 West Mexican Art: Secular or Sacred? *In* The Iconography of Middle American Sculpture, pp. 98–133. The Metropolitan Museum of Art, New York.

1974 Ethnographic Analogy in the Interpretation of West Mexican Art. *In* The Archaeology of West Mexico (Betty Bell, ed.), pp. 132–146. Sociedad de Estudios Avanzados del Occidente de México, A.C., Ajijic, Jalisco.

n.d. Shaft Tombs, Shell Trumpets and Shamanism: A Culture Historical Approach to Problems in West Mexican Archaeology. Unpublished doctoral dissertation, Department of Anthropology, University of California. Los Angeles, 1966.

HENTZE, CARL

1961 Das Haus als Weltort der Seele: ein Beitrag zur Seelensymbolik in China, Grossasien, Altamerika. Ernst Klett Verlag, Stuttgart.

KELLY, ISABEL

1974 Stirrup Pots from Colima: Some Implications. *In* The Archaeology of West Mexico (Betty Bell, ed.), pp. 206–211. Sociedad de Estudios Avanzados del Occidente de México, A.C., Ajijic, Jalisco.

LINNÉ, SIGVALD

1960 The Art of Mexico and Central America. *In* The Art of Ancient America: Civilizations of Central and South America (H. D. Disselhoff and S. Linné), pp. 13–134. Crown Publishers, Inc., New York.

LOS ANGELES COUNTY MUSEUM OF NATURAL HISTORY

1972 Anecdotal Sculpture of Ancient West Mexico (Hasso von Winning and Olga Hammer). Exhibition sponsored by the Ethnic Arts Council of Los Angeles at the Natural History Museum of Los Angeles County.

LUMHOLTZ, CARL

1900 Symbolism of the Huichol Indians. *Memoirs of the American Museum of Natural History*, vol. III, Anthropology II. New York.

1903 Unknown Mexico. 2 vols. Macmillan and Co., Limited, London.

MEIGHAN, CLEMENT W., and H. B. NICHOLSON

1970 The Ceramic Mortuary Offerings of Prehistoric West Mexico: An Archaeological Perspective. *In* Sculpture of Ancient West Mexico: Nayarit, Jalisco, Colima; the Proctor Stafford Collection, pp. 17–32. Los Angeles County Museum of Art.

PREUSS, KONRAD THEODOR

1912 Die Nayarit-Expedition: Textaufnahmen und Beobachtungen unter mexikanischen Indianern. Erster Band: Die Religion der Cora-Indianer. Druck und Verlag von B. G. Teubner, Leipzig.

STEPHEN, ALEXANDER M.

1936 Hopi Journal (Elsie Clews Parsons, ed.). 2 vols. *Columbia University Contributions to Anthropology*, vol. XXIII. Columbia University Press, New York.

TALAYESVA, DON C.

1942 Sun Chief: The Autobiography of a Hopi Indian (Leo W. Simmons, ed.). The Institute of Human Relations and Yale University Press, New Haven.

VON WINNING, HASSO

1969 Ceramic House Models and Figurine Groups from Nayarit. *In* Verhandlungen des XXXVIII. Internationalen Amerikanistenkongresses, Stuttgart-München, 12. bis 18. August 1968, vol. I, pp. 129–132. Kommissionsverlag Klaus Renner, München.

1972 Ceramic House Models and Figurine Groups Mounted on Slabs. *In* Anecdotal Sculpture of Ancient West Mexico (Hasso von Winning and Olga Hammer), pp. 17–30. Exhibition sponsored by the Ethnic Arts Council of Los Angeles at the Natural History Museum of Los Angeles County.

Post-Classic Mexican Death Imagery as a Sign of Cyclic Completion

CECELIA F. KLEIN

OAKLAND UNIVERSITY

THE importance of death in Post-Classic Mexican culture has long been noted; indeed, the prevalence of references to death and human sacrifice in Aztec art and literature has helped to gain for that people in particular a notoriety bordering on infamy. The Aztecs, it has been said, were a people obsessed with death, a people who forsook their reason in an ever-growing fanatical preoccupation with the ritual sacrifice of human lives. So important was the death cult in Aztec culture that the Post-Classic world view in general has been deemed obsessive and irrational. Such a people, as prevalent opinion would have it, could not have conceived of a coherent cosmos in which each god and creature had a logical place. This opinion has been supported by most modern studies of Post-Classic cosmology which reveal numerous seemingly unrelated concepts of space and time as confusing to the modern mind as the innumerable deities whose functions and attributes both conflict and overlap. Within such a framework the presumed irrationality of the Post-Classic death cult is indeed tenable.

Given this prevailing belief that Post-Classic Mexicans were incapable of rationalizing their universe, however, a specific group of Post-Classic death images deserves special notice, for these images manifest an inter-relationship and function, the nature of which, under examination, implies a remarkably coherent view of the cosmos. The conceptual patterns which emerge from this study render sensible many of the seemingly chaotic aspects of Post-Classic cosmology, including that of the diverse notions of time and space and their relation to specific members of the Mexican pantheon. Within this new cosmological framework, moreover, the infamous death cult is seen as resting on a highly rational cosmological base. Death and death imagery, in this case, become, not indicators of a chaotic concept of time and space, but rather the very opposite—indicators of a unified and consistent cosmic system.

Those death images which shed light on these perpetual problems exclusively represent deities. As is to be expected, the Aztec death god Mictlantecuhtli and his female consort, Mictecacíhuatl, are among them. However, it is instructive that Mictlantecuhtli is by no means the most important or most prevalent of the deities represented; he is in fact merely a relative or lesser variant of a far more pivotal deity, the female earth monster Tlaltecuhtli.

There are numerous Post-Classic images of Tlaltecuhtli, most of them two-dimensional and all of them depicting the goddess *en face*, that is, with her face and body directly confronting those of the viewer. In two-dimensional Post-Classic Mexican art, *en face* images are ordinarily extremely rare. The deity's form is thus invariably what is more commonly referred to in art historical jargon as "frontal," although she is typically depicted with her back to the viewer, her head upturned, in what might better be described as a dorsal view. What often reads for the modern viewer as the disconcerting loincloth of a male (e.g., Nicholson 1967: 85–6) is actually a cloth panel which decorates the back of the monster's skirt, as seen on the famous three-dimensional statue of Tlaltecuhtli's close relative, the definitely female earth goddess Coatlicue, in the Museo Nacional. Tlaltecuhtli further adopts the squatting posture assumed during native childbirth in which the legs are displayed and bent at the knees; so consistent is this posture among images of the female earth monster that Seler (1901–2: 103) identifies the pose as a major characteristic of that deity. Both her invariable frontal form and strictly feminine pose thus distinguish her clearly from the earth crocodile deity Cipactli, who was regarded as male and who always appears in profile form in two-dimensional Post-Classic images.

The female earth monster is relevant here because she is invariably accompanied by symbols of death. Monstrous profile faces with large teeth and round or ringed eyes—Mesoamerican signs of death (Thompson 1960: 45, 173; Seler 1904: 323; Seler 1963, I: 220)—typically adorn her joints and clawed extremities. Occasionally she carries Death's heads in her feet. Her skirt is often decorated with skulls and crossbones, as is that of her variant, Coatlicue, who further wears disembodied human hearts and hands, both symbols of death in Mesoamerica (Thompson 1960: 132). At times Coatlicue's head, like that of another of Tlaltecuhtli's variants, the Chichimec earth goddess Itzpapálotl, takes a human form with skeletal features. Both goddesses are frequently accompanied by spiders, scorpions, and other noxious creatures associated with the dead; both, like Tlaltecuhtli, frequently display a protruding tongue which takes the form of the flint knife used by Aztec priests to remove the hearts of sacrificial victims. Both protruding tongues and flint knives symbolized death (Proskouriakoff 1968: 248; Caso 1928: 34; Thompson 1960: 78). Because of their close relation to the female earth monster herself as the prime bearer of such symbols of death, moreover, both goddesses frequently adopt the *en face* dorsal form, displayed posture, and monstrous faces at the joints and clawed extremities which are diagnostic of that deity. So random is the distribution of these numerous elements among the three goddesses, in fact, that a precise identification is sometimes difficult. It appears that the deities were so closely related that their formal elements were fused and interchangeable.

As the principal Post-Classic Mexican representative of the earth itself, Tlaltecuhtli played a role of utmost importance. She was conceived of as a giant, reputedly amphibian, creature afloat in the center of a large ocean where her body formed the surface and bowels of the earth. Her upturned head, with wide open jaws, rested at the western horizon, her hind quarters presumably at the eastern horizon. All vegetation sprang from her body; thus she was the direct source of all life and its nourishment. As the archetype of fertility, birth, and nurture, she was logically conceived of as a female and a mother; such a concept accounts for the consistent appearance of the goddess in the displayed posture of parturition. Her sister-variant Coatlicue was regarded as the mother of the sun, the moon, and the stars, and was variously addressed as "our mother" and "mother mistress of the earth people" (Seler 1960–61, II: 1004–6). As Cihuacóatl, the "Mother Serpent," and the Chichimec earth goddess Itzpapálotl, she was patroness of the Cihuateteo, the souls of women dead in childbirth who escorted the descending sun to its daily setting in the west. Seler (1963, I: 121) described her close Huastec relative, Tlazoltéotl, as the "great parturient" ("la gran paridora"). Tlazoltéotl was further known as "Our Mother" and "Mother of the Gods," and was associated with sex, lust, fecundity, prostitution, and midwifery. Accordingly, Tlazoltéotl appears in the Aztec Codex Borbonicus, page 13, in the *en face* posture of delivery characteristic of Tlaltecuhtli and actually in the act of giving birth.

Tlaltecuhtli therefore clearly embodied the concept of fertility so important to an agrarian people. But the Mesoamerican belief that the bowels of the earth contained the underworld and the souls of the dead associated the goddess with death as well. In Mexican cosmography the entrance to the underworld lay in the west; here the female earth monster with her wide open jaws was believed to devour the setting planets and stars as well as the souls of dead humans. The dead descended from here to the navel of the monster at which was located Mictlán, the Aztec land of the dead, also known as *tlaxicco*, "the navel of the earth." Those who were to be reborn at the eastern horizon —the sun and the planet Venus, for example—apparently passed on to the deity's womb in the east. Death was therefore clearly a prerequisite for rebirth in such a system and Tlaltecuhtli herself required continual nourishment in the form of human hearts and blood. Individuals were frequently sacrificed in honor of her or her relatives to ensure the continuance of earthly life. The Codex Borbonicus image of Tlazoltéotl giving birth to the maize god, accordingly, portrays that goddess wearing the flayed skin of a victim sacrificed to increase the next crop. The appearance of death symbols on the great goddess of the earth is therefore explained by her function of receiving and housing the dead in exchange for the regeneration of life throughout time.

According to Aztec myth, Coatlicue cried out for her bloody repasts during the night (Seler 1960–61, IV: 13–15). The Cihuateteo were nocturnal creatures who not only escorted the setting sun to its daily demise in the west but also descended headfirst to the center of the earth at midnight on certain days of the year to foment trouble for children and pregnant women. Tlazoltéotl was as well a goddess of the moon and of earthquakes and as such was associated with nighttime and darkness. All of the numerous variants of the female earth monster were, in fact, creatures of darkness and night, affiliated with the stars and the moon and the hours of sunset and midnight.

Unlike her male counterpart, the earth crocodile Cipactli, who is invariably affiliated with the east in the Mexican calendar, Tlaltecuhtli is never associated with a specific world direction in the codices. We know only that her giant head was placed in the west, her womb apparently to the east. However, since the Mexicans arranged the five world directions in a sequence running east, north, west, south, and center, it follows that the monster's torso fell to the south and/or the center. It was at the goddess' navel that the dead encountered the land of the dead, Mictlán; and Mictlán, as Thompson (1934: 222–5) points out, was originally assigned to the south by the Aztecs. Durán (1964: 135–6) placed Coatlicue in the mythical land of Colhuacan, which was traditionally associated with the west, and Itzpapálotl governed the fifteenth week of the Mexican 260-day calendar under the day sign Calli (House), which according to Seler (1900–01: 108) symbolized "the dark house of the earth . . . the west." As Teteoinnan, Tlazoltéotl reigned in the mythic realm of Tamoanchan, "the house of descent," located in the west (Seler 1963, I: 106); as the goddess of earthquakes Tlalli iyollo, the "heart or center of the earth," and, as Ixcuina, a female consort of the death god Mictlantecuhtli at the "navel of the earth," she can further be associated with the southern and central world directions. Tlaltecuhtli and her sister-variants therefore all belonged to the west, the south, and/or the center of the universe, regions apparently associated in the Post-Classic Mexican mind with earth, darkness, fertility, and death.

The similarity and overlapping of the associations of the various earth goddesses surely accounts for the similarity and interchangeability of their forms and attributes in Post-Classic visual imagery. The remaining images in the group singled out for inspection here similarly display the characteristic iconographic features of the female earth goddess Tlaltecuhtli: all appear *en face*, several in dorsal form; those portrayed full-figure adopt the displayed female posture of childbirth; and most have monster faces at the joints and/or clawed extremities, large teeth, protruding tongues (one in the form of the sacrificial flint knife), round or ringed eyes, and other obvious references to death. Since the deities represented here also clearly adopt the diagnostic pose and attributes of Tlaltecuhtli, they, like Tlaltecuhtli's sister-variants, must bear a close conceptual relation to the female earth monster herself. It is an understanding of the nature of this relationship which makes possible the simplification and ordering of Post-Classic cosmology.

The Huastec earth goddess Tlazoltéotl, as noted earlier, appears in the Aztec Codex Borbonicus in the *en face* displayed form characteristic of Tlaltecuhtli; she appears many times elsewhere in the codices (e.g., Codex Borgia, page 74; Codex Vaticanus 3773, page 74) with frontal displayed body and profile head. Tlazoltéotl's relation to the female earth monster is evident; however, it is significant that she functioned primarily as a goddess of maize. According to legend she was the mother of the maize god Cinteotl, and Seler (1963, I: 121) regards her as a goddess of the mature maize crop. Tlazoltéotl therefore properly belongs to a separate category of Post-Classic deities whose specific function was to fertilize the crops. The intimate relation of such a role to that of the great female earth monster hardly need be expounded, and it can be no accident that every one of the major Post-Classic vegetation deities appears at least once in the two-dimensional art of the period in the *en face*, frequently displayed, form of Tlaltecuhtli. This is true of Xipe Tótec, whom Seler (1900–01: 100; 1960–61, IV: 120; 1963, II: 21) identified as a variant of Tlaltecuhtli and a god of the evening sky and the west; Chicomecóatl, known as "she who maketh all our food"; the water goddess Chalchiuhtlicue who lived in the west and south (Seler 1901–02: 22); another moon goddess, Xochiquetzal, at home in the west and south; and Xochiquetzal's male consort, Xochipilli, the Aztec "Lord of the South" (*ibid.*: 139).

The adoption of the form and posture of Tlaltecuhtli is particularly characteristic, however, of the major Aztec rain god, Tláloc. Tláloc frequently appears in frontal form, often with his legs displayed. He appears thus at least once, moreover, in an Aztec stone relief complete with the monster-faced joints and extremities of Tlaltecuhtli and in that goddess' dorsal form. Several times elsewhere he both wears and carries human skulls. In these instances his image, like Tlaltecuhtli's, frequently appears on the underside of a stone box or monument, a position which emphasizes his relation to that deity. In every case his eyes are ringed or banded, his teeth long and sharp.

Tláloc stored his rain underground in caves where all water was believed to originate. He left it in the care of his dwarfish assistants, the Tlaloques, who reportedly lurked at the bottom of every body of water (Krickeberg 1964: 148). Durán (1971: 154) reports that Tláloc's name means "Path under the Earth" or "Long Cave," and the *Histoyre du Mechique* refers to him as "Tlaloca teutli . . . , dieu de la terre" (Seler 1960–61, IV: 36). The Codex Ramírez refers to him as "the god of the lower regions" (Phillips 1883: 620). His features appear on the god Tlalchitonatiuh, "Sun near the

Earth," who, Tozzer (1957: 116) convincingly argues, represents the setting sun in the west. The deity's association with the earth is supported by the presence of the so-called Kan cross on the torso of several of the frontal displayed images of Tláloc and by the incorporation of the date 1 Tochtli (1 Rabbit) in the headdress of one of these. The Kan cross frequently appears on the forehead of the Maya earth monster Itzam Cab, while the date 1 Tochtli was an Aztec name for the earth itself.

The Kan cross originally symbolized the south among the Maya (see Thompson 1960: 112, 145, 251–2), and the date 1 Tochtli was invariably associated with the south in the Aztec calendar and legends. The Kan cross further symbolized the color turquoise, the color associated with Tláloc and his mythical realm of Tlalocan, the "house of turquoise," which Caso (1958: 60), among others, locates in the south. It would appear, therefore, that Tláloc's appearance in the pose and attributes of Tlaltecuhtli is entirely consistent with his role as an earth, death, night, and fertility deity inhabiting the southern portion of the universe.

The appearance of the date 1 Tochtli and the Kan cross on these images of Tláloc are, however, further revealing. The date 1 Tochtli not only served as a synonym for the earth itself but was the date of the legendary creation of the earth (Seler 1960–61, II: 794). Among the Aztecs and Mixtec, the 52-year "century," or cycle of 52 years, ended with the year 1 Tochtli. The Kan cross in turn was an important element of the *xiuhuitzolli*, a Zapotec symbol of the 365-day solar year which recurs on a cyclical basis (Thompson 1960: 252). Among the Maya it was interchangeable with the glyph for Yax, which meant "new" as well as "south," and with the most common Maya glyph for "completion" (*ibid*: 111–12, 276). The completion glyph was used to signify the end of a temporal cycle at which time the succeeding cycle would begin. The evidence therefore indicates that the Kan cross, like the date 1 Tochtli, signified a completed temporal cycle in some way associated with the earth, death, darkness, vegetation, and the southern world direction. On the frontal displayed images of Tláloc in the guise of the female earth monster, moreover, it is contained within the Aztec symbol for turquoise, the *chalchíhuitl*, which further symbolized the center of the world. Since space was organized in a sequence ending with the central world direction, the symbol implies a completed spatial cycle as well.

An examination of the remaining images in the group supports the implication that *en face* images referring to the female earth monster functioned as symbols of completed spatial and temporal cycles. A well-known Huastec relief from Tepetzintla portrays an *en face* figure in dorsal view, apparently descending headfirst with arms and legs displayed. It has sharp upper teeth and a protruding tongue; its hands and feet are clawed. The deity's face and torso are skeletal while its legs sport the paper bows worn by numerous earth and death deities in Post-Classic visual imagery. Comparison of this figure with various Post-Classic images of the god Xólotl, a variant of the god Quetzalcóatl, secures the popular identification of this deity as Xólotl. The figure, moreover, wears a border of Venus glyphs on its skirt, an attribute particularly pertinent to Xólotl who represented the planet Venus as the Evening Star.

The Post-Classic Mexicans divided the 584-day Venus cycle into four phases: that of the Morning Star, that of the planet's disappearance into superior conjunction, that of the Evening Star, and that of disappearance into inferior conjunction. Each phase was associated with a specific world direction, the Morning Star logically being affiliated with the east, where it appears, and the Evening Star being equally logically affiliated with the west. Superior conjunction was assigned to the north, inferior conjunction to the south. Both Mexican and Maya sources make it clear that the Venus cycle began with heliacal rising in the east and concluded with inferior conjunction in the south; thus Xólotl, as the representative of the Evening Star of the west who "dies" and disappears into inferior conjunction, clearly symbolized the latter phases of the cycle. He was accordingly charged with the responsibility for pushing the setting sun into the underworld at the western horizon and with leading the souls of the dead to their habitat at the navel of the earth in the south.

On page 58 of the Post-Classic Maya Codex Dresden, a similarly descending dorsal image, which also has been identified by Seler (1901–02: 166) as the Evening Star on the basis of the Maya glyph for Venus which forms its head, actually appears at the end of a series of tables of lunar eclipses. Thompson (1960: 232) notes that this figure differs from preceding profile images in the series in that it lacks numbers representing intervals between eclipses, and he concludes that the image "in fact has an entirely different function, for it appears to have served primarily to mark the conclusion of the cycle."

If the above *en face* images of Venus-bearing attributes of earth and death deities can be assigned to the concluding phases of that planet's cycle, then the same must be suspected of the famous Toltec so-called "Morning Star" reliefs at Tula and Chichén Itzá. These Early Post-Classic reliefs portray a frontal human face in the open jaws of a feathered reptile, viewed head-on, which has clawed feet and a protruding bifid tongue. The deity's eyes are frequently ringed; death symbols, such as cross-hatching, often decorate the monster itself. Although he ultimately identifies the image as the Morning Star deity of the east, Tlahuizcalpantecuhtli, Seler (1960–61, I: 693–4) observes that the images found on Mausoleum III at Chichén Itzá are accompanied by the date of the conclusion of a so-called "Great Venus Cycle" of 151,840 days. Since the image accompanies the date of completion of the cycle, and since the Venus cycle is known to have ended with inferior conjunction in the south, it follows that the image actually refers to the planet in its final phase of inferior conjunction in the south.

Support for this argument comes from a possibly Aztec version of the same image which carries on its reverse side a relief of a kneeling profile figure carrying on his back the date 11 Calli (11 House) by means of a looped cord or rope. Among the Mexicans, as among the Maya, temporal cycles were regarded as burdens which were carried on the backs of divine beings by means of a looped cord. At the end of each cycle the bearer of the current temporal cycle paused to rest while a successor shouldered the burden of the following cycle (Thompson 1960: 59–61; Nicholson 1966; Sahagún 1951–70, v: 100). Since the Aztec image closely resembles Classic Maya images of the divine bearers of time resting at the end of their labors, Nicholson (1966: 143) suggests that it similarly refers to the end of a temporal cycle. The appearance of the image on the back of a relief, clearly derived from the Toltec so-called Morning Star reliefs, thus lends credence to the hypothesis that all such images refer to the end of temporal cycles.

The Post-Classic use of an *en face* image of a deity affiliated with death, darkness, and the female earth monster to signify the completion of a spatio-temporal cycle is best demonstrated by the famous Aztec Calendar Stone. According to the generally accepted interpretations of Beyer (1921), Seler (1960–61, II: 796–9), and Caso (1958: 31–3), this giant relief from the Aztec capital of Tenochtitlan is a graphic symbol of the Aztec concept of time. The Aztecs believed that the universe had passed through four cyclical ages, each of which was associated with a specific world direction, and each of which had ended with the violent destruction of man, the world, and the sun. The Aztecs themselves were living in the fifth and final era, or "sun," which was also expected to be destroyed—this time by earthquakes—at midnight on the day 4 Ollin (4 Earthquake) at the end of the Aztec "century," or cycle of fifty-two years. The first age had corresponded to the east, the second to the north, the third to the west, and the fourth to the south. The present and final age or sun was associated with the center of the world (Seler 1963, II: 31).

The Calendar Stone itself accordingly depicts a giant disk decorated with pointed projections, which in Post-Classic iconography invariably represents the sun. The outer rim consists of two serpents, or Xiuhcóatls, meeting at the tails and heads, who symbolized the daily course of the sun through the sky and underworld. The inner ring depicts the complete sequence of the twenty day signs of the Mexican calendar. The central image is framed by the Mexican sign for Ollin, meaning "earth" or "earthquake," accompanied by four small circles which convert the sign into the date 4 Ollin (4 Earthquake), the date of the expected destruction of the world by earthquakes at the end of the present and final sun. In the four angles of the Ollin sign are four dates which represent the four previous epochs or suns. Since the central image is surrounded by symbols of completed temporal cycles and by the date of the anticipated completion of the present cycle, it is logical to assume that the image itself refers to the completion of the fifth and final era or sun at midnight at the center of the universe.

The iconography of the central image of the Calendar Stone supports this assumption. The figure, clearly representing a deity, appears *en face*. Its open mouth reveals large teeth and a protruding tongue which takes the form of a sacrificial flint knife. The outer edges of its eyes are decorated with double bands and its outstretched hands, which are clawed and which clutch human hearts, take the form of devouring monster heads. The deity clearly is portrayed as dead; its relation to the female earth monster is unmistakable.

Scholars have persisted in identifying the Calendar Stone deity as Tonatiuh, the sun god of the daytime sky, who in the codices is always associated with the eastern world direction. However, as I have demonstrated elsewhere (Klein n.d.: 98–114), the image actually represents Tonatiuh's counterpart, Yoaltonatiuh, the Night Sun, the dead sun in the dark bowels of the earth and underworld at the center of the world. Yoaltonatiuh was also known as Yohualtecuhtli, "Lord of the Night" (Sahagún 1951–70, III: 202), the very name given to the star whose appearance in the center of the sky at midnight on the final day of the 52-year cycle proclaimed for the Aztecs the successful completion of that cycle and the beginning of a new one. A full-length figure in Codex Borgia, page 40, identified by Seler (1963, appendix: 40) as Yohualtecuhtli, actually assumes the parturient posture of Tlaltecuhtli with upturned, albeit profile, head and anthropomorphic sun disks at its joints and clawed extremities. The appearance on the Aztec Calendar Stone of a sun god associated with earth, death, darkness, and the central world direction is consistent with its context of the end of the world and the death of the sun at midnight on the last day of the era assigned to the center of the universe.

The Aztec Calendar Stone image shares with the Toltec and Aztec Evening Star reliefs a head-on pose, and it shares with numerous codical profile images of other deities affiliated with the "dead" planet Venus the double bands around the eyes, the bi-colored facial painting, and the peculiar form of the jewelled fillet on its head. There is considerable evidence, in fact, that the central image of the Calendar Stone refers simultaneously to the Night Sun and the planet Venus in inferior conjunction. Such a dual reference is understandable in light of the fact that the end of the Venus cycle coincided with that of the solar cycle every eight years and with the end of the 52-year cycle every other "century." The date accompanying the Evening Star reliefs of Mausoleum III at Chichén Itzá refers to the completion of an even larger period comprised simultaneously of eight 52-year cycles and 260 revolutions of Venus (Seler 1960–61, I: 693–4). The coincident endings of the two respective cycles and the incorporation of attributes of the Evening Star deity in the Calendar Stone image of the Night Sun thus implies an intimate relation between those two deities.

Among the Yucatec Maya the Evening Star was in fact known as Ah p'iz akab, or "Lord of the Night." The Mexican Evening Star deity, Xólotl, who was believed to push the setting sun to its demise at the western horizon, "in some way . . . actually represented the sun," according to Thompson (1960: 79). Xólotl ruled the seventeenth day-sign Ollin (Earth, Earthquake) in the Mexican calendar and co-ruled the sixteenth week with the critical date 4 Ollin. The commentator of Codex Vaticanus 3773 states that the date 4 Ollin was merely another name for Xólotl; according to the commentator of Codex Vaticanus 3738, it was on a day 4 Ollin that the god Quetzalcóatl disappeared into the sea to be later reborn as the Morning Star (Caso 1967: 197). An Aztec jade figurine of Xólotl displays on its back a relief of a feathered reptile bearing an image of the sun. Throughout Aztec mythology and the various Post-Classic codices, moreover, there is substantial evidence that both the Night Sun and the Evening Star were even further fused in the Post-Classic mind with the moon. Both of the principal Aztec moon goddesses—Tlazoltéotl and Xochiquetzal—were, as indicated earlier, similarly related to the female earth monster Tlaltecuhtli.

The intimate relation between the various deities who reigned at the navel of the earth extends, finally, to the death gods themselves. Chavero remarks that the sun which has set at the western horizon is converted into Mictlantecuhtli, the "Lord of the Underworld" (Fernández 1959: 224–5). The *Histoyre du Mechique* further refers to the death god Mictlantecuhtli as one "Yoaltentli" whom Seler (1960–61, IV: 36) identifies with Yohualtecuhtli, the "Lord of the Night," who simultaneously represented the Night Sun and the Evening Star. Like Yohualtecuhtli, Mictlantecuhtli is repeatedly associated in the codices with the hour of midnight and with the southern and central world directions. His habitat, the land of the dead known as Mictlán, was located at the navel of the earth. Like the Evening Star and the Night Sun, moreover, the death god had stellar associations; in Codex Telleriano-Remensis, the *Histoyre du Mechique*, and Codex Vaticanus 3738 he is identified as a Tzitzimime, a stellar manifestation of the soul of a dead warrior. The Tzitzimime were the male counterparts of the Cihuateteo, the souls of women dead in childbirth, and like them were believed to descend periodically headfirst to the center of the earth at midnight. Both the Evening Star and Yohualtecuhtli, as well as a moon god, Achitumetl, are similarly listed as Tzitzimime; at the end of the fifth and final epoch or sun, the Tzitzimime were expected to descend to devour the living. The similarity of associations and attributes among the Evening Star, the Night Sun, and the death god therefore creates yet a third category of deities affiliated with the female earth monster Tlaltecuhtli—that of the great stellar night lords of the underworld.

In accord with their close relation to Tlaltecuhtli, both Mictlantecuhtli and his female consort, Mictecacíhuatl, are portrayed in the codices as skeletal creatures with ringed eyes, protruding tongues, and clawed extremities. In Codex Borgia, page 56, and Codex Vaticanus 3773, page 76, the *en face* head of Mictlantecuhtli is substituted for that of Tlaltecuhtli as a symbol of the terrestrial regions. A Post-Conquest image of Mictecacíhuatl in Codex Magliabecchi, page 64, depicts the death goddess *en face*, here full-figure with legs and arms displayed, her round eyes ringed, her tongue protruding, her chest and head adorned with human hearts and hands, and her joints and clawed extremities taking the form of monstrous faces. Durán (1964: 180, 183), in the course of describing the funeral ceremony of the Aztec emperor Tizoc, reports that a man impersonating the "lord of the underworld" wore "masks" on his shoulders, knees, elbows, and stomach. Such an obvious reference to the female earth monster appears again in the Codex Borgia image of Iztli (page 32), a god of obsidian and the sacrificial knife, usually associated with the east, who here, according to Seler (1963, appendix: 32), is depicted in the underworld located in the south. Since the deity is presented in the act of giving birth to the god Tezcatlipoca, he logically assumes the *en face* female posture of childbirth. His hands and feet are clawed, his joints are decorated with anthropomorphic flint-knives reminiscent of the monster-faced joints of Tlaltecuhtli. On his wrists and ankles he wears the paper bows symbolic of earth and death deities. Itzli's formal resemblance here to the female earth monster is surely due to his role in this particular instance of a parturient god/goddess of death inhabiting the navel of the earth.

The appearance of the various stellar night lords of the underworld, the vegetation deities, and the numerous earth goddesses in the pose and attributes of the great female earth monster Tlaltecuhtli suggests that all of these deities were conceptually related to the extent that their associations actually merged. This suggestion has been supported by the foregoing study of those associations: all of the relevant images examined depict deities affiliated with the earth, death, and darkness; all belong to the western, southern, and/or central world directions. Several of the images definitely refer to the end of a spatio-temporal cycle. So intimate, in fact, is their interrelationship that they would seem to comprise a self-contained group exclusive of the remaining major deities of the Post-Classic pantheon. The remaining deities—Quetzalcóatl, Huitzilopochtli, Tezcatlipoca, and Xiuhtecuhtli, for example—were all nonagrarian deities of creation, fire, war, and the hunt. They were almost exclusively male; all were traditionally regarded as celestial rather than terrestrial and most as diurnal rather than nocturnal. All were associated with the world directions of east and north; none with the west or south. This observation holds true for Cipactli, the male counterpart of Tlaltecuhtli, the Morning Star deity Tlahuizcalpantecuhtli, counterpart of Xólotl the

Evening Star, and Yoaltonatiuh's day sun counterpart, Tonatiuh, as well. These gods never assume the frontal form of Tlaltecuhtli nor do they at any time exhibit her displayed posture and insignia. Moreover, like the numerous deities affiliated with earth, death, and darkness their various associations and functions can be demonstrated to have merged and overlapped among themselves (Klein n.d.: 154–73).

This formal and associational distinction between two groups of Post-Classic Mexican deities reveals a remarkably coherent division of the entire Post-Classic pantheon into two complementary halves. This division was clearly based on a presumed opposition between sky and earth, light and darkness, male and female, and life and death. But since the gods of the day sky were further invariably assigned to the east or north, and those of the night sky and underworld to the west, south, or center, the divided pantheon simultaneously implies the concept of a dualistic cosmos as well. Such a concept would associate the east and north with the sky and daytime, the west, south, and center with the earth and the night. Within a culture that conceived of space and time in terms of ever-recurring cycles, such a concept would have important ramifications for an understanding of the death cult in Post-Classic Mexico.

We know from the researches of Krickeberg (1950) and others that the Post-Classic Mexicans did in fact divide the universe vertically into two complementary halves: sky and earth. The sky was conceived of in the form of five or seven superimposed layers which decrease in length as they proceed upward. Depicted graphically in two dimensions, they form a stepped triangle with its apex at the top. The earth was similarly disposed in a series of five layers which two-dimensionally took the form of an inverted stepped triangle. The bottommost layer was the site of Mictlán, the land of the dead, also said to be located at the navel of the earth. The concept of the female earth monster Tlaltecuhtli was therefore synonymous with this inverted triangle.

Physical space, however, has depth and the Mexican concept of a layered universe must have incorporated the third dimension as well. Conceived as volume, the layered universe must have assumed the form of an upright and an inverted stepped pyramid joined at the base at the surface of the earth. Such pyramids would logically have been either conical in shape or four-sided to emphasize the four world directions. The latter concept is directly analogous to the actual form of the four-sided stepped temple-pyramid in Post-Classic Mexico which often is comprised of exactly five or seven layers. Krickeberg (1950) points out that the Mexican temple-pyramid was thus almost certainly modeled after the vertical concept of the universe.

The Mexicans, we know, further conceived of space as it would appear on a horizontal plane. This horizontal concept frequently took a form resembling a Maltese cross, as seen in the famous so-called "world-direction chart" of Codex Fejérvary-Mayer, page 1. Each arm of the cross corresponded to one of the four world directions

—east, north, west, and south—the area of their point of intersection representing the fifth and central world direction. Depicted graphically, the schema markedly resembles a four-sided pyramid viewed from above; possibly it derives from the concept of such a pyramid "flattened out" on a horizontal plane. The center of the cross thus corresponds to the temple-platform of the standard temple-pyramid and to the bottom layer of the cosmic inverted pyramid at which was located Mictlán, the land of the dead, and the center of the earth.

So well integrated were these various notions of the structure of cosmic space that the Mexicans were able to fuse the vertical concept of space with their concept of the world on a horizontal plane. When the cosmic cross was depicted two-dimensionally, it was conceived of as being upright as well as prone. That arm of the cross corresponding to the east was placed at the top, that of the west at the bottom. The east was thereby associated with the "above" and the sky, while the west was associated with the "below" and the earth (Soustelle 1940: 58). The present-day Mixtec inhabitants of Mitla still refer to the east as "up" and the west as "down" (Parsons 1966: 491). The north and south were relegated to the left and right side arms of the cross, respectively, a position which similarly accords with native references to them today as "the sides of heaven" or the "left hand" and "right hand" of the universe (Laughlin 1969: 175; Corona Núñez 1957: 12).

The north and south, in fact, were comparatively unimportant in Mesoamerican thought and were frequently allied with the more important world directions of east and west. Invariably at such times the north was associated with the east, the south with the west (see Seler 1960–61, IV: 81). The north thereby shared with the east the connotations of the sky and the "above," while the south, like the west, represented the earth and the "below." Therefore, were the graphic axis dividing the "sky" from the "earth" to be on a true horizontal, the cross would have to be turned clockwise at a 90° angle. That the Mexicans understood this is demonstrated by the frequent substitution in the codices of a square divided into four or five comparable segments in which both the east *and* the north appear at the top, and both the west *and* the south at the bottom. The central world direction was believed to penetrate both the sky and the earth, and thus to provide access from one to the other. In the vast majority of literary and codical references to the five world directions, however, the center of the universe is associated with the earth and is often interchangeable with the south. This basically dual orientation of the cosmic cross explains the recurrent association of gods of the sky with the east and north, and deities of the earth and underworld with the west, south, and center.

The dualistic structure of the Post-Classic pantheon implies a temporal division of the cosmos as well. All of the deities who assume the pose and attributes of the female earth monster in visual imagery were associated with the nighttime, many with the hours of sunset and midnight in particular. We know that time was conceived of in terms of ever-recurring cycles in Post-Classic Mesoamerica and that each cycle was traditionally divided into four segments or phases. The standard division of the cyclic structure of time was based on the twenty-four-hour course of the sun, the four major segments corresponding to sunrise, high noon, sunset, and midnight, respectively (see Durán 1971: 119). However, as Soustelle (1940: 85) points out, time in Post-Classic Mexico was essentially indistinguishable from space; thus the cyclic concept of time corresponded to the Mexican concept of cosmic space. When this temporal concept was superimposed upon the spatial concept, sunrise was logically aligned with the east and sunset with the west. Since the Post-Classic spatial sequence of the five world directions invariably ran east, north, west, south, and center, high noon must have corresponded to the north and midnight to the south and center. There is considerable evidence that the south and center were associated with midnight; as has been seen, virtually all of the deities assigned to those world directions were associated with midnight as well. Conflicting calendrical information from the Aztecs regarding the temporal affiliations of the north suggests that the pattern had become somewhat obscured by the end of the Post-Classic period.

In the Mexican codices temporal cycles almost always begin with that phase of the cycle which corresponds to the east and end with that which corresponds to the south. This is true, for example, of the 260-day cycle which began with the day 1 Cipactli (1 Earth Crocodile), named after Tlaltecuhtli's counterpart, the male earth monster of the east, and which concluded on a day Xóchitl (Flower) associated with the south. As has been seen, it was equally true of the 52-year "century" which began with an Ácatl (Reed) year of the east and ended in a year Tochtli (Rabbit) belonging to the south. The Venus cycle similarly began with the phase of the Morning Star of the east and concluded with inferior conjunction in the south; Seler (1963, II: 18) presumes that the lunar cycle followed this pattern as well. Since these cycles all began with the phase corresponding to the east, it follows that they began at the moment of sunrise or of first appearance of the planet as well. We know that the Venus cycle did in fact begin with the moment of heliacal rising at dawn. Moreover, since the cycles ended with the phase which corresponded to the south, they must have ended at—or sometime after—the hour of midnight. Cristóbal del Castillo states that the Aztec day ended at midnight, and Caso (1967: 115) accepts his report. It was at midnight, when Yohualtecuhtli appeared in the center of the sky, that the ritual New Fire was drilled at the end of each Aztec year and century to signify the successful completion of a cycle.

Once understood, therefore, the cosmological schema of the Post-Classic Mexicans is coherent and rational. The various concepts of space and time were logically related to one another and to the vast pantheon which inhabited the cosmos. The universe was divided into two critical halves: the first being affiliated with the sky, the day, and the world directions of east and north; the second with the earth, the night, and the world directions of west, south, and center. The various spatio-temporal cycles began with dawn in the eastern sky and ended around midnight in the dark bowels of the earth in the west, south, and center of the world. Since the earth further housed the land of the dead, the end of a cosmic cycle was likened to the end of the life cycle itself. The great stellar bodies which periodically disappear at the western horizon were believed to "die" upon entering the open jaws of Tlaltecuhtli. This association of death with the concept of cyclic completion accounts for the Post-Classic use of images of deities represented as dead to signify the completion of cosmic cycles. Such images in turn must be recognized as having had a profound cosmological significance to the men who made them.

Without necessarily condoning the vast number of human sacrifices performed in the Post-Classic period, therefore, one must appreciate the rationality of the foundation upon which their perpetuation rested. To the Post-Classic Mexican mind the renewal of space and time could not take place without the successful completion of the current spatio-temporal cycle, and such completion required the intervention of death itself. Without human blood the female earth monster Tlaltecuhtli would have lacked the phenomenal energy required to give rebirth to the forces which sustain the universe; without death, time and space themselves would come to a terrifying end. The conclusion of a cosmic cycle in Post-Classic Mexico created a moment of crisis which only death could resolve. The tremendous importance of the death cult at that time and place was thus due to the belief that the very existence of all things desired was ultimately dependent upon death.

BIBLIOGRAPHY

Beyer, Hermann

1921 El llamado "Calendario Azteca:" descripción e interpretación del cuauhxicalli de la "Casa de las águilas." Verband Deutscher Reichsangehöriger, México.

Caso, Alfonso

1928 Las estelas zapotecas. *Monografías del Museo Nacional de Arqueología, Historia y Etnografía.* Talleres Gráficos de la Nación, México.

1958 The Aztecs: People of the Sun. (Trans. by Lowell Dunham.) University of Oklahoma Press, Norman.

1967 Los calendarios prehispánicos. *Serie de Cultura Náhuatl, Monografía 6.* Instituto de Investigaciones Históricas, Universidad Nacional Autónoma de México, México.

Corona Núñez, José

1957 Mitología tarasca. Fondo de Cultura Económica, México.

Durán, Fray Diego

1964 The Aztecs: The History of the Indies of New Spain. (Trans. by Doris Heyden and Fernando Horcasitas.) Orion Press, New York.

1971 Book of the Gods and Rites and the Ancient Calendar. (Trans. by Fernando Horcasitas and Doris Heyden.) University of Oklahoma Press, Norman.

Fernández, Justino

1959 Coatlicue: estética del arte indígena antiguo. Segunda edición. Instituto de Investigaciones Estéticas, Universidad Nacional Autónoma de México, México. (Primera edición 1954.)

Klein, Cecelia

n.d. Frontality in Postclassic Mexican Two-dimensional Art. Unpublished doctoral dissertation, Columbia University. New York, 1972.

Krickeberg, Walter

1950 Bauform und Weltbild im alten Mexico. *In* Mythe, Mensch und Umwelt, *Paideuma, Mitteilungen zur Kulturkunde*, vol. iv, pp. 295–333. Bamberger Verlagshaus Meisenbach & Co., Bamberg.

1964 Las antiguas culturas mexicanas. Segunda edición. (Trans. by Sita Garst and Jasmin Reuter.) Fondo de Cultura Económica, México. (Primera edición 1956.)

Laughlin, Robert M.

1969 The Tzotzil. *In* Handbook of Middle American Indians (Robert Wauchope, ed.), vol. 7, pp. 152–194. University of Texas Press, Austin.

Nicholson, H. B.

1966 The Significance of the "Looped Cord" Year Symbol in Pre-Hispanic Mexico: An Hypothesis. *Estudios de Cultura Náhuatl*, vol. vi, pp. 135–148. Instituto de Investigaciones Históricas, Universidad Nacional Autónoma de México, México.

1967 A Fragment of an Aztec Relief Carving of the Earth Monster. *Journal de la Société des Américanistes*, n.s. vol. lvi, pp. 81–94. Paris.

Parsons, Elsie Clews

1966 Mitla, Town of the Souls, and Other Zapotec-Speaking Pueblos of Oaxaca, Mexico. University of Chicago, Chicago. (First published 1936.)

PHILLIPS, HENRY, JR.

1883 Notes upon the Codex Ramirez, with a translation of the same. *Proceedings of the American Philosophical Society*, vol. XXI, pp. 616–651. Philadelphia.

PROSKOURIAKOFF, TATIANA

1968 The Jog and the Jaguar Signs in Maya Writing. *American Antiquity*, vol. 33, no. 2, pp. 247–251. Society for American Archaeology, Salt Lake City.

SAHAGÚN, FRAY BERNARDINO DE

1951–70 Florentine Codex: General History of the Things of New Spain. (Trans. by Arthur J. O. Anderson and Charles E. Dibble.) 13 parts. *Monographs of The School of American Research*, no. 14. The School of American Research and the University of Utah, Santa Fe.

SELER, EDUARD

1900–01 The Tonalamatl of the Aubin Collection. An Old Mexican Picture Manuscript in the Paris National Library (Manuscrits Mexicains No. 18–19). Published at the Expense of His Excellency the Duke of Loubat, Berlin and London.

1901–02 Codex Fejérváry-Mayer: An Old Mexican Picture Manuscript in the Liverpool Free Public Museums (12014/M). (Trans. by A. H. Keane.) Published at the Expense of His Excellency the Duke of Loubat, Berlin and London.

1904 Wall Paintings of Mitla: A Mexican Picture Writing in Fresco. *In* Mexican and Central American Antiquities, Calendar Systems, and History (Charles P. Bowditch, ed.). *Smithsonian Institution, Bureau of American Ethnology, Bulletin 28*, pp. 243–324. Government Printing Office, Washington.

1960–61 Gesammelte Abhandlungen zur Amerikanischen Sprach- und Alterthumskunde. 5 vols. Akademische Druck- und Verlagsanstalt, Graz. (Reprinted from 1902–23: A. Asher & Co. and Behrend & Co., Berlin.)

1963 Comentarios al Códice Borgia. 2 vols. plus appendix. Fondo de Cultura Económica, Mexico.

SOUSTELLE, JACQUES

1940 La pensée cosmologique des anciens mexicains (représentation du monde et de l'espace). *Actualités Scientifiques et Industrielles 881, Ethnologie*. Hermann & Cie., Éditeurs, Paris.

THOMPSON, J. ERIC S.

1934 Sky Bearers, Colors and Directions in Maya and Mexican Religion. *Carnegie Institution of Washington, Publication 436, Contributions to American Archaeology*, vol. II, no. 10, pp. 209–242. Washington.

1960 Maya Hieroglyphic Writing: An Introduction. Second edition. University of Oklahoma Press, Norman. (First published 1950: Carnegie Institution of Washington, Washington.)

TOZZER, ALFRED M.

1957 Chichen Itza and Its Cenote of Sacrifice: A Comparative Study of Contemporaneous Maya and Toltec. *Memoirs of the Peabody Museum of Archaeology and Ethnology, Harvard University*, vols. XI, XII. Cambridge.

Death and the Ancient Maya

MICHAEL D. COE

YALE UNIVERSITY

This people had a great and excessive fear of death. . . . When in time they came to die, it was indeed a thing to see the sorrow and the cries which they made for their dead, and the great grief it caused them. During the day they wept for them in silence; and at night with loud and very sad cries, so that it was pitiful to hear them. And they passed many days in deep sorrow. (Tozzer 1941: 129)

So Diego de Landa described Maya attitudes towards death in late Pre-Conquest Yucatán, an outlook which, as Ruz (1968: 76) points out, was very different from the stoic fatalism of the Central Mexican peoples. It suggests that, for the Maya, the fact of human mortality might have been a major preoccupation of their culture, a conclusion amply born out by the testimony of archaeology and ethnohistory.

BURIAL PRACTICES

The rich archaeological data on Maya burial practices have been documented in the magnificent study by Ruz mentioned above. On the other hand, ethnohistory provides only scanty information. This, however, makes it certain that these practices differed greatly according to the social status of the individual concerned. Landa tells us that, in Yucatán, a commoner was buried in a shroud and his mouth filled with maize dough and "some of the stones which they use for money, so that they should not be without something to eat in the other life" (Tozzer 1941: 130). Such persons were buried at the rear of the house, beneath the floor, a pan-Maya trait known for both Classic and Post-Classic times. The house was usually abandoned following interment, unless there were enough persons in the house to enable them to overcome their dread of the spirit of the departed one. On the other hand, nobles and "persons of high esteem" were cremated. Over the urns which contained their ashes pyramid-temples were built. For some, they only burned part of the body, burying the rest; in this case, the ashes were placed in hollow pottery statues. For the Cocom overlords was reserved the custom of preserving the front part of the skulls, which were built up with bitumen to look natural and which were fed on ritual days. Thus, the Mexicanized rulers of Yucatán distinguished themselves from their underlings even in death by following Mexican mortuary customs.

Fairly detailed information on burial practices comes from the Pokomán Maya of Verapaz and the Guatemalan highlands (Miles 1957: 749–50), but this is confined to funerary ceremonies among the lords themselves. According to Fuentes y Guzmán, a lord was placed in a great olla which had been set in the earth, along with his wealth and finery. A mound was constructed over the place, its size depending upon the social and political status of the deceased; a statue of the lord was placed on the mound and worshiped. Among the northern Pokomán in Verapaz, according to data gathered by Las Casas, the dead ruler was dressed in his finery and jewels, and was seated upon a dais, thus simulating a position which he would have taken in his palace in real life. To the funeral came friendly lords or their surrogates, bringing slaves and offerings. The dead man was then placed in a box of stone or wood, seated cross-legged; with him were put gold, folded mantles, and other wealth. This box was lowered into a tomb carved out on a mountain top. The slaves were then dispatched and placed around the box. If the slave had been an agriculturalist, they put farming implements with him; if he were a hunter, then he was accompanied by bows and arrows. With the female slaves were *manos* and *metates* to grind maize, pottery vessels for cooking and food preparation, drinking vessels, and plates and bowls. Above the tomb, they erected a small altar of masonry "on which they commonly burned incense and offered other sacrifices" (Miles 1957: 750).

These data, sparse though they are, accord very closely with what we know of mortuary customs among other peoples of Mesoamerica on the eve of the Conquest. First, among the southern Maya, as with the Aztecs and Tarascans, there was the clear-cut concept that the tomb must replicate the palace, so that the ruler could continue to enjoy those prerogatives which were his in life. In a way, the palace, with its slaves and servants and complex division of labor, must be "sent" to the other world. Secondly, great lords were honored by having some sort of permanent structure built over their final resting places, whether mounds or altars, which continued to be the focal point of worship by their successors and followers. And, finally, there was a marked cleavage between how ordinary persons and those of high rank were treated after death.

MAYA CONCEPTS OF DEATH AND THE UNDERWORLD

In speaking of the Yucatec Maya, Landa says, "This people has always believed in the immortality of the soul, more than many other nations" (Tozzer 1941: 131), an assertion which we shall later examine. He goes on to claim, however, that the Maya believed in a good and bad future life. For those whose lives had been virtuous, their souls went to a kind of heaven where there were all sorts of good things to eat and drink, and where there was a great ceiba tree under which they would have perpetual rest. For evil persons, there was a hell called Metnal, where souls would be "tormented in it by the devils and by great extremities of hunger, cold, fatigue and grief" (Tozzer 1941: 132). The devil, or prince of all the devils, ruled over the place, and was the source of all diseases and, ultimately, death. His name is given by Landa as "Hunhau," a name that I will show is of great significance.

Both Ruz and Tozzer have shown how incongruent this account of the other world is when compared with non-Maya concepts in Mesoamerica, and it is certain that it has a strong Christian bias, derived perhaps from the self-serving testimony of Gaspar Antonio Chi. If the Maya were like other Mesoamericans, then it is quite likely that the underworld was the destination of all those who "died in bed," a nine-layered and four-directioned realm down through which the soul passed on a long and perilous journey. Landa's statement that suicides went to the Maya heaven (Tozzer 1941: 132) suggests that this was reserved for those who suffered unusual deaths, such as slain warriors, women who died in childbirth, and those who perished from drowning. Again, this would have been multi-layered.

There are two Maya words for the underworld in the dictionaries. One is Metnal or Mitnal, believed by Tozzer (1941: 132, fn. 617) to be derived from the Nahuatl Mictlan. The other is Xibalba, found both in the highlands and lowlands, and derived from the root *xib*, meaning "fear, terror, trembling with fright," a definition which recalls the Yucatec Maya horror of death. Most of the Maya believed that the entrance to the underworld was a cavern in the Alta Verapaz. From this entrance or hole came a stench of rotting corpses and clotted blood. It was the duty of the Maya medicine man to send back through this hole the diseases inflicted by the underworld rulers on the race of men; the Ritual of the Bacabs contains long incantations to this end.

According to several dictionaries and other sources of ethnological information, the lowland Maya had another term for the ruler of the underworld: Cizin, a name derived from *cizin*, meaning "flatulence" or "breaking of wind," attesting to the Maya view of his realm as a world of putrescence and corruption. More enigmatic is the supernatural being called Mam among many of the southern Maya. This is an essentially evil deity who lives beneath mountains and who causes earthquakes. Thompson (1950: 173) convincingly links him with the Mexican god Tepeyollotl, who plays a similarly sinister role and who is guised in the form of a jaguar.

THE POPOL VUH AND THE HERO TWINS

A far more profound view of the Maya concept of death and the underworld is contained in the Popol Vuh; the story of the Hero Twins and their triumph over death is of supreme importance, as recognized by Ruz (1968: 49). Although the Popol Vuh is the sacred book of the Kavek dynasty which ruled the Quiché Maya at the time of the Conquest (Edmunson 1971: vii), the contents of its early sections were widely disseminated and may have been commonly held knowledge over much of Mesoamerica.

In view of its significance, the story bears recapitulation. It actually concerns two sets of brothers. The first set, offspring of the old creator couple, Ixmucané and Ixpiayacoc, consists of 1 Hunahpu and 7 Hunahpu. While these youths are playing a ball game on the surface of the earth, the Lords of the Underworld, angered at the noise, summon them into their presence. Taking leave of their mother, they descend to the underworld, where they are subjected to a series of humiliations by the Lords and proceed to fail a series of magical tests. They meet their final defeat in a ball game and are sacrificed. The head of 1 Hunahpu is hung up in a calabash tree, but one day the daughter of one of the Lords happens to be passing beneath it; 1 Hunahpu's head spits into her hand, and she becomes pregnant. Now, it has long been recognized that 1 Hunahpu is equivalent to the lowland Maya tzolkin day 1 Ahau, the starting point of the Venus calendar, when the Morning Star has a heliacal rising. 7 Hunahpu or Ahau is just 240 days later; 1 Hunahpu or Ahau is just 20 days later in the tzolkin than 7 Ahau. Thus, it is highly likely that we are dealing with an astral myth concerning the Morning and Evening Stars.

To continue with the story, the girl is expelled from the underworld and goes to live with the youth's mother, Ixmucané, where she gives birth to the Hero Twins. These are named Hunahpu and Xbalanque, and grow up to be great hunters with the blowgun. They play ball, and again the noisy game infuriates the arrogant underworld Lords, who summon them by means of sinister messenger owls. In a journey which is obviously cognate to the voyage of the soul after death, the Twins descend some very steep stairs, pass between steep hills and ravines, and cross rivers of blood and corruption by floating in their blowguns. At last they arrive at the meeting of roads of contrasting colors, and take the black road which leads to the court of the underworld. Here they begin to best the Lords, for they send along the road a mosquito, which, by biting each of the Lords, causes them to reveal their names. There are twelve of these, headed by 1 Death and 7 Death; the names of the others are those of diseases.

The Twins best the Lords in a game played in the same ball court in which their father and uncle had suffered defeat. Then they undergo the same trials in each of five underground chambers or "houses," but manage by subterfuge to triumph over all but one. For instance, in the House of Gloom the Twins are given cigars, and told to keep them lit all night; instead, they fix fireflies to the tips to fool the Lords. Eventually, they are overcome in the House of Bats, presided over by the dread Cama Zotz, or Killer Bat; but their death is only temporary. They reappear disguised as dancers and magicians before the underworld Lords. Their final act of legerdemain was for each Twin to cut the other to pieces with a knife and bring him back to life. Both 1 Death and 7 Death were beside themselves on seeing this feat, and asked that it be performed on them. It was, and they perished forever. Hunahpu and Xbalanque had triumphed over death and the underworld. Rising in triumph, they reached their apotheosis in the heavens as the Sun and the Moon.

Do we have here a paradigm for the death and apotheosis of Maya rulers? It should be here stressed that the Hero Twins and their story was definitely not confined to the Quiché. Among the Maya of Verapaz, both Hunahpu and Xbalanque were worshipped as gods under the names of Hunahau (which the Las Casas account misspells as Hunaha) and Exbalanquen (Miles 1957: 748). The former was listed as one of the sons of Ixchel and Itzamná, who surely correspond to the old creator couple in the Quiché legend. The latter was said to have descended to hell via one of the entrance caves near Cobán and to have made war on the king and people there.

In dictionaries of the Pokomán language, Hunahpu is given as "one of the most principal idols," but Xbalanque is not mentioned. However, Fuentes y Guzmán (1932, I: 266), in speaking of the funeral of great lords among the southern Pokomán, says that the corpse was buried at night, after a two-day wake and after offerings had been made to Xbalanque so that this god would accompany the deceased.

It will be remembered that, in Landa's garbled account, "Hunhau," or 1 Ahau, is given as a "devil" presiding over hell, a logical choice since Hunahpu triumphed over the underworld. But, even more significant, one of the esoteric riddles which aspirants to high office in Yucatán had to answer (as given in the Book of Chilam Balam of Chumayel) concerned the trick of putting a firefly on the end of an unlit cigar.

Thus, there is ample ethnohistoric evidence that the Hero Twins cult was widespread over the Maya area, that they were intimately involved with the underworld, and that in some way they were the supernatural, mitigating force between the living and the dead, at least as far as the hereditary nobility was concerned. The question now is, can this complex of beliefs be found in the archaeological remains?

DEATH SYMBOLISM AMONG THE PRE-CONQUEST MAYA

Alberto Ruz (1968: 47) makes the sound observation that the Maya, as opposed to the Mexicans, seem less obsessed in their art with real, human death, but that this is compensated for by a greater presence of death in abstract form, especially in symbols, which appear with high frequency. I will briefly describe these symbols, since the identification of certain scenes as funerary depends upon their recognition. Some fall into the category of what I will call overt symbols—motifs which are either universally recognized as connected with death, such as human skulls, or which appear with such frequency with these representations that their meaning cannot be missed. These are to be distinguished from esoteric or allegorical symbols, in which the mortuary aspects can easily be overlooked by those without the occult knowledge to understand their import.

The first of these overt symbols is the human skeleton, or, more properly, the skeletalized corpse itself. This functions as a deity, known as God A in the codices. In his fullest form, he is seated upon a throne of human bones (Fig. 1), although he is seen in the codices in a variety of other activities, and even has a female counterpart (Fig.

Fig. 1 (left) *God A on his throne of human bones.* Dresden Codex, p. 53a.

Fig. 2 (center) *God A's female counterpart.* Dresden Codex, p. 9c, right.

Fig. 3 (right) *Death spots, closed eyes, and open mouth of dead goddess.* Dresden Codex, p. 53b.

2). It would be wrong, however, to consider God A as *the* Death God. Skulls and human bones, often crossed, also function as death symbols.

Less obvious are the black spots which appear on the bodies and cheeks of God A, dead divinities, and persons in general; these are the blotches which identify decomposing corpses (Fig. 3). Another bodily indication of death is the presence of closed eyes, usually accompanied by an open mouth. One of the stranger death symbols is the "division-sign" appearing on the cheek, or sometimes in the headdress, of divinities with mortuary aspects (Fig. 4). Death-eyes are disembodied eyes with the nerve stalk attached, and are closely identified with God A and other death figures. In the codices and on funerary ceramics, one often sees a death collar, consisting of human eyes separated by what Thompson has called "death hairs" (Fig. 5); this is worn by prisoners in the Dresden Codex (Fig. 6), and recalls the collars of wood and cords placed around the necks of offenders in the account of Gaspar Antonio Chi. I have speculated that it stands for death by decapitation (Coe 1973: 16).

As a good example of esoteric, allegorical symbolism, I will point to the divinity known as the Jaguar God of the Underworld (Fig. 7). This has long been recognized as the Sun on his night journey through the underworld, with his jaguar ears, Roman nose (over which a crullerlike twist can often be seen), filed frontal incisors or "egg-tooth," and bound hank of hair. Where such a representation appears, we can be sure we are dealing with the underworld. It is no accident that this fearsome visage most often decorates war shields in Classic Maya reliefs, alternating with the "division-sign" of death or with the number seven (this god presiding over that numeral). He also appears with high frequency on tubular pottery incense burners from the Tabasco-Chiapas area.

One could extend this esoteric symbolism, as Thompson (1950) has done. For in-

Fig. 4 *"Division-sign" on cheek of death god seated before temple. Death-eyes surmount the headdress.* Dresden Codex, p. 28b.

stance, jaguar, water, and water-lily associations can be convincingly shown to be part of the repertory of underworld art.

MAYA FUNERARY CERAMICS

Let us now turn to a great body of Classic Maya art which, in my belief, represents not only a deep concern with Maya ideas about the afterlife, but also demonstrates that the Maya lords accepted the concept of death and apotheosis contained in the Hero Twins myth. For many years now, it has been an accepted dogma that the subject matter of pictorial Maya ceramics was mainly the here and now, a depiction of every-

Fig. 5 *Death-eyes (upside-down) on the wings of the Killer Bat. Chamá polychrome vase.* Private collection. Photo by Justin Kerr.

Fig. 6 *Decapitated god (God CH) wearing death collar and death spots.* Dresden Codex, p. 2a, left.

day life among the elite with perhaps a few gods and decorative motifs thrown in for diversion. It was also a majority opinion that the artists who painted or carved these vessels were illiterate and totally ignorant of the complex intellectual life led by their employers.

After long and careful study of the matter, I have been led to exactly opposite conclusions. Maya pictorial ceramics deal exclusively with the underworld and life after death, and the overwhelming majority of texts painted on them are meaningful and refer to the same esoteric material. The justification for this view is fully presented elsewhere (Coe 1973), but let me here present an example. A polychrome vase from Dumbarton Oaks (Fig. 8) is painted with an elaborate palace scene. Like all other examples of pictorial pottery, it was once placed in a tomb, and thus by its very function must have a mortuary aspect. In this scene, the ruler and some of his subordinates are painted black, the color not only of war but also of death. On the pilasters of the palace

Fig. 7 *The Jaguar God of the Underworld. Temple of the Sun, Palenque* (after Thompson 1950: Fig. 12, *14*).

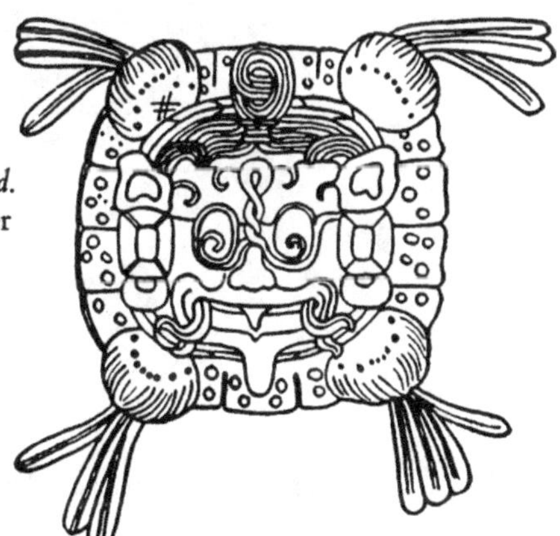

Fig. 8 *Polychrome vase.* Dumbarton Oaks, Washington.

are the fearsome masks of the Jaguar God of the Underworld, surely an indication that this is taking place elsewhere than in our world. To confirm the identification, note the death's head off to one side of the scene. Now, in this kind of representation, none of the participants can be identified as gods; would not, then, the reasonable explanation be that we are looking at a depiction of that palace and its retinue which Mesoamerican lords were so anxious to project into the underworld on their demise?

In fact, death symbolism, both overt and esoteric, is all-pervasive on pictorial pottery. I have discovered that the iconography of the underworld is tremendously complex, with a bewildering variety of gods and mythological scenes, most of which represent myths not recorded in any ethnohistoric documents and, therefore, beyond our ken. I will confine myself here to a demonstration of the "Harrowing of Hell" theme explicit in the Hero Twins story.

First of all, it has become clear from my study, which includes the examination of several hundred unpublished vessels, that the two principal rulers in the underworld are those deities known in the codices as God L and God N. Curiously enough, they rarely, if ever, appear together. God L is perhaps best known on the east side of the entrance to the Sanctuary of the Temple of the Cross at Palenque (Fig. 9): an old, cigar-smoking personage with a Moan bird and/or Moan-bird feathers in his headdress. I have no idea who he really is. God N (Fig. 10) is another aged divinity, usually with a snail-shell on his back, although sometimes this is a turtle carapace. There is excellent reason to believe that he also functioned as god of the Uayeb days at the end of the year, and that he is identical with Mam, the old under mountain god of the southern Maya, and with Pauahtun of the Yucatec Maya. These two, along with the Jaguar God of the Underworld, appear with high frequency on Maya ceramics.

Another common representation on the pottery is a pair of handsome, richly attired Maya youths (Fig. 11), a motif which I have called the Young Lords. These usually have "god-markings," and are thus deities; they almost always wear a headdress with a jawless "Zip Monster" in front. This is not just a question of double symmetry on a particular pot, for they generally are slightly differentiated from each other, and occasionally appear together in larger scenes. I believe that the pair of young gods who are seen to wear headbands are the same; since I identify the Young Lords as the Hero Twins, so the "Headband Gods" might be one aspect of these in the underworld.

On a bowl said to be from Quintana Roo (Blom 1950), the Twins are seen in their most renowned role, that of blowgunners, shooting at a fantastic bird. The death spots on their bodies, however, indicate that they could be in the underworld. A remarkable carved vase from the Chocholá area of Yucatán (Coe 1973: no. 64) contains, I think, an explicit reference to the Twins' approach to the underworld rulers: a fantastic Mosquito God is in the act of stinging God N, who lies cringing in his shell.

Fig. 9 *God L smoking a cigar. Temple of the Cross, Palenque* (after Maudslay 1889–1902, IV: Pl. 72).

Fig. 10 *God N crawling from his shell. Carved vase, possibly from Guatemala.* Private collection. Photo by Justin Kerr.

Fig. 11
The Young Lords. Polychrome vase from highland Guatemala.
Private collection.
Photos by Justin Kerr.

Ball-game scenes, which I do not illustrate, are far from rare on Maya pottery. But particularly ubiquitous, especially in the Chamá area, are vessels referring to the various "Houses" in which the dread trials took place. Young Lords, or Headband Gods, are often shown smoking cigars (as are other underworld deities), and on a fine vase in the Museum of Primitive Art (Coe 1973: no. 45) is an underworld ritual scene in which can be seen what I take to be a Maya pun on the cigar incident: a little firefly carries a cigar, instead of the other way around.

Finally, the denouement approaches. In the Popol Vuh, the Twins are killed by the Killer Bats, but reappear in the court of the underworld. There are many representations of Young Lords dancing and even tumbling; one vase in the Museum of the American Indian shows them performing before God N and possibly God L. Among the rest is a Chamá pot (Coe 1973: no. 15) showing the Armadillo Dance mentioned by our great Quiché source. The climax of the drama, when the Twins cut up the ruling Lords, can be seen on no less than three vases known to me, the most dramatic being a Chamá vase from the collection of Gillett Griffin, on which a Young Lord conceals a sacrificial knife behind his back while pulling God N from his shell (Coe 1973: no. 16).

I am not claiming that everything we see on pictorial ceramics of the Classic Maya can be explained by the Popol Vuh. Far from it! It seems to me that what we have is only a surviving fragment of a far larger original which has disappeared for all time, and which explained in the greatest detail what the dead person was going to see and experience in the other world. The Primary Standard Text which appears on these vases, as I have explained elsewhere (Coe 1973: 18, 21–22), is probably a long funerary chant which was sung over the dead or dying man to direct him to and through this perilous place. But what I do feel is that the Hero Twins story, by occupying a prominent place in this artistic repertory, suggests that the ultimate fate of the Maya lords was not extinction but apotheosis to the heavens, where they might take their place among the stars. Alberto Ruz (1968: 56) notes that the mythical first four men of the Quiché tribe, after receiving premonitions of their impending death, promised to their wives and followers that they would return, presumably to be worshiped as gods by their people. There is some evidence from archaeology that the Classic Maya rulers thought likewise.

TOMBS, TEMPLES, AND PYRAMIDS

Some years ago I published a paper entitled "The Funerary Temple among the Classic Maya" (Coe 1956). In this article, I concluded from an examination of many excavation reports that the primary function of the pyramid that supported a temple substructure was to house the tomb of a ruler or other important personage, and that this was the reason for its construction in the first place. Alberto Ruz, who seems to have been about the only scholar to read the article, came to an opposing thesis, namely, that it was the presence of the temple-pyramid which attracted the tomb or tombs. He considered his discovery of the crypt in the Temple of the Inscriptions, obviously built before the pyramid, a notable exception.

I have seen little in the ensuing years to change my original hypothesis. True, there are many tombs and graves found near the surface of temple-pyramids in intrusive contexts, but there have been precious few investigations into the bases of pyramids at ground level; of these, almost but not quite all have encountered primary tombs of great size and magnificence. I believe this shows that the ethnohistoric evidence that the Maya erected important structures and even pyramids over the tombs of their rulers can be extended back into Classic times.

Be that as it may, Ruz himself suggests (1968: 186–7) that the great Palenque tomb which he discovered represents not only death but also the spiritual resurrection of the dead king which it housed. Not only the treasure trove of jewelry which accompanied this lord in his sarcophagus, but also the soul duct, or "psychoduct," leading up the passageway to the surface from it, implies some sort of hope for life in the hereafter. Ruz even goes so far as to suggest that the scene carved in relief upon the sarcophagus lid expresses resurrection. Notwithstanding the fact that I do not agree with some of the identifications which he makes of specific elements in this tableau—for instance, the world tree above the youth as a corn plant—I do think that the general theme has been correctly identified. This would suggest to me that the reclining youth is one of the Hero Twins, the very embodiment of the theme of death and transfiguration. There has been a tendency, ever since Seler's day, to think of these world trees, which we find not only here but also in the Temples of the Sun, Cross, and Foliated Cross, as placed on earth to hold up the sky. I wonder whether they are not instead growing in the underworld to hold up the earth? I also question the easy identification of the surrounding band with supposed celestial symbols as a "sky band" representing the heavens. Might not this band just as well represent the night sky, which is, after all, closely tied to the underworld?

In my 1956 article, I also note the high incidence of graves, intrusive certainly, in what have been called "palaces." Given these facts, then, might not the primary and secondary purposes of most of the mountainous piles of architecture which we see at a Classic Maya site have been to house the honored dead? Perhaps we should be talking of "necropolises" instead of "ceremonial centers."

MORTUARY CENTERS AMONG THE MAYA

Setting aside the possible mortuary nature of individual Maya buildings, there is some slight evidence that entire sites might have had some kind of occult connection with the dead and the underworld. Jaina immediately comes to mind: a tiny, calcareous islet off the Campeche coast, separated from it by a tidal inlet. Its ceremonial center is minuscule and unimportant compared to those on the mainland—for example, Uxmal and Kabah—and cannot explain the presence of many thousands of richly stocked graves that have been found over its surface. Most of these contained hollow, whistle-figurines of the highest artistry, better than any found in more famous sites. It has generally been felt that the best of these are portraits of living rulers; I doubt this. A comparison should be made between these and those personages who look *least* like gods on Maya funerary ceramics. I would guess that many detailed correspondences in costume and even physical features with specific deities will be found, and that many or most will, in fact, eventually be identified as gods or demigods in the underworld drama.

Be that as it may, Jaina cannot be explained on its own terms. It must have been the focus of a mortuary cult that brought dead and dying persons from the richer and more highly populated Puuc area for final interment in a kind of "Isle of the Dead" in the western sea, where the sun sets into the ocean and the underworld.

I also wonder about Palenque and Copán. The Emblem Glyphs of both have strong underworld connotations: Bone (T.570) and Skull (Jaguar Skull?) for Palenque, and Bat (T.756) for Copán. It may be significant that both sites stand at the extremes of the Maya area, in border territories which might have been the scenes of continual war with outsiders. And, at Copán, several of the stelae depict rulers garbed as underworld rulers, such as Stela I, in which the lord is embellished with the trappings of the Fish God, GI of the Palenque Triad.

CONCLUSIONS

There can be little doubt that a major concern of the Maya, or at least of their elite, was the world of the dead. Much of their architecture and all of their pictorial ceramics were dedicated to this end. The social and political nature of this obsession cannot be avoided: basic to all Maya life is ancestor worship, and to the ancient Maya this meant worship of the departed rulers, apotheosized as divinities, from whose race they sprang in the first place. Regardless of what happened to the commoners after death, the souls of the elite were immortal, having followed that perilous journey to hell and back which was first traversed successfully by their predecessors, the glorious Hero Twins.

BIBLIOGRAPHY

Blom, Frans

1950 A Polychrome Maya Plate from Quintana Roo. *Notes on Middle American Archaeology and Ethnology*, vol. iv, no. 98, pp. 81–84. Carnegie Institution of Washington, Cambridge.

Coe, Michael D.

1956 The Funerary Temple among the Classic Maya. *Southwestern Journal of Anthropology*, vol. 12, no. 4, pp. 387–394. University of New Mexico Press, Albuquerque.

1973 The Maya Scribe and His World. The Grolier Club, New York.

Edmonson, Munro S.

1971 The Book of Counsel: The Popol Vuh of the Quiche Maya of Guatemala. *Middle American Research Institute, Tulane University, Publication 35*. New Orleans.

Fuentes y Guzmán, Francisco Antonio de

1932 Recordación Florida: discurso historial y demostración natural, material, militar y política del Reyno de Guatemala. 3 vols. Sociedad de Geografía e Historia, Guatemala.

Maudslay, A. P.

1889–1902 Biologia Centrali-Americana: Archaeology. 1 vol. text, 4 vols. plates. R. H. Porter and Dulau & Co., London.

Miles, S. W.

1957 The Sixteenth-Century Pokom-Maya: A Documentary Analysis of Social Structure and Archaeological Setting. *Transactions of the American Philosophical Society*, n.s. vol. 47, part 4, pp. 731–781. Philadelphia.

Ruz Lhuillier, Alberto

1968 Costumbres funerarias de los antiguos mayas. Universidad Nacional Autónoma de México, Seminario de Cultura Maya, Mexico.

Thompson, J. Eric S.

1950 Maya Hieroglyphic Writing: Introduction. *Carnegie Institution of Washington, Publication 589*. Washington.

1970 Maya History and Religion. University of Oklahoma Press, Norman.

Tozzer, Alfred M. (ed.)

1941 Landa's Relación de las Cosas de Yucatan: A Translation. *Papers of the Peabody Museum of American Archaeology and Ethnology, Harvard University*, vol. xviii. Cambridge.

Death-Associated Figures on Mochica Pottery

ELIZABETH P. BENSON

DUMBARTON OAKS

THE Mochica lived in irrigated valleys on the north coast of Peru, between desert, mountains, and sea. I have elsewhere (Benson 1972: 27–32) postulated a major deity (one god, who is also two or three gods in one—father and son, and perhaps father and twins), descended[1] from the ancient mountain god of Chavín and characterized by snake earrings, snake appendages on the belt, and a fanged mouth (the fanged mouth not being restricted to the deity, but used as a symbol for supernatural power in a number of creatures). This deity was, in one sense or manifestation, a *deus otiosus*, a creator god, who dwelt in the mountains and was a deity of the mountains, the seat of the older civilization and the source of the water that irrigated the coastal valleys. In another form the deity was an active god. If god-the-father was the mountain god in the east, he was also probably a sun god, and the active god was a manifestation that came down to the coast each day. This coastal deity is always shown in action, with knees bent, and was perhaps a culture hero of the people who were dependent on the sun and the water from the mountains. The Mochica were also dependent on the sea for livelihood, and this deity is most often shown in sea scenes: in a boat, fishing, fighting a fish monster, impersonating or fighting a crab. Moreover, the sun—that is, the sun god—coming from the mountains in the east, sank into the sea in the west each evening. This god was probably thought to have died in the sea and been reborn in the morning. I believe that there was a Mochica otherworld or afterlife that was probably entered through the sea, but was on the other side of it; that many Mochica pottery representations have to do with sacrifice, funeral rites, passage to—and life in—the afterworld; and that these themes are related to concepts of fertility, the rebirth of the sun, and the continuation of Mochica power.

1. There is, of course, no evidence for any direct lineage between the Mochica and Chavín, but certainly there was a cultural inheritance, as there was throughout much of Peru. The Mochica were not the only heirs of Chavín, but motif complexes, archaizing pots, etc., indicate that they felt a particularly strong identification with the earlier civilization.

Fig. 1 *Roll-out drawing of a painted pot in the Art Institute of Chicago* (after Kutscher 1954: Pl. 25B). Drawing by Wilhelm v.d. Steinen.

There are a number of scenes on Mochica pottery that deal with sacrificial beheading and amputation. In these, certain figures and elements recur: pottery, houses, women, cormorants, and male figures in certain garments. In Figure 1 the major figure, in a loincloth and log-shaped ear ornaments, has his hands held by two women in dark garments with contrasting waistbands, and is surrounded by the amputated legs, arms, and head that must be his fate. To the right is a simple structure with a seated figure in a white garment, a dark shawl around the shoulders, and a headdress with a diagonal line at the side. This figure is minimally rendered, but these details are made quite clear. He sits in "prayer pose" before a stirrup-spout pot and a jar with a tie on it.

In scenes of the afterlife represented on pottery, some of the same elements appear. In Figure 2 a couple—a woman and a dead man—are seated on a striped base (an indication of importance in Mochica iconography) with a variety of pots and tied offerings painted at their feet. The Mochica convention for representing the dead was to show socket eyes (if not a skeletal head) and, in some cases, a skeletal ribcage, but an otherwise normal body. Certainly sex organs never died.

Pottery is a common ingredient of scenes that depict sacrifice or show the dead. In fact, I was led into a study of funerary scenes by an attempt to analyze the contexts in which pottery appears. Pottery representations fall into several types in these scenes. In a number of scenes, an important figure holds a cup or goblet (Figs. 22b, 24, 28), so it is evident that libation with chicha is a part of this complex.[2] This use of pottery

2. Bird, Dwyer, Furst, and Grossman (Benson n.d.b) have commented on the use of chicha in various funerary rites in Peru, Chile, and Ecuador, and of fermented liquids in Mexico and Guatemala.

Fig. 2 *Skeletal man in a cape being fondled by a woman. The body of the pot forms a stepped or striped platform, on the top of which various pottery shapes are drawn.* Photo courtesy of the Museum of the American Indian, Heye Foundation, New York.

may be specific to scenes related to sacrificial ceremonies. A scene on a pot in the Museum für Völkerkunde, Munich (Kutscher 1950a: Fig. 62), shows a gathering of mythical—probably godly—creatures, two of whom jointly hold a goblet. They are separated, by what must be a sky band, from a scene below in which two nude, seated figures with bound hands are about to be decapitated.

Jars appear, usually at least two of them, in frieze designs clearly representing the afterlife (Figs. 7, 9, 11, 16; Kutscher 1954: Pls. 30B, 31A), and singly—or with a stirrup-spout pot—in sacrifice scenes in front of a simple structure which may have a figure inside (Figs. 1, 19, 25). These jars usually have a tie around the neck, and sometimes a sprig in the tie.[3] Tied objects are an important part of the funerary complex. What we may assume to be prisoners-of-war were brought in with the victor holding the end of a rope tied around the prisoner's neck (Kutscher 1954: Pl. 24). The rope was then left around the neck and is depicted simply dangling there (*ibid.*: Pl. 23; Larco Hoyle 1965: 70). In Figure 1 the decapitated head and amputated limbs are tied with rope.[4] Bowls of offerings are usually tied together in pairs (Figs. 26, 27), and sometimes panpipes that are being played are tied together (Fig. 7). Not only are funerary jars depicted with a tie around the neck, but many actual jars of this shape (Ubbelohde-Doering 1954: Pl. 169; Larco Hoyle 1966: Pls. 40, 41)—as well as stirrup spouts (Ubbelohde-Doering 1954: Pls. 174, 175) and "cruets" (Schmidt 1929: 192), which are imitations of the jar shape—have a tie painted or modeled on them, arguing against the assumption that the tie is merely a practical handle or carrying device. The tie seems to be symbolic of offering or sacrifice; I believe that tying is an integral part of the funerary ritual, and that the jar with the rope around the neck is the purest funerary symbol. The tied jar is perhaps in some way equivalent to the prisoner figure or the sacrificed limb or head.

A large number of jars of the shape depicted on the pottery exists in the collection of the Museo Larco Herrera, Lima, many of which are decorated with the tie or tie-shape. Forty-odd of these jars have a stirrup-spout pot depicted in relief on the jar, often repeated four times, with the "tie" hanging between the pot representations. Other motifs that appear on these jars are maize and various animals, but these are

3. Peter Furst has pointed out (Benson n.d.b) that the Huichols of northern Mexico tie a sprig to a jug of fermenting liquid to keep the dead away until it is fermented. Robert Sonin (*ibid.*) has noted that in modern Peru a branch is hung outside houses in which chicha is sold.

4. I know of no archaeological evidence from the North Coast for this sort of thing, but Penteado Coelho (n.d.) illustrates a number of buried, severed Nasca heads which have a cotton rope tied through a hole in the forehead. I am grateful to Junius Bird for calling my attention to this publication.

not as plentiful as the stirrup-spout designs. Many of these pots also have a wave motif at the top.

The stirrup-spout pot, when it is alone, is usually shown with the deity or on a raised, striped platform or with the most important person in the scene (Figs. 3, 12). It appears to be associated with the deity and/or power, and it seems to occur only in scenes that have to do with death. The stirrup spout is a very ancient form in the Andes —pre-Chavín, and an important form in Chavín times for the most lavishly decorated pottery. It is likely that the stirrup-spout pot was a cult image, associated in the Mochica mind with the old mountain deity and the Chavín religion, hence with the Mochica deity. It was possibly the most important cult object the Mochica made; as a depicted form it would have had strong symbolic value.

In addition to jars, women also appear in the preparation-for-death and afterlife scenes, both in elaborate painted and relief pottery and on modeled pots. An example of the latter in the Museo Larco Herrera shows a large central prisoner figure with a rope around his neck and, at either side, a small woman clasping the figure's arm. The woman's role in death ceremonies and the afterlife probably explains the meaning of some of the erotic scenes which show a live woman, or sometimes a dead woman or two women, with a dead man (Figs. 2, 11, 12). I suspect that many of the modeled pots that are often described as "mother and child" (e.g., Kutscher 1950a: Pls. 25, 30; Anton 1972: Pl. 148) actually depict a woman bearing off a probable sacrificial victim, since many of the figures with the women are shown with the haircut of a victim or prisoner-of-war (Kutscher 1950a: Pl. 30). These women are usually oversized, which may indicate a great earth-mother or sea-mother, or at least the mythical aspect of the woman. (The fact that some of the women in the erotic scenes are also oversized [Larco Hoyle 1965: 38, 39, 46, 47, 119] is one argument against the male figures' being child victims, although the scale variance of figures in erotic scenes is a subject for separate investigation.) Another group of pots shows the deity attacking—in much the same way that he attacks sea monsters—a woman carrying a small figure in a shawl on her back, with a jar, which functions almost like a badge of office, at her waist (Ubbelohde-Doering 1954: Pl. 191; Kutscher 1954: Pl. 55A). One could hypothesize a myth in which one of these women (or this particular supernatural woman), instead of bearing the victim to the god's realm as she was supposed to do, tried to take him off for herself and was caught by the deity.

Another possibility is that the little figure so carried in the attack scenes was the offspring of the deity and the woman, for another genre of scenes in which women appear shows the deity making love (Fig. 3; Larco Hoyle 1965: 109, 113, 140), perhaps to the same woman depicted as being attacked by him. Here a number of elements from the sacrificial scenes are shown, indicating a death association for this subject.

Fig. 3 *Roll-out drawing of a relief pot showing the deity making love* (after Baessler 1902–3, III: Pl. 119).

With minor variations, the following motifs occur: amputated limbs and "trophy" head; a simple structure with two women, who appear to have long braids (women also frequently appear in pairs in scenes with skeletal or sacrificial figures); the deity and his woman in another structure, with a stirrup-spout pot in front of the deity's head; an anthropomorphic cormorant making chicha while another seems to be pouring from a jar onto the deity,[5] these figures usually having a pronged headdress, which Barbara De Mott (n.d.: 10) has called the "fisher" headdress (similar but more elaborate headgear is sometimes worn by the deity as fisherman); and the deity's "lizard helper" standing in prayer pose, watching. Most versions of this scene show a row of waves below, suggesting that the scene takes place in or under the sea, or on a shore. A number of other erotic pots also have this wave motif on the base (Larco Hoyle 1965: 30, 39), although even more frequent is the striped motif (Fig. 2; Larco Hoyle 1965: 38, 48, 124, 125, 134, 135), like that seen on pyramid bases.

In yet another group of scenes, the deity is apparently being led to the underworld, accompanied in some cases by anthropomorphic cormorants (Fig. 4; Baessler 1902–3, III: Pl. 123)—these deep-plunging birds would be excellent guides into the sea—and, in other, rarer cases, by a cormorant and a woman (unpublished pot, Museo Nacional, Lima) or a cormorant and a lizard (Museo Larco Herrera). The deity in these depictions wears the headdress of the mountain god, "god-the-father." I tend to call this the "sunrise" headdress, but, in this case, I think it is the "sunset" headdress. (The active deity wears a variety of headgear, but most commonly a brimless hat with a jaguar head and paws.) Women and anthropomorphic cormorants are sometimes inter-

5. Junius Bird (Benson n.d.b) has noted that in northern Chile the last offering given before covering a burial was a mixture of chicha and corn meal, which was poured over the body.

changeable in scenes where they seem to give some comfort and succor to sacrificial victims (Fig. 24), and effigy cormorants are sometimes depicted holding a tied jar (Baessler 1902–3: Pl. 54). Cormorants, however, do not appear in scenes of the afterlife, thus strengthening the argument that the afterlife is on the other side of the sea, beyond the realm of cormorants, who are useful only in the passage from one world to the other. To some extent, there are, in Mochica thought, equivalences between human beings and anthropomorphic animals, but a distinction between sacrifice scenes and scenes in the afterlife is that anthropomorphs do not appear in the latter.

In some of the sacrifice scenes, as well as in certain other ritual and afterlife scenes, there are figures which seem to represent what might be called priests. The garments of these figures vary somewhat and suggest different types of priests or different functions or moments in a ceremony. Some of the same figures are depicted on modeled pots, both full-figure (Fig. 5) and as portrait vessels (Anton 1972: Pl. 169). They wear a simple basic garment, usually white, which often has lines—suggesting fringe—at the

Fig. 4 *The deity being supported by two caped anthropomorphic cormorants on a platform with a step motif, a symbol of importance.* Photo courtesy of the Art Institute of Chicago.

Fig. 5 *Globular pot with the head of a blind man with a wrinkled face. He wears a garment with a "badge" and a headdress with "rick-rack" decoration.* Photo by Helmut Jäger, courtesy of the Übersee-Museum, Bremen.

bottom, and sometimes a "badge" at the neck; the garment may also have a motif at the cuff ("S's"—which, I believe, are a symbol for "sea"—or circles or a stepped fret). Very often a cloth like a cape or shawl or scarf goes over the shoulders and is tied at the chest or goes around the waist. On modeled pots the garment tied around the body is often rounded out, as if there were something inside. (Women may carry a jar or a small figurine in a shawl, but these are not attributes of the males.) There is a headdress that may or may not go under the chin, but usually has a tie on top that often forms a diagonal line at the side; sometimes the headdress has a serrated design. If the headdress does not tie under the chin, the wearer may have "log" ear ornaments; these are worn in other contexts, but the figures discussed here rarely wear any other kind of ear ornament. I suspect that the use of tied-on garments, both on the body and on the headdress, has to do with a hierarchy in the priesthood or with the function of the priest or with a given time or role in his duties, as well as being a meaningful entity in itself.

All of these figures depicted on the modeled pots have some physical disability: blindness, lameness, old age, or traces of disease, such as leishmaniasis or verruga—a disease with symptoms similar to leishmaniasis (cf. Weiss 1961; Coury 1969; Grand Rounds 1000 Years before Columbus; Lastres, Muelle, and Farfán 1943: Pl. 1). One figure has a walking stick because he has no toes on one foot (Lothrop 1964: 173). Some have heavy swollen faces and hold cups (Osborne 1968: 40). Many have abnormal dentition (Schmidt 1929: 145, left). It seems evident that the priests were chosen for their office—which I presume had to do with death—because they had a

Fig. 6 *Globular pot with a skeletal head, a headdress tied on top, a garment over the shoulders, and lines at the bottom of the shift.* Photo courtesy of the Museum für Völkerkunde, Berlin.

physical deformity.[6] They were associated with the dead by a sympathetic magic. Faces which have been affected by leishmaniasis or verruga look like mummified faces; blind faces have the blank look of the dead.

Sometimes these figures are dead. A globular pot of a person, with a headdress tied on top, a cape, a white shift with lines, badge, and S's on the sleeves, has a skeletal face and holds panpipes (Fig 6). A painted frieze showing life in the otherworld has a similar figure at the left, playing a quena (Fig. 7). He has a dark garment looped around the shoulders—this is surely meant to represent something tied around the neck, but it appears to be superimposed, probably because it was thought of primarily for its symbolic meaning rather than as a real object. Despite all that is said of Mochica realism, what the Mochica were most interested in was not naturalistic rendering but what we would call symbolic motifs. For example, I believe that the lines at the bottom of these priests' garments are also symbolic. This motif appears on short or long shifts, drawn above or below the hem, but it is always carefully drawn, even on relatively crude relief scenes. The design must be a kind of shorthand for something it suggests. It may indicate something like the ragged edge of a vow of poverty or purification. It may define some spiritual status difference between its wearers and, say, the deity, who often has a jagged bottom to his shirt, or, at least, such a motif where the shirt ends (Kutscher 1954: Pls. 53, 62, 63, 64A). It may have a meaning related to raveling, unfinished ends, or possibly to the use of raveled threads to make ritual ties for death ceremonies.

In the painted scene (Fig. 7) there are also two women: one large, dressed in a dark garment and holding a cup, the other small and wearing a light garment. Both have a braid or rope from neck to waist and a curious scarification on the cheek. Three other

6. I am grateful to Johannes Wilbert for pointing out Pedro Weiss's (1961) paper on the association between leishmaniasis, verruga, and the potato. The two diseases are endemic in certain valleys in the Andes which today produce the best potatoes in Peru; those who suffer from this disease are the guardians of the crops (*ibid.*: 68). Hence, there is not only an association between disease and fertility, but another between disease and the highlands. "On the coast," writes Weiss, "the potato is associated with leishmaniasis, verruga, lizards, and felines" (*ibid.*: 73; author's translation). Other authors, notably Larco Hoyle (1965: 87–92, 123–8), have argued that many of these faces are those of "castigados" who have been deliberately mutilated as punishment for crimes, specifically sexual crime. I cannot agree with this. In the first place, I think that the subjects that were important enough to be depicted on the finest pottery have to do with cosmology, belief, ritual, and offering, and were not moralizing examples for human beings. Moreover, most of the malformed faces are clearly the result of disease and not of surgery. If there were deliberate mutilation, I suspect that it would be in imitation of a sacred illness. Weiss (*op. cit.*: 68) notes that in certain villages those suffering from leishmaniasis were accustomed to corrode the nose of the statue of the patron saint to imitate the lesions of the illness.

Fig. 7 *Roll-out drawing of a painted pot in the Museum für Völkerkunde, Berlin* (after Kutscher 1954: Pl. 30A). Drawing by Wilhelm v.d. Steinen.

Fig. 8 *Detail of a painted pot in the collection of Guillermo Ganoza, Trujillo.* Photo by the author.

Fig. 9 *Roll-out drawing of a relief-decorated pot in the Museum für Völkerkunde, Berlin, showing a frieze of figures in the afterlife* (after Kutscher 1954: Pl. 31B). Drawing by Wilhelm v.d. Steinen.

figures—a pair of twin panpipers and a figure in a "rickrack" headdress topped with feathers—have shirts with lines at the bottom. A tiny quena-player is dressed like the two pipers; all three of these figures have hooded capes and a tie around the neck.

Musicians do not appear in many categories of scenes: they are not shown in sacrifice scenes, presentation-of-prisoner scenes, or battle scenes. Certain pots with musicians may represent a pre-battle ritual. In Figure 8 a procession of figures in warrior's gear forms a spiral design, at the top of which is a man in priest's garments; in addition to the warrior figures there are also three quena-players and two drummers. A similar pot (Muelle 1936: Fig. 2; Jiménez Borja 1955: 120) shows a procession of warriors, at the nucleus of which is a man in priest's garments playing a quena and a man with a knife headdress playing a drum. I believe, however, that these are versions of the afterlife scene. The hand-holding trait is seen in afterlife scenes (Figs. 7, 9, 11, 16), and scenes of the afterlife do sometimes have figures in warrior's dress (Fig. 16; Kutscher 1954: Pl. 31A). Musical instruments appear in almost every afterlife scene and on many modeled skeletal pots; they are frequently held or played by priest figures. The evidence is strong that they are death-associated and that at least some of them indicate the otherworld, or the preparation for it.

In Figure 9 a panpiper in bird headdress faces a piper in jaguar headdress, with a small drummer between them; this motif is repeated further along in the scene. (Pipers tend not only to be represented in pairs, but in pairs of pairs.) At the far right is a figure with an under-the-chin headdress and a cloth tied around the waist; there are two jars tied with ropes behind him, and a small figure facing him holds a cup. A figure in the center has a cloth tied around the shoulders. All of these figures have skeletal heads.

A status order in the instruments seems to be indicated in these scenes. The deity is shown playing panpipes (Larco Hoyle 1945: 22), and panpipers in general tend to be bigger than other musicians in the scene—in most cases, if they are small figures, the other figures do not have instruments. Panpipes are sometimes shown with a head or hand on the end, possibly suggesting ceremonial amputation and decapitation (Fig. 10; Disselhoff 1967: 105). All four musicians in Figure 10 have lines at the bottom of their garments, this time hanging like fringe. They all wear shifts and capes, some with vertical stripes. The two small trumpet-players have the headdress tied on top. The panpipers are not only larger, but more elaborately dressed. They have jaguar and bird headdresses like those in Figure 9, probably emulating the deity and his lizard helper who wear jaguar and bird headdresses, respectively (Fig. 30). The lizard helper, however, is never depicted playing a musical instrument. This creature, who, I believe, is part sea-lizard, frequently has a thick tie around the waist and most often wears a vertically striped garment. The vertically striped shirt is sometimes worn by

Fig. 10 *Roll-out drawing of a painted pot in the Museum für Völkerkunde, Berlin, depicting panpipers and quena-players* (after Kutscher 1950a: Fig. 32). See Schmidt 1929: Pl. 196 for a view of the entire pot.

the deity in scenes where he is attacking the woman (Ubbelohde-Doering 1954: Pl. 191) or where he is attacking sea creatures (Bushnell 1957: Pl. 25), although it is one of his least frequently worn garments. It occasionally appears on the death-priest figures (Kutscher 1950a: Pl. 26); it is sometimes worn by small male figures with oversized women (Ubbelohde-Doering 1954: Pl. 232); and it sometimes appears on dead men in erotic scenes (Larco Hoyle 1965: 134). A pot published by Larco Hoyle (*ibid.*: 80) shows a man with a skeletal head, a diagonal line on his headdress (which also occasionally appears in the erotic scenes), and a vertically striped garment. He is holding panpipes with one hand, and, with the other, he is embracing a woman whom he is tongue-kissing. Figures in erotic scenes often hold panpipes, but rarely play them (Fig. 11). I believe that panpipes existed as a symbol, almost like a word, perhaps signifying death as well as status.

In Figure 12 two women are shown with a kind of tie around the neck. Strong and Evans (1952: 152) found in the burial of the Warrior Priest at the Huaca de la Cruz site the burials of two women, one of whom had a cotton sash tied around the neck,

Fig. 11 *Roll-out drawing of a pot with a modeled skeletal couple on top (he is holding panpipes) and a frieze of painted skeletal figures with pots below* (after Baessler 1902–3, III: Pl. 127).

Fig. 12 *Roll-out drawing of a pot in the Museo de Arte, Lima* (after Kauffman Doig 1971: 302).

suggesting garroting. Burial 5 at Huaca de la Cruz was a woman whose hair "had been combed into two large ropes, one on each side of the face, bound with cotton string and hanging below the shoulders" (*ibid.*: 142). Burial 6 had an identical arrangement. The women depicted on pots sometimes seem to have tied hair, whereas sometimes a garroting cord may be indicated. In either case, it seems clear that these women, who may have succored the dying, also went along with the dead. The women in Figure 12 both have skeletal faces; one of them is embracing or dancing with a skeletal figure with a rope coming from his neck. At the left side is an enthroned figure with a cape and a long garment with S's at the cuff. In front of him is a stirrup-spout pot, and, above one of the women, panpipes are suspended in space. The use of both of these objects seems highly symbolic, both here and elsewhere.

The enthroned figure is unusual. Its garments suggest the death-priest, but the stirrup-spout pot is usually shown with an enthroned figure that, if it is not the deity, is at least wearing elaborate garments. Here I suspect that it is the power of the deity that is invoked, the association of the priest with the deity. Figures on modeled erotic pots are also sometimes enthroned, particularly in fellatio scenes.

This particular enthroned figure has the step motif on the cheek. The step, a provocative Mochica motif, is basically a sign of importance. It may derive from a simplified diagram of mountains, and may have as one meaning "mountains." It is frequently combined with the scroll motif, which may signify "sea." This double motif, which appears often and in various forms, would then combine the significance of the two most important elements in the Mochica world. The step motif appears alone on litters and the approaches to pyramids (the pyramid itself being, of course, a step motif); it appears doubled on the roofs of houses and on the headdresses of certain human and owl warriors; and it also appears as an isolated motif (Figs. 11, 21). A square-based pot in the Museo Larco Herrera has an erotic couple on top (he is skeletal, she is alive), and, painted on the side of the pot, are a stirrup-spout pot and two tied, topped jars beside a stepped triangle. These are drawn, not as a scene, but as glyphic elements. The step motif also appears on the faces of the important dead. Larco Hoyle (1965: 87) believes it to be a sign of castigation resulting from punishment by flaying. Faces may have been flayed (although there is little pictorial evidence for this), but one must keep in mind that the step motif is one of importance. I believe that it is not a sign of punishment, but is evidence of the importance of the dead after they no longer wore the garments that would identify their status. If the step motif does signify something like "mountains" and all that that implies, it is possible that people so marked, who have gone through the sea to the afterlife, are still stamped as "mountain people," inheritors of the importance or divinity of the mountains. One reason for the dominant status of panpipes may have been that their shape naturally forms a step motif.

Fig. 13 *Death-priest playing a quena.* Photo courtesy of the British Museum, London.

Quenas and/or trumpets are usually played by smaller figures in the afterlife friezes (Fig. 10), although, among the modeled figures, quenas seem to be to some extent interchangeable with panpipes. I do not believe, however, that there are any skeletal modeled figures playing quenas. Quena-players are usually dressed in the priest's garb (Fig. 13; Schmidt 1929: 142) and, again, have blind or diseased faces. Two quena-players (Fig. 13; d'Harcourt and d'Harcourt 1924: Pl. 45, right) have a design of beans

Fig. 14 *Pot in the Museo de Arqueología de la Universidad Nacional de Trujillo.* Photo by the author.

on their headdresses.[7] Another figure with a bean headdress is blind and seems to be playing an ocarina and holding seeds, beans, or corn kernels in his hand (Tello 1938: Pl. 36, right). Quenas and panpipes are sometimes played by anthropomorphic vegetables (Anton 1972: Pl. 108; Tello 1938: Pl. 32; Montell 1929: Fig. 7), and one potato figure with a diseased face and a headdress tied under the chin holds what may be a quena (Sawyer 1966: Fig. 77). Music thus ties in with fertility as well as with death and sex in the afterlife; all of these things are part of a closely woven system of beliefs.

Curved trumpets have been found in burials, and they are sometimes pictured with funerary offerings (Fig. 15a). The clay instruments are often richly decorated with

7. Another effigy pot of a priest figure (Larco Hoyle 1938–39, I: Fig. 32) has beans on the headdress, but plays no instrument. Still another bean headdress is worn by a figure lying along the back of a llama on a pot in the Linden-Museum, Stuttgart (Disselhoff 1967: 98).

elaborately dressed figures or felines on the ends. One (Disselhoff 1967: 105) depicts a figure playing panpipes.

Another apparent musical instrument is the "rattlepole" (Figs. 14, 15b). Rattlepole carriers, like pipers, tend to appear in pairs, but they are rarer than the latter. A pot in the Museo de Arqueología de la Universidad Nacional de Trujillo (Fig. 14) shows an effigy drummer on top and two painted figures below, with offerings between them, who wear white shifts and dark shoulder ties; each of them is holding a rattlepole. A pot in the Museum für Völkerkunde, Berlin (Schmidt 1929: 203; Kutscher 1950a: Fig. 34), shows skeletal rattlepole carriers larger than figures playing quenas. On a pot in the Museum für Völkerkunde, Munich (Fig. 15b), there are three small figures, one of whom is carrying a mace, and the other two, rattlepoles with trophy heads on top. These figures wear characteristic priestly headdresses; two have a slinglike object tied over the shoulders; the third has lines at the bottom of his garment; and at least two of them wear loincloths. Behind them are panpipers wearing capes and jaguar headdresses (the facing figures on the other side of the pot wear bird headdresses). There are also warriors in the procession, and burial offerings (Fig. 15a) are shown on the top. (For other views of this pot, see Ubbelohde-Doering 1954: Pls. 170, 171.) The elements in this scene—garments, instruments, and tied pottery—indicate that it is a funeral rite.

The other important instrument in these scenes is the drum.[8] Drums are most frequently played by skeletal figures or men with diseased faces in fairly simple versions of the priests' dress (Fig. 16; Anton 1972: Pl. 113; Benson 1972: Fig. 6-5). The modeled figure on top of the pot from which Figure 7 is taken is a skeletal drummer in priest's dress with strange face-markings (Ubbelohde-Doering 1954: Pl. 182). Many of these drummers have a garment tied around the waist. At least one of these figures, with a skeletal face, on a vase in the Museum für Völkerkunde, Munich, wears the vertically striped garment (Staatliches Museum für Völkerkunde 1968: Abb. 58). Drums are sometimes depicted without a figure, but, in such cases, they are not shown as a symbol or word, as panpipes are, but as part of a group of offerings, probably grave goods, along with pots and food (Rautenstrauch-Joest-Museum 1959: Pl. 58). Actual drums of clay also exist, but these may be effigy instruments (Ubbelohde-Doering 1954: Pl. 187, bottom; Kroeber 1925: Pl. 67a).

Panpipes and quenas are played by vegetables, but not by anthropomorphs. Drums are not played by vegetables, but are played by anthropomorphic cormorants (Fig. 17) and seals (Fig. 18). These two creatures, of course, indicate a strong sea association.

8. The conch shell also appears as an instrument in Mochica scenes, but seems to be related to a different iconographic complex.

Fig. 15a,b *Fragment of a painted pot.* Photos courtesy of the Museum für Völkerkunde, Munich.

Fig. 16 *A priest-drummer on top of a pot with an afterlife frieze in relief below.* Museo Nacional de Antropología y Arqueología, Lima (after d'Harcourt 1924: Pl. 45).

Fig. 17 *Anthropomorphic cormorant playing a drum.* Museo Nacional de Antropología y Arqueología, Lima. Phot by the author.

Fig. 18 (right) *Anthropomorphic seal playing a drum.* Photo courtesy of the Museum für Völkerkunde, Berlin.

Fig. 19 (below) *Roll-out drawing of a pot showing a seal hunt in the Museum für Völkerkunde, Munich* (after Kutscher 1950a: Fig. 18).

Although they do not appear in afterlife scenes, they seem to be interchangeable with skeletal human drummers. Cormorant drummers often wear the garments of the priests, so they are not only equivalents of the women assistants in sacrificial scenes, but also, to some extent, of the priests. Curiously, cormorant drummers tend to be more elaborately dressed than their human drummer counterparts, in garb equivalent to that worn by human quena-players. (Human—or divine—pipers and quena-players are often more richly dressed than human drummers.) Most seal drummers have a strap under the chin and a modified two-prong headdress (Fig. 18) of the type seen on anthropomorphic cormorants (Figs. 3, 17) and on a fish monster (Fig. 30). There are also anthropomorphic cormorants that hold a jar (Schmidt 1929: 178, left) or simply stand and do nothing. Depictions of pure cormorants are rare, whereas seals appear often in effigy form, but rarely as anthropomorphs unless they are drummers. Non-anthropomorphic painted cormorants in some scenes—sometimes with the deity—are shown tied together in a row, suggesting that they were used for fishing (unpublished pots, Museo Larco Herrera).

A group of scenes showing seal hunts shares a number of motifs with the sacrificial scenes. In addition to the seals and the hunters, there are also several smaller figures in these scenes: a figure in prayer pose, a little figure in a simple house, and a tied jug or jugs (Fig. 19; Benson 1972: Fig. 4-5; Disselhoff 1967: 37). The seal hunt also deals with death, of course, and was a ritual with death trappings.[9] The major figures in seal-hunt scenes wear garments similar to those of the death-priests. These scenes seem fairly consistent in having two or more hunters in a short white shirt with lines at the bottom and one figure in a vertically striped shirt. The vertically striped shirt is proportionately rare in the death-priest figures. (The deity himself occasionally wears a vertically striped shirt.) The garments here are shorter than those of most of the counterparts in the death scenes, which may simply have to do with the nature of their wearers' occupation—they use short garments to go into the water in active pursuit of the seals. These hunters also have a cloth tied around the waist, much like that seen around the shoulders of priest figures, that seems to bulge slightly at the widest part. The men who hunt seals wear the pronged headdress that is often worn by seal drummers. There is an identification between hunter and victim, between priest and supernatural seal.

Another kind of hunting scene shows snail-gatherers, some of whom are dressed

9. Baessler (1902–03: Pl. 126) reproduces drawings of two low-relief pots which are not actually seal hunts, but which show together seals, tied jars, and figures in prayer pose. One pot includes also a skeletal figure with panpipes and a hooded cape; the other has a large drummer with a fanged mouth on top.

like seal-hunters (Kutscher 1950a: Fig. 19; Yacovleff and Herrera 1934: Fig. 38), with pronged headdress, a vertically striped shirt, and a fat garment tied around the waist. Others have tied garments and a short shirt with lines (Fig. 20). It seems to me that there is a symbolic opposition to the seal and snail hunts. Seal-hunters went to sea, to the guano islands, which look like mountains, where they may have killed the seals as guardians of guano, a fertilizer that they undoubtedly used for land crops (see Kubler 1948; De Mott n.d.). Seals, of course, are sea animals which look like land animals. On the other hand, the snail hunters went to the real mountains to gather what looks like something from the sea.

Deer-hunters usually wear more elaborate dress than is seen on figures in the seal- or snail-hunt scenes (Jiménez Borja n.d.; Kutscher 1950a: Figs. 13, 15), but in some deer-hunting scenes there are small figures similar to those in the death and seal-hunt scenes,

Fig. 20 *Pot representing snails and snail gatherers in the Museo Nacional de Antropología y Arqueología, Lima.* Photo by the author.

and sometimes these are major figures (Fig. 21). All hunting scenes may have been considered as sacrifices and were certainly ritual. Modeled effigy pots of seated anthropomorphic deer with a rope around the neck (Lothrop 1964: 174) reinforce this idea, for human prisoners or victims (Larco Hoyle 1965: 70) are similarly represented; on both, the genitals are emphasized. Another sexual association is that deer hunts are often depicted on "cornpoppers" (Tello 1938: Figs. 44, 45), a form that not only sometimes shows erotic motifs (Larco Hoyle 1965: 22, 23), but also may be derived from, or chosen for, its combination of sex-organ shapes. The cornpopper form is depicted on effigy pots representing certain variant death-priest types who also hold either a rolled object (Sawyer 1966: Fig. 54) or a stirrup-spout pot (Schmidt 1929:

Fig. 21 *Painted pot showing a deer-hunt scene in the Museo Nacional de Antropología y Arqueología, Lima.* Photo by the author.

Fig. 22a,b *Pot showing a painted "badminton" scene in the Museo Nacional de Antropología, y Arqueología, Lima.* Photos by the author.

Fig. 23 *Roll-out drawing of a painted pot* (after Jiménez Borja n.d.). Drawing by Wilhelm v.d. Steinen.

144) in one hand and the cornpopper in the other. A further fertility association for the deer-hunt scenes is that they usually have vegetation depicted on them.

Another kind of scene which involves some of the same characters discussed here is what Kutscher (1958), in reproducing three of these scenes, has described as a ceremonial "badminton" game, where spears appear with "badminton birds" attached. In each of the two scenes reproduced here (Figs. 22, 23), there is a major figure who has a fanged mouth, and in one case (Fig. 22), there is also a figure facing him who holds a cup. On a smaller scale there are figures wearing the priests' shift, with lines at the bottom. Some have a dark cloth tied around the shoulders; others have a light cloth tied around the waist (see Kutscher 1958: Fig. 2 for roll-out drawing). These figures have the two kinds of priestly headdress: that which goes under the chin and is tied on top, and that which does not go under the chin but emphasizes the diagonal line. In Figure 22b one very small seated priest facing two funerary jars looks very much like the figure in the amputation scene (Fig. 1). Kutscher (*ibid.*: 426) notes about this pot that "two individuals in the top row of the painting have closed eyes, as is characteristic of sleeping and also of dead men. Equally as puzzling as these two figures who may represent blind men is the small figure representing a man with amputated arms on top of the vase." This figure on top also has a headdress with a diagonal line, a short white garment with lines at the bottom, and a dark garment tied around the waist.

Another version of this scene (*ibid.*: Fig. 1) shows richly dressed figures as well as tied jars and priest figures with ties around their shoulders. Figure 23 depicts a prominent figure, who looks even more like the deity than the figure shown in Figure 22, standing on a platform with jars at the bottom, and surrounded this time by what may be animal equivalents of some of the figures in the other scenes: anthropomorphic foxes, a hummingbird, and, facing him, a lizard. An unpublished version of the "badminton" scene in the Museo Larco Herrera shows the game being played by anthropomorphic birds, one of whom holds what looks like a sort of net seen in the deer-hunt scenes.

This "badminton game" may be a ritual preparatory to a deer hunt. Deer were hunted with spears. The figures in the "badminton" scenes do not have warriors' accoutrements other than the spears and spearthrowers. Moreover, some of the garments of the more richly dressed figures in these scenes are similar to those worn in deer-hunt scenes, notably a kind of pleated kilt and a "collar" with a double snake design. (A pair of snakes is an attribute of god-the-father.) If the hunt were part of the sacrifice-death-fertility complex, then the related elements would be tied together in these scenes.

In front of the major figure in Figure 23, on another plane, stands an anthropomorphic owl wearing the priest's garments—the shift with lines at the bottom, a pale slinglike garment at the shoulders, and the headdress going under the chin and tied on top. In one hand the owl holds an object that looks like a whip, but which is probably again a ritual tie. Owls have an important and complicated role in Mochica belief, and certain aspects of the anthropomorphic owl overlap the subject discussed here. An owl appears in the same guise as in Figure 23 in a scene with anthropomorphic hummingbird, fox, and other animal runners, standing in front of a deitylike figure on a platform (Kutscher 1954: Pl. 72). The runner scenes do not normally have any of the common ingredients of the sacrifice-afterworld complex, but here, although there are no funerary jars, there is a stirrup-spout pot hanging in space in front of the major figure, and, of course, there is the anthropomorphic owl in priest's dress. This might suggest that the runner scenes, one of the most common Mochica subjects, may have some relation to the death complex.

On a pot in the Peabody Museum, Harvard University (Tello 1938: Pl. 70),[10] a modeled anthropomorphic owl, in the hooded cape commonly worn by skeletal figures, has in front of it a still life of various painted and modeled objects (reminiscent of a shaman's *mesa*), including a *florero* with vertical stripes and a bowl containing something. Next to these are painted a warrior's helmet and shirt. Below is a spotted creature with a deer tail, tied to a stump with a rope around its neck. Beside it are horizontally striped funerary jars (these stripes suggest the alternating dark and light steps of platforms on which the deity or an important personage appears). At the bottom right there is, sitting in prayer pose on a platform, a figure with a distorted mouth, wearing a dark garment and a headdress tied under the chin. On top of the pot, at the side of the owl, is a small modeled figure of the deity, wearing the sunrise headdress and lying under a blanket with plus signs on it. (The blanket with plus signs also appears on some of the "family" pots in the erotic scenes [Larco Hoyle 1965: 124, 125]. The plus motif is also sometimes associated with the cornpopper form. I suspect that it may symbolize stars or night.)

There are a number of possible interpretations of this scene, which seems related to, but essentially different from, other complexes discussed here. One may be that the anthropomorphic owl, a nocturnal creature, is the guardian of the deity at night. The cormorants would take the deity into the sea, undoubtedly with other priestly help; the owl would bring him back at sunrise. The jugs may have to do with the funerary rites of the god or possibly the "death" of the owl at dawn or the sacrifice of the deer, which may have been necessary for the god's revival. The other objects may also have to do with the sustenance and resuscitation of the god.

10. There is a similar, but less complicated, pot in the Museo de América, Madrid.

One of the most complicated and best-preserved of the sacrifice scenes contains a number of the elements discussed in this paper (Fig. 24).[11] Three nude men are being borne in litters by other nude figures. The scene on the lowest level, with trophy heads at either end, and the scene at the top, where a figure is shown being decapitated by monsters, probably indicate the fate of these figures. They are being attended by a woman with a jar carried in a shawl and by anthropomorphic cormorants. Other anthropomorphic cormorants appear in the background, three of whom hold a sling or tie, and all of whom are wearing the same garments. On the upper level, in the most modest house, two women with braids or ropes face another, smaller woman holding a cup, who stands in front of a nude prisoner or victim. The second house, with a step-motif foundation and war clubs on the roof, contains a warrior with a cup, faced by an anthropomorphic bird. The major structure, in the central zone, has a striped pyramidal base with a richly dressed figure inside, and in front of him is a little figure, holding what is probably a ritual tie and wearing a loincloth and a serrated headdress with three prongs or feathers; he is dressed very much like the hunters of seals and snails.

One obvious question is: who is the richly dressed figure on top of the pyramid? Perhaps he is the lord to whom the prisoners are being presented before they are sacrificed (other scenes suggest that these are prisoners-of-war; see Kutscher 1954: Pl. 23). It is even possible that he is the chief priest, who does not soil his hands with the dirty work but who oversees the whole procedure. I think that there is also another possibility, which I would like to explore later.

I have been mentioning, without discussion, structures that appear in sacrifice, love-making-of-the-deity, and seal-hunt scenes. The house with jaguars or war clubs on the roof and a striped, stepped platform below it certainly has as one level of meaning importance, power—secular and/or sacred—and perhaps association with the deity. But there are also a number of smaller, more modest structures, usually inhabited by a seated priest and funerary jars. Very often the two types of structure appear in the same scene. Both may have funerary associations. In the main scene in Figure 25, the quena-players, the small figure in front of the major figure holding what appears to be a shallow bowl, and the four figures holding ties might clue us in to the funerary content of this scene, but the real clincher is at the side: the modest structure with trophy head and jars seems to stamp the death association clearly upon the scene. Again, these elements are used as almost-glyphic symbols.

Houses appear as the major motif on a number of Mochica pots (e.g., Tello 1938: Pl. 74; Baessler 1902–3: Pl. 13). A modeled pot in the Linden-Museum, Stuttgart

11. Another pot with much the same iconography is partially published in Larco Hoyle 1966: Pl. 48.

Fig. 24 *Roll-out drawing of a painted pot* (after Kutscher 1950b: Fig. 4).

(Disselhoff 1967: 17, top left), presents a priest in prayer pose, with a thick garment tied around his shoulders, kneeling at a house with a stepped roof. There is another caped figure in front of the house and three jars on the other side. This pot is published next to one which shows both types of houses: on top, the elaborate, modeled house with stepped roofcomb, and the simple house painted below. A pot similar to the Stuttgart one is published by Larco Hoyle (1938–9, II: Fig. 218). In front of the house are two skeletal figures wearing vertically striped shirts. One of them holds a "stick" in front of the door. Another unpublished pot in the Museo Larco Herrera has a roof with a step motif and painted war clubs. Below, on either side of a door is a modeled skeletal figure playing panpipes. Still another house with a stepped roof has an open

Fig. 25 *Roll-out drawing of a scene on a painted pot* (after Baessler 1902–3, I: Pl. 48).

door flanked by tied jars with lids. This pot also has the paired snakes that appear on the "collars" of deer-hunters and in some of the sacrifice scenes.

The simple house seems to be a funerary symbol, the locus of the death-priest. But the more solid house may also be funerary. Where the simple house may be compared to the tied jar, the solid house may be compared to the stirrup-spout pot. In a recent report on Chan Chan, the later Chimú site in the Moche Valley, Moseley and Mackey (1973: 344) state that "each of the nine divine rulers of Chan Chan constructed his own compound to serve as palace, royal coffer, and mausoleum. When he died, apparently no sacrifice of wealth or human life was too great to ensure his return to the celestial pantheon. His compound became a great and sacred shrine, tended by royal relatives and retainers. Meanwhile his chief heir—the new lord of Chimor—founded his own high-walled domain, repeating the cycle." An earlier stage of this development may have been part of Mochica custom. Certainly house structures seem to have had important independent symbolism related to the funerary complex.

A number of pots suggest two different kinds of priests involved in funerary ceremonies (Figs. 26, 27). One or both of these priests seem to be in charge of the preparation of ritual goods and offerings. Figure 26 shows a modeled figure with a rather battered face, a slightly unusual headdress, and a white shift with a dark garment tied around the middle, sitting above a scene which has, on one side, a woman with a braid or rope, and, on the other, a man with something tied around his neck which goes out from his body and seems to contain beans, kernels, or seeds. This is a possible indication of the meaning of the fat garments tied around a number of other figures: these garments may have contained offerings being ritually carried. The garment that is tied around the waist like a backwards apron is often associated with scenes in which there are offerings. Perhaps the garment, when it contains offerings, is worn around the shoulders or waist, and, after the offerings have been presented or laid out, is straightened out and retied around the body. Between the two figures on this pot is a large fish which looks as if it were alive and swimming, and behind them are offerings.

Another pot with two different priest figures (Fig. 27) shows a caped, modeled figure on the top who wears a chevron-design headdress that is sometimes seen on figures in afterlife scenes (Fig. 7). On the body of the pot, along with jugs, food offerings, and a stirrup-spout portrait vase, is a painted figure with a conventional priest's headdress but a body that looks like a sack of potatoes. It has a textile design, and I think that it is meant to be a mummy bundle. Again, there may be the idea of the priest imitating the dead or an indication that these priests were actually killed with the man who was being buried. Both of these ideas seem implicit in the Mochica funerary complex.

One of the most interesting scenes related to this material shows women weaving

Fig. 27 *Priest seated above a painted offering scene.* Photo by Rolf Wunderlich, courtesy of the Museo de América, Madrid.

Fig. 26 *Priest seated above a painted offering scene.* Photo by Didoni, courtesy of the Linden-Museum, Stuttgart.

(Fig. 28). Pictures of artisans are virtually non-existent in Mochica art, and this weaving scene surely was not painted to show how weaving was done, to immortalize the weavers, or to depict a sort of seventeenth-century Dutch genre scene. Textiles, of course, have a sacred meaning throughout the Andes and were plentiful in grave offerings. I believe that this pot shows a preparation for an important funeral. Further evidence is given by the pots floating in the air by each loom, and particularly by the two scenes showing priest figures. In one scene a figure sits in a structure, wearing a light garment with a striped cloth tied around the waist. He has the priest's badge,

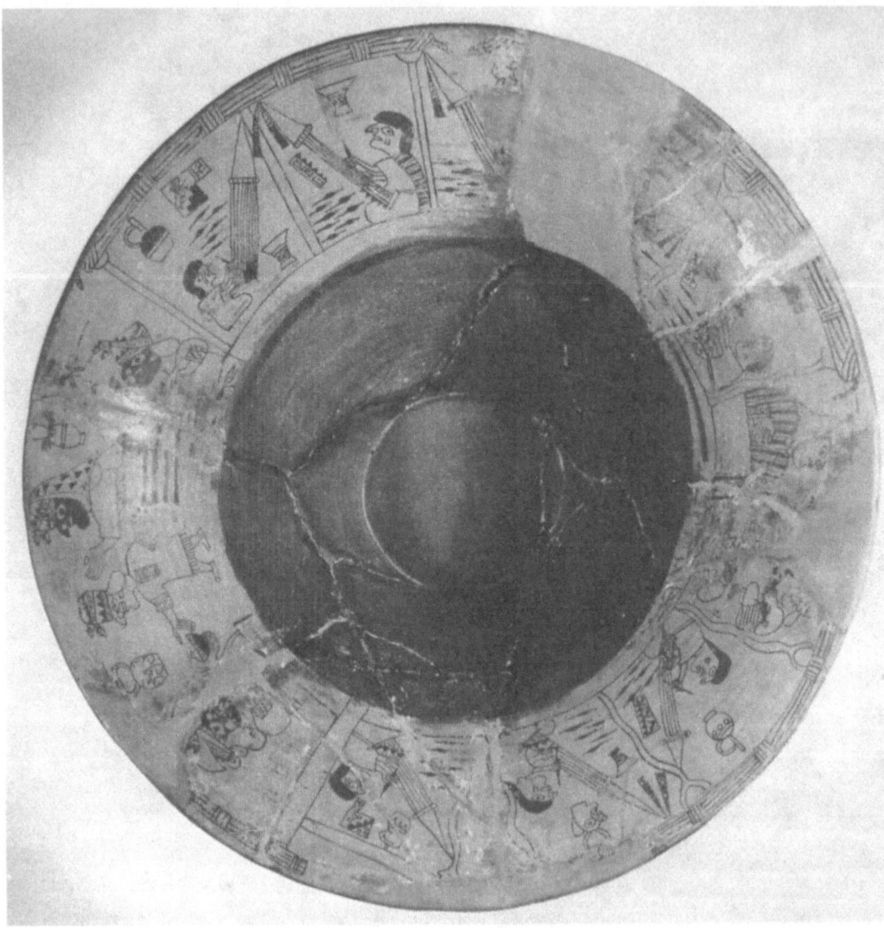

Fig. 28 *Vessel with scenes of women weaving*. Photo courtesy of the British Museum.

Fig. 29 *Roll-out drawing of an elaborate offering scene* (after Larco Hoyle 1938–9, II: Lám. XXXI).

serrated headdress, and log ear ornaments; he holds out a cup to a smaller figure, also wearing priestly garments. Between them a stirrup-spout pot floats. To the right of them are two similarly dressed figures, two funerary jars, and a fish. The other priestly scene shows a figure, in a vertically striped shirt and a headdress tied under the chin, facing a figure with a diagonal tie on the headdress and a garment tied around the waist. The pot has been damaged here, but there seem to be offerings between them. There are funerary jars below. These figures and the weaving women are all shown in modest structures.

Another elaborate scene (Fig. 29) shows a richly dressed figure sitting on a striped, stepped platform in a house, with a *florero* on the ground in front of him and a stirrup-spout pot floating in the air. He is facing a priest who seems to be presenting plates, one on top of the other and tied together, with food in them. At the other side of the scene, in a simpler house, sits another richly dressed figure, who may be the same person shown again. Behind him is a figure in a serrated headdress, white garment, and dark cape, and another small seated figure with a headdress going under the chin and tied on top. Two other similarly dressed small figures at the end of the scene hold ritual ties. The offerings here are not only plentiful, they are also supernatural: the dishes and jars have feet, and some of the jars are pouring themselves.

I have raised the question of who the richly dressed person might be. In the scenes where prisoners are being presented, one might think that this is some sort of *jefe* at the top of the power structure reviewing the captives. It is possible that here it is a lord or chief-priest whose approval of the offerings is needed. But I am inclined to think that this is actually the dead man, the man whose burial is being celebrated. Certainly the offerings indicate a burial of great importance, and the man on the platform looks important. I think that he is already dead, but not so depicted. We do not understand enough about when the Mochica depicted people as alive and when as dead. (There may have been a belief that a chieftain like this did not die, but became immortal.) Nor do we understand enough about the exact moment in time when these scenes took place or in what realm.

I have come to the conclusion that the death-priests were not only in charge of preparations in this world, but were sacrificed with the dead as part of the escort to the other world. They were not only major-domos but victims. The duty of a guide to the afterlife was a serious one. A bit of archaeological evidence for this comes from the burial of the Warrior Priest at the Huaca de la Cruz site, where, on top of the Warrior Priest's cane coffin a skeleton was found which had "very heavy and massive bones.... The skull... [had]... extremely pronounced muscular attachments and an unusually prominent basal occipital torus" (Strong and Evans 1952: 152). Of this burial, which was just above that of the two women described previously, Strong and Evans also note that "the ankles and knees were tied together with sashes of cloth . . ." (*ibid.*). A great chieftain probably had buried with him not only two women and one or more death-priests—the man in Figure 29 may have had five; the Warrior Priest had four accompanying bodies—but, to celebrate his conquests, may have had prisoners-of-war, or certain parts of them (Fig. 1), interred with him also. (Uhle [1913: 106–7] notes the burial of extra skulls and bones at the Huaca de la Luna, Moche.) A chieftain took with him to the otherworld his entourage—and also perhaps some of his enemies' power.

A modeled pot in the Museo Larco Herrera shows that even what we presume to be a prisoner-of-war had an entourage. This pot shows an unadorned prisoner figure with a rope around his neck, led by a death-priest with his headdress tied on top in front to form a diagonal line. Behind this death-priest is another, and at either side are two smaller figures with diagonal headdresses and log ear ornaments, who are holding with both hands the arms of the prisoner figure, so that they look a little like the anthropomorphic cormorants supporting the god on other pots.

I have also come to the tentative conclusion that what has heretofore been called the deity's "lizard helper" should be called the "lizard-priest," for this creature is probably a kind of personal psychopomp for the deity. The lizard-priest is always seen with the deity and is associated with no one else. He wears the vertically striped garment, has the thick tie around the waist, and is almost always seen in prayer pose (Fig. 30), a common gesture of the priests at certain moments. Jiménez Borja (1955: 122) publishes a pottery fragment in the Museo Nacional de Antropología y Arqueología, showing the deity receiving a cup from the lizard-priest. On his other side the deity is holding hands with a human figure, whose other arm is also outstretched, as if he were holding hands with the now-vanished figure behind. This hand-holding motif is, of course, seen in afterlife scenes.

Fig. 30 (above) *Drawing of the deity and the lizard-priest on a painted pot* (after Kutscher 1950a: Fig. 64).

Fig. 31 (right) *Pot representing the deity and his slain lizard-priest.* Photo courtesy of Arnold I. Goldberg.

A Mochica II pot in the collection of Arnold I. Goldberg (Fig. 31) shows the deity standing over the decapitated body of the lizard-priest. In one hand the deity holds a knife; in the other he holds the decapitated head, held in a slinglike contraption or harness, which may explain the object held in the hand of other death-priests. On other pots, the lizard-priest appears in the scene in which the deity makes love, a scene which has been included here because of its numerous funerary ingredients. The lizard-priest, as an aquatic creature, also accompanies the deity on many of his sea ventures. If the afterworld is on the other side of the sea, then the suggestion is that the lizard-priest is with the deity, say, in the afternoon, when the sun (the deity) is on the water, until the deity kills the lizard when he himself is taken through the farthest depths of the sea. One of the pots showing the deity with the two anthropomorphic cormorants (Valcárcel 1937: Pl. 4) has, beneath this group, a painted box, on the front of which the lizard-priest is shown with funerary paraphernalia—a cup in hand, jars at its feet—facing what is probably an anthropomorphic fox with a jaguar headdress, who is holding a drum.

The creatures involved with the deity are more various than those related to the core of this complex, indicating that this is a universe in which there are certain rules for the depiction of human and animal forms, and that there are at least two different aspects of this universe: an otherworld, perhaps in part a transitional world, in which anthropomorphic animals and vegetables exist, and an afterlife in which they do not. The involvement of sea creatures in the scenes discussed here implies a transit through the sea, but other complexes of scenes—touched on here in descriptions of the deity's milieu—suggest a more complicated otherworld, inhabited by all the anthropomorphs who appear on the pots. Cutting through this whole structure, there seems to be a fairly rigid "class" stratification among human and supernatural beings, among musical instruments, buildings, and pottery shapes.

The intertwining of sex and death, and certain patterns of representing vegetable matter with the elements of these scenes, suggests rites of fertility for the race and the valleys that supported it. The burial ritual and beliefs were surely not just for individual glorification, but expressed a means of continuation for the Mochica people as well. The chieftain undoubtedly received some of his power from the deity, so in his burial there must have existed some notion of offerings to the deity in his nocturnal realm and a relationship between death-ritual beliefs and the daily passage of the sun. Judging from the complications encountered in the iconography of the pots, ritual and symbolism were complex, many-leveled, and pervasively important.

* * *

As an epilogue, I would like to cite a recent article by Douglas Sharon (1972), an account of a *curandero*, who was an artist in charge of frieze-reconstrúction at Chan Chan, which, of course, lies in the heart of Mochica territory. A number of photographs accompanied this article. The *curandero* was shown wearing a knitted cap while he drank beer or made copies of ancient pots or prepared the artifacts for his *mesa*. While preparing his herbs, he wore a straw hat. But he was also pictured during a healing session (*ibid.*: 47), fighting off the spell of a sorcerer that had disturbed the session. For this activity he wore what appeared to be a large handkerchief around his head, tied at the top so that it formed a diagonal line at the side.

BIBLIOGRAPHY

Anton, Ferdinand

1972 The Art of Ancient Peru. G. P. Putnam's Sons, New York.

Baessler, Arthur

1902–03 Ancient Peruvian Art: Contributions to the Archaeology of the Empire of the Incas from his Collections. (Trans. by A. H. Keane.) 4 vols. A. Asher & Co., Berlin, and Dodd, Mead, & Co., New York.

Benson, Elizabeth P.

1972 The Mochica: A Culture of Peru. Praeger Publishers, New York and Washington.

n.d.a Pottery as Symbol in Mochica Art. Lecture presented at Dumbarton Oaks, February 24, 1972. Washington.

n.d.b Death, Sex, and Pottery in Mochica Art. Paper presented at the University Seminar on Primitive and Pre-Columbian Art, Columbia University, October 6, 1972 (also Minutes of Meeting No. 13). New York.

Bushnell, G. H. S.

1957 Peru. Frederick A. Praeger, New York.

Coury, Charles

1969 La médecine de l'Amérique précolombienne. Appendice sur les Codices Mexicains par M. D. Grmek. Les Éditions Roger Dacosta, Paris.

De Mott, Barbara

n.d. The Guano Island Wood Figures and Their Ritual Cult. Ms. New York, 1972.

Disselhoff, Hans Dietrich

1967 Daily Life in Ancient Peru. (Trans. by Alisa Jaffa.) McGraw-Hill Book Company, New York/London/Toronto/Sydney.

Grand Rounds a Thousand Years before Columbus

1965 *Pfizer Spectrum*, vol. 13, no. 2, cover, pp. 25–29. Chas. Pfizer & Co., Inc., New York.

d'Harcourt, R. and M.

1924 La céramique ancienne du Pérou. Éditions Albert Morancé, Paris.

Jiménez Borja, Arturo

1955 La Danza en el antiguo Perú (Época pre-inca). *Revista del Museo Nacional*, tomo xxiv, pp. 111–136. Lima.

n.d. Moche. Prólogo de Hildebrando Castro Pozo. Editorial Lumen, Lima.

Kauffmann Doig, Federico

1966 Mochica, Nazca, Recuay en la arqueología peruana. Universidad Nacional Mayor de San Marcos, Lima.

1971 Arqueología peruana: visión integral. Ediciones Peisa, Lima.

Kroeber, A. L.

1925 The Uhle Pottery Collections from Moche. *University of California Publications in American Archaeology and Ethnology*, vol. 21, no. 5, pp. 191–234. University of California Press, Berkeley.

Kubler, George

1948 Towards Absolute Time: Guano Archaeology. *In* A Reappraisal of Peruvian Archaeology (Wendell C. Bennett, ed.), *Memoirs of the Society for American Archaeology*, no. 4, pp. 29–50. Menasha.

KUTSCHER, GERDT

1950a Chimu: Eine altindianische Hochkultur. Verlag Gebr. Mann, Berlin.

1950b Iconographic Studies as an Aid in the Reconstruction of Early Chimu Civilization. *Transactions of the New York Academy of Sciences*, Series II, vol. 12, no. 6, pp. 194–203. New York.

1954 Nordperuanische Keramik: Figürlich verzierte Gefässe der Früh-Chimu. *Monumenta Americana, Herausgegeben von der Ibero-Amerikanischen Bibliothek zu Berlin*, I. Verlag Gebr. Mann, Berlin.

1958 Ceremonial "Badminton" in the Ancient Culture of Moche (North Peru). *In* Proceedings of the Thirty-Second International Congress of Americanists, Copenhagen, 8–14 August 1956, pp. 422–432. Munksgaard, Copenhagen.

LARCO HOYLE, RAFAEL

1938–39 Los Mochicas. 2 vols. Casa Editora "La Crónica" y "Variedades" and Empresa Editorial "Rimac," Lima.

1945 Los Mochicas (Pre-Chimu, de Uhle y Early Chimu, de Kroeber). Sociedad Geográfica Americana, Buenos Aires.

1965 Checan: Essay on Erotic Elements in Peruvian Art. Nagel Publishers, Geneva/Paris/Munich.

1966 Peru. (Trans. by James Hogarth.) The World Publishing Company, Cleveland and New York.

LASTRES, JUAN B., JORGE C. MUELLE, and J. M. B. FARFÁN

1943 Representaciones Patológicas en la Cerámica Peruana. *Publicaciones del Museo Nacional.* Lima.

LOTHROP, S. K.

1964 Treasures of Ancient America: The Arts of the Pre-Columbian Civilizations from Mexico to Peru. Skira, Geneva.

MONTELL, GÖSTA

1929 Dress and Ornaments in Ancient Peru: Archaeological and Historical Studies. Elanders Boktryckeri Aktiebolag, Göteborg.

MOSELEY, MICHAEL E., and CAROL J. MACKEY

1973 Chan Chan, Peru's Ancient City of Kings. *National Geographic*, vol. 143, no. 3, pp. 318–345. National Geographic Society, Washington.

MUELLE, JORGE C.

1936 Chalchalcha (Un análisis de los dibujos muchik). *Revista del Museo Nacional*, tomo V, no. 1, pp. 65–88. Lima.

OSBORNE, HAROLD

1968 South American Mythology. Paul Hamlyn, London.

PENTEADO COELHO, VERA

n.d. Enterramentos de cabeças da cultura Nasca. Tese de Doutoramento appresentada ao Departamento de Comunicações e Artes da Escola de Comunicações e Artes da Universidade de São Paulo, 1972. 2 vols.

RAUTENSTRAUCH-JOEST-MUSEUM, KÖLN

1959 Schätze aus Peru von Chavin bis zu den Inka. Verlag Aurel Bongers, Recklinghausen.

SAWYER, ALAN R.
1966 Ancient Peruvian Ceramics: The Nathan Cummings Collectiòn. The Metropolitan Museum of Art, New York.

SCHMIDT, MAX
1929 Kunst und Kultur von Peru. Propyläen-Verlag, Berlin.

SHARON, DOUGLAS G.
1972 Eduardo the Healer. *Natural History*, vol. LXXXI, no. 9, pp. 32–47. American Museum of Natural History, New York.

STAATLICHES MUSEUM FÜR VÖLKERKUNDE, MÜNCHEN
1968 Altamerikanische Kunst: Mexico—Peru. Katalog zur Ausstellung des Staatlichen Museums für Völkerkunde, München.

STRONG, WILLIAM DUNCAN, and CLIFFORD EVANS, JR.
1952 Cultural Stratigraphy in the Virú Valley, Northern Peru: The Formative and Florescent Epochs. *Columbia Studies in Archeology and Ethnology*, vol. IV. Columbia University Press, New York.

TELLO, JULIO C.
1938 Arte Antiguo Peruano: Album fotográfico de las principales especies arqueológicas de cerámica existentes en los Museos de Lima; Primera Parte: Tecnología y morfología. *Inca*, vol. II. Museo de Arqueología, Universidad Mayor de San Marcos, Lima.

UBBELOHDE-DOERING, HEINRICH
1954 The Art of Ancient Peru. Frederick A. Praeger, New York.

UHLE, MAX
1913 Die Ruinen von Moche. *Journal de la Société des Américanistes de Paris*, n.s. vol. X, pp. 95–117. Paris.

VALCÁRCEL, LUIS E.
1937 Dioses, hombres y bestias. *Cuadernos de Arte Antiguo del Perú*, no. 5. Museo Nacional, Lima.

WEISS, PEDRO
1961 La Asociación de la Uta y Verruga Peruana en los Mitos de la Papa, Figurados en la Cerámica Moshica y Shimu. *Revista del Museo Nacional*, tomo XXX, pp. 65–77. Lima.
1969 Significado del motivo enfermedad en el arte figurativo precolombino. *Amaru: Revista de artes y ciencias*, no. 9, pp. 26–34. La Universidad Nacional de Ingeniera, Lima.

YACOVLEFF, E., and F. L. HERRERA
1934 El mundo vegetal de los antiguos peruanos. *Revista del Museo Nacional*, tomo III, no. 3, pp. 243–322. Lima.

The Paracas Cemeteries: Mortuary Patterns in a Peruvian South Coastal Tradition

JANE POWELL DWYER
BROWN UNIVERSITY

EDWARD B. DWYER
RHODE ISLAND SCHOOL OF DESIGN

ACCORDING to the accounts and chronicles of sixteenth-century Spanish observers, the funerary customs of the native peoples of Peru consisted of elaborate ritual. One eyewitness description of burial practices on the Peruvian south coast is worth repeating in part:

> In these valleys the custom is very general of burying precious things with the dead, as well as many women and the most confidential servants possessed by the chief when alive. In former times they used to open the tombs, and renew the clothes and food which were placed in them; and when a chief died the principal people of the valley assembled, and made great lamentations. . . . They had, and still have, the custom of mourning for the dead before the body is placed in the tomb, during four, five, or six days, or ten, according to the importance of the deceased, for the greater the lord the more honour do they show him, lamenting with much sighing and groaning, and playing sad music. They also repeat all that the dead man had done while living, in their songs; and if he was valiant they recount his deeds in the midst of their lamentations. When they put the body into the tomb, they burn some ornaments and cloths near it, and put others with the body.
>
> Many of these ceremonies are now given up . . . because by degrees these people are finding out the errors of their fathers, and how little these vain pomps and honours serve them. They are learning that it suffices to inter the bodies in common graves, as Christians are interred, without taking anything with them other than good works. In truth, all other things but serve to please the devil, and to send the soul down to hell more heavily weighted. (Cieza de León 1864: Ch. LXIII)

Cieza de León was describing the end of a tradition which appears to go back nearly two thousand years in this region of Peru. Archaeological investigation has shown that among the ancient south coastal peoples it was the custom to wrap the dead with cloths to form a conical fardel or mummy bundle sometimes reaching more than a meter and a half in diameter. Offerings were then placed within the tomb, including food, jewelry, fancy and plain pottery, extra clothing, and ritual paraphernalia. Within this general pattern there were variations in emphasis upon the kind or style of grave goods from valley to valley and through time, but archaeologists can always define the existence of a burial elite on the basis of both the quality and quantity of offerings within a set of comparable tombs.

When we consider the various south coastal occupations, all of which are known mainly from the excavations of cemetery sites, there is one group that is unique in that several of its burial grounds were excavated almost completely by archaeologists. This is the Paracas culture whose elite members, or at least their souls, were foremost, as Cieza might have described them, in having to cope with the grievous weight of the burial offering. We cannot determine their destination in the afterlife, but the Paracas dead went accompanied by some of the most elaborately decorated textiles known to New World archaeology.

Much of this Paracas textile material consists of finely embroidered pieces with an iconography which most probably interprets the spiritual world to which the deceased would travel, and which sheds light upon the religious, social, and even economic systems of the living. The textile iconography, coupled with the large numbers of excavated tombs and the recorded archaeological context of the discovery, has drawn attention to the Paracas culture and presents intriguing potential for the interpretation of mortuary practice.

While the Paracas cemeteries and their well-preserved contents are justly famous, it is surprising to realize how little has been written about the people who were buried there. We are reporting on research which was started in 1968 and which has continued intermittently, both here and in Peru, until the present. Our intention in this paper is twofold: first, to present a more coherent picture of Paracas mortuary patterns by integrating archaeological data from the cemeteries on the Paracas peninsula and from related sites in the neighboring areas with new information on artifact associations and implications derived from a more precise chronology of Paracas cultural development; and second, to use ethnohistoric data from the immediate Post-Conquest period to seek some key to the understanding of Paracas mortuary custom.

The Paracas peninsula, located some 286 kilometers south of Lima, juts out into the Pacific Ocean from an area of cool, foggy desert between the Pisco and Ica valleys (see Craig and Psuty 1968: 78–90). Its mushroom shape forms two bays: Bahía de Paracas to the north is a protected deep water harbor, and Lagunillas to the south is more open and faces into the prevailing winds. The land surface is of beach and sand dunes along the bay frontage and bare hills rising to bluffs overlooking the open ocean on the extremities of the peninsula.

Although *huaqueros* (professional grave robbers) had been looting sites in the area since the last quarter of the nineteenth century, the first and still most extensive scientific archaeology was undertaken by Julio C. Tello, beginning in 1925. Tello excavated several different sites and carried out a wide area survey. His best-known discoveries were made in several parts of a zone called Cerro Colorado. Here, overlooking the Bahía de Paracas, he found an area of architectural features, extensive habitation refuse, and some tombs, which he called Cabeza Larga because of a characteristic head deformation seen in the excavated skeletal material. About one kilometer to the south, on the summit of Cerro Colorado, he located a series of deep shaft or bottle-shaped tombs which he called Cavernas, or caverns. Finally, on the north slopes of the same hill, between Cavernas and Cabeza Larga, he located a mass burial containing several hundred funerary bundles at a spot he named the Necropolis.

As yet, only the merest part of Tello's notes and findings has been published. Besides several articles in the Lima newspapers and a notice given at the XXII International Congress of Americanists (Tello 1928), his most important work on the subject, *Paracas, Primera Parte* (Tello 1959), was published from his manuscripts posthumously. It contains descriptions of selected items from the Cavernas tombs and from several Necropolis bundles, representing only a small fraction of the total discovery. The exact excavation associations are still a mystery.

This has resulted in a literature which has treated the Paracas textiles as art objects devoid of context. There has been some interest in the nature of the message conveyed in the embroidered designs, especially on the more elaborate specimens, with speculation running from calendar systems to recorded history. Unfortunately, this speculation has necessarily treated the Paracas textile material generally, and has not used the grave lot or mummy bundle as an analytic unit. It has, therefore, missed what must be the most important feature of burial furniture: that specific items were included with each deceased individual for reasons which not only make sense—that is, had meaning for the living members of the society—but which also sort the dead in ways which should become meaningful to the archaeologist.

The Tello Archive in Lima contains his notes and drawings on 51 of the more than 429 Necropolis funerary bundles he excavated. It is extremely important for our understanding of the Paracas culture that this material be made available for study. The Museo Nacional de Antropología y Arqueología in Lima has the majority of the Paracas textiles excavated by Tello in storage, and the courtesy and help of the museum staff have made this study possible. Our research has consisted of photographing textiles of known provenience or bundle association in order to reconstruct the grave lot unit. Our documented sample now consists of textiles and associated items from Cavernas tombs 1 to 5 and thirty-seven tombs from Cabeza Larga, most of the textiles and associated items from forty-one Necropolis funerary bundles in the Lima museum, two other bundles in the Museo Arqueológico de la Universidad San Antonio Abad, Cuzco, one in the Peabody Museum in Cambridge, and notes on still another in the American Museum of Natural History, New York.

It is interesting that Tello has notes on over twenty Necropolis bundles which we could not locate, and we have recorded sixteen to eighteen bundles which are not mentioned in his notes, according to the inventory of his papers (Valcárcel 1966). Some of the latter must have been opened after Tello's death and are not included in his notebooks for this reason. Still, there are at least 360 bundles unaccounted for, many of which may have never been opened.

It was obvious from the mass of documented material that the Paracas sites represented an extensive population and a fairly long time period which could be ordered in a developmental sequence. Using the associated textiles and other material in the Lima museum, specimens from museums in the United States and Europe, as well as all available evidence of stratigraphy and artifact association in the Pisco-Paracas area, a style sequence was established consisting of six distinct phases. These roughly correspond to the temporal phases Early Horizon Epochs 9 and 10 and Early Intermediate Period Epochs 1 and 2, as defined on the basis of pottery in the Ica Valley by Menzel, Rowe, and Dawson (1964) and as outlined in the Introduction of Rowe and Menzel (1967). This corresponds to about 600 B.C. to 150 B.C.—a 450-year period. In the Paracas area, decorated textiles were more useful than pottery to establish the sequence because the design changes which occur in the latter at this time do not lend themselves to fine seriation.

The sequence works roughly as follows. In the earliest phases, specific stylistic and technical features include a predominance of loom-woven ornamentation and the use of a narrow color spectrum in which bichromatic, even monochromatic, components are emphasized. Stylistically, there is a preference for overall patterning, or, where an individual theme is represented, the design is very large, angular, and composed of wide and narrow outline bands. At first, there is very little use of embroidery. Through time, however, embroidery becomes the preferred means of decoration. There is also clear evidence of wide experimentation with different dying techniques to obtain a completely new spectrum of colors and with juxtaposition of color areas to create specific visual effects. Development moves toward more realistic or naturalistic depiction. Rounded and foreshortened forms appear, and each design figure is rendered in greater detail. In the latter part of the sequence, the artist seems to start observing carefully the world about him and to strive toward depictions that are as naturalistic as possible within the general limits of the style.

This seriation and the chronological placement of Paracas textiles, which has been discussed at greater length elsewhere (Dwyer n.d.), establishes some order in the great mass of artifactual material. It enables us to take a new view of the Paracas sites themselves, and it provides a schema with which to look at these sites and their materials in relation to other contemporaneous sites on the south coast in order to compile data on widespread variation and change in funerary observance. Finally, it also allows us to investigate not only the development of iconographic themes and styles, but also the specific forms and function of Paracas funerary offerings and burial patterns.

Let us first consider the archaeological contexts. It is important first to consider the Paracas Peninsula sites themselves, and then to look at evidence which can be brought to bear upon them from related sites in neighboring areas. Up to now many archaeologists concerned with Paracas culture have discussed Cavernas, Cabeza Larga, and Necropolis as separate sites, and have traditionally considered the Cavernas and Necropolis style remains as evidence of two distinct cultures. An alternate hypothesis is that the three sites are different functional and chronological components of a single culture. If this were the case—and we feel that it is—then the changes we see in the material remains would reflect responses to existent cultural variation and the evolution of that variation through time.

That we are dealing with variability within a single continuum is strengthened by even a casual examination of the surface of the Cerro Colorado zone. Apparently it was a very large settled area. There is now considerable refuse (including stone tools, broken pottery, textile fragments, and assorted plant, animal, and shell remains) extending almost two kilometers from the northern slopes of the hill of Cerro Colorado down to the bay shore. This continuous refuse area connects the Necropolis and Cabeza Larga zones. There is little direct surface evidence for segregating the area. However, the separation of the cemeteries, as well as the variation in the grave offerings, does suggest a temporal order and a social distinction between the burial grounds.

Some material from the Cavernas tombs may date to Early Horizon Epochs 7 and 8. The greatest quantity, however, is from the succeeding Epochs 9 and 10, after which burials ceased at Cavernas. The earliest material in the Necropolis dates to Epoch 10 of the Early Horizon, and this location was used for burial through Epochs 1 and 2 of the following Early Intermediate Period. Burials at the Cabeza Larga zone seem to be contemporary with those at the Necropolis. Thus, while there is a shift through time from Cavernas to Necropolis and Cabeza Larga, there is one point in time, Early Horizon Epoch 10 (actually only the earlier part of this epoch, or 10a), when the three areas were simultaneously used, and the choice of burial site must have depended solely upon social factors.

Some of the Cavernas tombs, described by Tello as deep shafts or bottle-shaped chambers, contained from thirty to forty individuals. These remains were reported to include male, female, and infant populations, with females predominant in the tomb groups (Tello 1959: 53). Tello indicates that he felt that the Cavernas remains were those of individuals belonging to different social classes, since some were very poorly wrapped in only a rough cotton sheet, others were wrapped with one or two ordinary mantles and simple ornaments, and, finally, other skeletons were more elaborately wrapped in two or three mantles decorated with patterns in double cloth or, more rarely, with embroidered borders (*ibid.*: 55). In general, there was a relative paucity of grave offerings here in comparison to burials in the Necropolis.

The method of interment at the Necropolis, the kind and quantities of funerary offerings, and apparently the individuals who were buried there differ remarkably from the mostly earlier Cavernas complex. Tello indicates that remains were interred in house foundations, not in deep shaft tombs, and that mummy bundles were grouped together, a central large bundle being flanked by several medium-sized bundles. Many still smaller bundles were placed on top of the group (*ibid.*: 56). Both the excavator and later writers inform us that the bundles contained primarily the remains of elderly males and, of course, very rich offerings of often as many as several hundred textiles.

At the same time that these fancy interments were taking place at the Necropolis, other individuals were being buried at Cabeza Larga. The latter interments are never as rich and sumptuous as the majority of the Necropolis specimens. At Cabeza Larga, the dead were buried individually or in groups within the habitation area. Lanning reports the excavation of a group burial of individuals, each wrapped in a single plain cloth and without other offerings (Lanning n.d.: 464). This evidence suggests that the poorer members of the society, poorer either in wealth or social status, utilized the Cabeza Larga area, while at the same time the Necropolis was reserved as a cemetery for the richest of individuals and their attendants, or those deceased toward whom the living felt the most extreme obligation.

Other important evidence bearing on the Paracas material comes from a site in the middle Pisco Valley called Chongos, excavated in 1962 by the Museo Regional de Ica. Decorated textiles associated with funerary bundles, indistinguishable in style from those found at Cabeza Larga and the Necropolis, were recovered from a number of Chongos tombs. Some of the refuse from this site can be dated to Epoch 10 of the Early Horizon, but most of it belongs to Epoch 1 of the Early Intermediate Period. According to Alejandro Pezzia, who directed the excavations, the tombs were found in a roughly rectangular area measuring approximately 120 by 200 meters, and containing several different types of interments (Pezzia 1969: 36). The first type, found in simple cylindrical graves, consists of an individual in a funerary bundle made up of various mantles, some decorated with the elaborate embroidery of the Paracas style. Typically, one of the mantles is folded and sewn on the upper portion of the bundle to form a pillow or headlike form. Some of the human remains in this type of burial were evidently covered with a black resin or bituminous substance before the wrapping of the body. The second type of Chongos burial is more curious. The body is found wrapped in a single mantle which is covered with a thick layer of clay. According to Dr. Pezzia, this gives it the appearance and consistency of a large adobe brick. He also noted that at least two of these "adobe" burials contained females (personal communication, 1973). The third type of burial found at this site consists of individuals interred without any protective covering at all. Pezzia is not clear as to whether offerings were associated with this form of interment. Finally, as a fourth type of Chongos burial, the remains of children were placed in ceramic urns.

The great variety in burial practice seen at Chongos is important when compared to that of the Paracas peninsula. The Chongos burials are contemporary with many of those found at the Necropolis cemetery, and, if we take similarities in the iconography of the burial mantles into account, the two peoples shared some levels of their art and belief systems. Still, the Paracas site seems to represent a richer community with far fewer categories of treatment of the dead.

The most elaborate of all of the Paracas-style burials come from the Necropolis. It is clear that the individuals buried there were given the most intensive care and attention in the burial preparation. Efforts by the living to produce burial offerings, especially the decorated textiles, must have represented an astronomical number of man-hours. Since this most elaborate cemetery was first used well after the Paracas tradition had been established, and since the Cavernas had been the burial site used previously, it appears that considerable change occurred both in the amount of effort the living were willing to spend in honoring the dead and in the location for that honor. These changes occurred at the same time and can be dated to Epoch 10 of the Early Horizon.

The accounts of those who took part in the opening of Necropolis bundles, and our own notes on textile and other artifact associations of those bundles, show that there was a definite pattern established in the original wrapping procedure. Upon opening a mummy bundle, one usually finds an outer protective mat of reeds, then a very long cotton winding sheet sometimes twenty meters or so in length. This winding sheet may cover one or several large embroidered mantles or other larger garments. Below these finely decorated cloths there is usually another coarse protective wrapping and then a mass of fine textiles, often of smaller size than the upper mantles. Not all bundles were treated equally, however. In our sample, several of the richest bundles—that is, those with the greatest number of decorated cloths—contain textiles among the outer wrappings that are stylistically later than those in the inner mass of decorated ones. Perhaps some kind of renewal offering was made to certain bundles long after their main portions had been put together. There is, of course, the possibility that stylistically distinct textiles woven over a long temporal period—perhaps a lifetime—

were placed in the bundle at the time of interment, but it seems unlikely that this procedure would account for the most recent textile's always occurring in the outermost layers of the funerary bundle. Bennett long ago suggested four phases of wrapping (Anonymous 1938). We believe that there was simply a periodic renewal of offerings—each consisting of no more than one or two new textiles—by descendants of the deceased or by some other interested group which dealt with particular bundles.

The literature on Paracas also often notes the existence of a carbonized layer of cloth somewhere in the bundle or on the body itself. This may have been due to some substance, such as bitumen, which was applied to the corpse in certain categories of high-status burials at Chongos. However, no materials in our sample showed this charring, and the literature is confusing as to whether it is the body of the deceased which is charred or the textile layers themselves. Tello (1928: 689) reports this carbonized or burned layer near the body. He also described what he believed to be a process of "mummification" or preparation of the Necropolis corpse which took place before wrapping. Most authors are skeptical of his reports that this included the removal of the soft parts of the body (such as the lungs, intestines, brains, etc.), but there seems to be somewhat more evidence for the drying or smoking of the body over a fire, or coating it with a chemical substance (bitumin at Chongos) to give it a carbonized appearance. If such reports on pre-interment preparation are valid, they merely attest to the amount of intense effort which went into funerary preparation among the surviving members of Paracas society.

From the evidence at hand, what inferences can we make about the reasons for such elaborate mortuary rites and about Paracas funerary procedures in general? We have already mentioned the status differences among the various contemporary cemeteries, with the richest tombs at the Necropolis. There is also a size difference among the Necropolis bundles, and this shows up clearly in our sample. The largest of these bundles, for example, have two to three times the number of decorated cloths and total artifact specimens as the others. It is evident that certain individuals were singled out for even greater mortuary attention than the rest of this elite portion of the Paracas population. There are only one or two of these considerably larger Necropolis bundles in each style phase. If absolute dating for this part of Peru were on a firmer basis, we would be tempted to suggest that these largest bundles occurred about once every generation and represented primary leaders of the community.

In a comparison of the contents of these several large bundles with other smaller ones of the same time period, a number of interesting facts were revealed. First, one or more cloths bearing a specific motif, called here the "conventional flying Oculate Being" (Fig. 1), were contained in almost every elite Paracas bundle complex, apparently a necessary component of the funerary offering. One or several such cloths were always

Fig. 1 *Conventional flying Oculate Being motif, embroidery.* Fardo 421-104. (The hyphenated number indicates the bundle followed by the specimen within that bundle, as assigned by Tello. All specimens are in the Museo Nacional de Antropología y Arqueología, Lima. All photographs are by the authors.)

included in the smaller Necropolis bundles, but in the larger bundles up to one-third of the total number of decorated textiles depict this Oculate Being figure. This creature, which is characterized by very large eyes, is shown with its body drawn horizontally as if flying. It has a wide smiling mouth, a trophy head in one hand, a knife in the other, and streamers or appendages winding out from its body. The addition of these appendages is one of the important conventions used by Paracas artists to illustrate the mythical character of specific motifs in contrast to other non-mythical figures.

The Oculate Being motif goes back to Early Horizon Epoch 8 in pottery designs. It was the predominant mythical figure in Early Horizon Epoch 9 and can be seen as the primary figurative motif on decorated textiles from the Cavernas. Over time, there is extensive stylistic and iconographic innovation in Paracas textile decoration, but this motif is retained, in many ways unchanged from its original early prototype. This kind of design conservatism is almost exclusively used for this one particular figure. It may be that its significance is of the utmost importance in Paracas ritual and belief and that the inclusion of numerous textiles bearing its representation adds greater supernatural power to the larger bundles. Perhaps, as is frequent in other religious systems, the most conservative form of the symbol was considered to be the most sacred and effective.

The Oculate Being figure provided a point of departure for many iconographic innovations in the depiction of mythical, as well as non-mythical, figures in Paracas art.

Fig. 2 *Flying Oculate Being figure with feline spots, embroidery.* Fardo 410–56.

In the early phases of the development of Paracas iconography, the Oculate Being, in addition to its conventional form, was depicted with added attributes, such as the ears and spots of a feline (Fig. 2) or the wings and tail of a bird (Fig. 3). It could even take on a human aspect and be shown standing front face or in profile (Fig. 4). These different aspects—bird, feline, and human—later became the basic categories of Paracas iconography, categories which, although later subdivided and more clearly identified, are almost always symbolized by carnivorous creatures. The generalized bird becomes the condor or hawk; a killer whale, often shown with wings, is added to the repertory; and it is possible that specific felines can be identified. All of these creatures are hunters, and it is important to note that the human form of the Oculate Being is also a hunter, associated with human trophy heads. The Paracas artists themselves frequently illustrate death by showing the corpse or severed trophy head close to the mouth or "being eaten" by one of these predatory animals (Fig. 5). The flesh-eating connotation of this symbolism is clearly apparent.

Another curious aspect of the Necropolis bundles was brought out by an iconographic comparison of their contents. In many of these bundles a significant proportion of the decorated textiles depicts a series of interrelated themes or overlapping motifs which seem to belong to a symbolically coordinated design system. In one late

Fig. 3 (above) *Oculate Being figure with bird wings and tail, embroidery.* Fardo 147-13.

Fig. 4 (above, right) *Oculate Being figure in human-like pose holding trophy heads, embroidery.* Fardo 410-?.

Fig. 5 (right) *Flying mythical figure with bird wings holding trophy body to its mouth, embroidery.* Fardo 262-15.

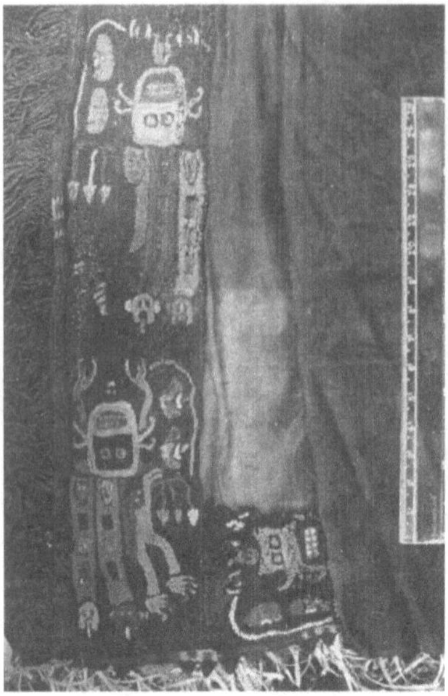

Fig. 6 *Mythical felines with associated beans and trophy heads, embroidery.* Fardo 378-58.

Early Intermediate Period Epoch 1 bundle (Fardo 378), for example, the designs on thirteen of the seventeen decorated textile specimens are the interrelated forms of the spotted feline, beans, and the trophy head. The body of the feline may be represented as a bean, or its spots can be equated with trophy heads or beans, or beans may alternate with trophy heads on the feline's streamers; in some way the three forms are united in the various designs (Fig. 6). The rest of the decorated specimens from this bundle seem unrelated to the feline/bean/trophy-head theme and establish new minor thematic relationships for the bundle. There are a number of other bundles which show the same feline/bean/trophy-head relationship but which have different sets of minor themes. Other frequently associated major themes are: (1) the feline, the cat-bird, and the falling human figure; (2) several different elaborately dressed warrior figures associated with the Oculate Being; and (3) the feathered killer whale and condor (Figs. 7 and 8).

The meaning of these consistent associations is not yet clear, but we might begin to speculate about them. The warrior figures may stand for the individual kings or heads of distinct lineages, all of whom are supported, in their social opposition to one another, by their relationship to a single all-powerful deity, here symbolized by the Oculate Being. On the other hand, perhaps they are successive rulers, who, like the

Fig. 7 *Feathered killer whale holding trophy head, embroidery.* Fardo 256-54.

Fig. 8 *Mythical condor holding long-necked bird and trophy head, embroidery.* Fardo 318-8.

Fig. 9 *Part of an embroidered border showing ten different human figures. The figure on the right wears the wings and headdress of a condor.* Fardo 190-17.

Incas, were each heads of corporate groups. The deity figure, a supernatural, is clearly associated with head-hunting, and the religious-secular elite must also be related to this activity. Other iconographic relations are evocative of the connection of the living and the dead with mythical animals. For instance, we might consider killer whale, feline, or cat-bird clans each having the relationship between the living and the ancestors graphically depicted in the textile art. The clans could consist of living groups whose rights and obligations were symbolized by mythical animal spirits, which could be impersonated by human beings for ritual purposes (Fig. 9). This might explain the impersonation scenes which sometimes occur in textile motifs. The various combinations of the themes in the bundles or on specific textiles may tell a story of the ancestry or history of the individual/clan/supernatural relationship which, unlike the well-known situation on the northwest coast of North America, seems at Paracas to be more important to the dead than to the living.

It is also interesting to look at the range of embroidered textiles in each funerary bundle for examples of the work of different artists in order to get some idea of how many individuals might have contributed to it. The quality and uniformity in style throughout the sample of textiles suggest a group of specialist embroiderers. Among these there are a number whose work is so distinct that it can be picked out. Stylistically, the larger bundles may represent the work of from eight to twenty individual artists, each contributing from one to six or so different cloths to the bundle. When comparing different contemporaneous bundles, we found that the work of what seems to be one artist is often either identical or related—in terms of the thematic system mentioned above—from textile to textile or from bundle to bundle. In view of the large number of artists contributing to the Necropolis bundles—at least to the larger ones—we would suggest that there was some kind of mortuary obligation on the part of several kin groups or other social divisions within the community to contribute a certain number of textiles. This would account for the predominance, in a single bundle, of motifs relating to a specific theme, as well as for the lesser number of other cloths which do not seem to bear theme relationships to the main body of textiles but which enter new themes of their own. It might also explain the wide diversity of motifs found among the textiles in the very large bundles. If these represented the remains of leaders, a broader segment of the community would have been obliged to make a funeral contribution to these bundles than in cases where the individuals were of lesser rank; even more social groups would be involved, and, hence, more tex-

Fig. 10 *Part of the same embroidered border as Figure 9 showing costumes depicted in fine detail. Note the fringe on the striped tunic on the figure to the right.* Fardo 190-17.

tiles, more artists, and more themes and associated groups of themes would be present as well.

It would appear that the Paracas culture is unique in its extreme emphasis on textiles as burial offerings. Why such care for costume rather than for the more traditional pottery in the grave furniture? Among the ancient peoples of Paracas, costume seems to have played an important part in defining an individual's social category. Costume may have indicated his ceremonial role or status level. It was also of such importance that the artists who created the Paracas textiles were very careful to indicate what kind of costume, headdress, and other emblems their tiny embroidered figures were wearing (Fig. 10), and each different costume assemblage seems to be an essential part of the visual definition of a particular motif. It is significant that those authors concerned with the Paracas textiles--primarily the Necropolis and Cabeza Larga examples—report that there were no signs of wear on the clothing found in the bundles. Among the several thousand textiles we examined, we could not see much indication of wear either. Also, many of these specimens are clearly unfinished. Perhaps these new garments were offered to the corpse as marks of its new status as deceased.

We might also note that cloth, per se, had tremendous ceremonial significance in Inca times (Murra 1962), and that its special relationship to the dead of the Paracas culture may simply reflect a long-term relationship between fancy textiles and important people. We have suggested that the Paracas cemeteries show a stratified society with a variety of burial patterns for different social groups. Most of our work has concentrated on the elite Necropolis cemetery and the design themes included in the bundles found there. Even in this single cemetery there is great variation in funerary pattern. There is still much more to be done with the little data we have gathered in terms of both analysis and interpretation. We are just now starting to try to correlate the burial record from Paracas with other events in the prehistory of the south coast.

It is clear that there is information to be derived from the existing evidence of ancient burial practices, but only insofar as the associations and contexts of the grave assemblage are known. Paracas textile art has been known and admired for many decades, but only a small beginning has been made thus far to interpret this art in its proper context.

ACKNOWLEDGMENTS The authors wish to acknowledge the cooperation of the staffs of the Museo Nacional de Antropología y Arqueología, Lima; the Museo Regional de Arqueología Ica; the Museo Arqueológico de la Universidad San Antonio Abad, Cuzco; the Brooklyn Museum; the Museum of Fine Arts, Boston; the Peabody Museum of Archaeology and Ethnology Cambridge; and the American Museum of Natural History, New York. We especially want to thank our colleagues in Peru: Julio Espejo, Carlos Galimberti, Luis Lumbreras, Jorge Muelle Alejandro Pezzia, and Sra. Teresa Zuniga de Arce. They made the research possible.

BIBLIOGRAPHY

ANONYMOUS (WENDELL C. BENNETT)

1938 If You Died in Old Peru. *Natural History*, vol. XLI, no. 2, pp. 119–125. American Museum of Natural History, New York.

CIEZA DE LEÓN, PEDRO DE

1864 The Travels of Pedro de Cieza de Leon, A.D. 1532–50, Contained in the First Part of his Chronicle of Peru. (Trans. and ed. by Clements R. Markham.) The Hakluyt Society, London.

CRAIG, ALAN K., and NORBERT P. PSUTY

1968 The Paracas Papers, Studies in Marine Desert Ecology, vol. 1, no. 2: Reconnaissance Report. *Occasional Publication No. 1 of the Department of Geography*, Florida Atlantic University, Boca Raton.

DWYER, JANE POWELL

n.d. Chronology and Iconography of Late Paracas and Early Nasca Textile Design. Unpublished doctoral dissertation, University of California. Berkeley, 1971.

LANNING, EDWARD PUTNAM

n.d. Chronological and Cultural Relationships of Early Pottery Styles in Ancient Peru. Unpublished doctoral dissertation, University of California. Berkeley, 1960.

MENZEL, DOROTHY, JOHN H. ROWE, and LAWRENCE E. DAWSON

1964 The Paracas Pottery of Ica: A Study in Style and Time. *University of California Publications in American Archaeology and Ethnology*, vol. 50. University of California Press, Berkeley and Los Angeles.

MURRA, JOHN V.

1962 Cloth and Its Functions in the Inca State. *American Anthropologist*, vol. 64, no. 4, pp. 710–728. American Anthropological Association, Menasha.

PEZZIA ASSERETO, ALEJANDRO

1969 Guía del mapa arqueológico-pictográfico del Departamento de Ica. Editora Italperú, Lima.

ROWE, JOHN HOWLAND, and DOROTHY MENZEL (eds.)

1967 Peruvian Archaeology: Selected Readings. Peek Publications, Palo Alto.

TELLO, JULIO C.

1928 Los descubrimientos del Museo de Arqueología Peruana en la Península de Paracas. *Atti del XXII Congresso Internazionale degli Americanisti, Roma, Settembre, 1926*, vol. I, pp. 679–690. Rome.

1959 Paracas. Primera parte. Publicación del Proyecto 8b del Programa 1941–42 de The Institute of Andean Research de New York. Empresa Gráfica T. Scheuch S.A., Lima.

VALCÁRCEL, C. D.

1966 El Archivo Tello. Tipografía Peruana S.A., Lima.

Eschatology in a Participatory Universe:[1] *Destinies of the Soul among the Warao Indians of Venezuela*

JOHANNES WILBERT

UNIVERSITY OF CALIFORNIA, LOS ANGELES

THE Warao have an anthropocentric world view. They conceive of themselves as living in the center of the terrestrial disk and at the foot of the world axis that connects the earth with the zenith and the cosmic vault. Thus, when a Warao baby emerges from the womb of his squatting mother, he falls right into the heart of the universe. Throughout his entire existence, and especially during adulthood, he shares this universe not only with his fellow men but also with a host of spirits who expect him to interact with them according to time-honored patterns of reciprocal behavior. There exists a relationship of compelling mutuality between mankind and the supernaturals, and neither the gods nor the mortals are free to disengage themselves from this entelechial purpose of life. The gods are forever affecting mankind, while man exists perennially before the curtains of eternity. This paper describes the Warao universe with its different places of ultimate destiny of the human soul, and, at the same time, explores the dynamics of interaction between heaven and earth.[2]

1. "Participatory universe" is a concept I borrow from Princeton Professor John A. Wheeler, who, as a physicist, believes that "we are going to come to appreciate that the universe itself in some strange way depends on our being here for its properties" (Helitzer 1973: 32). This is, from an ideological point of view, essentially similar to what the Warao think of the interdependence or mutuality that exists between man and the supernatural world.

I am grateful to Drs. Donald W. Lathrap and Irving Rouse for commenting on this paper and to Dr. P. T. Furst for editing it.

2. The data for this paper were gathered in the course of frequent fieldwork (since 1954) among the Winikina-Warao. While I use the generic tribal designation "Warao," it is well to bear in mind that regional variations in cultural patterns do exist among the hundreds of local groups of the tribe and that the facts as described in the present paper best fit the Winikina. Furthermore, the information contained in this paper is the result of interviewing many different religious practitioners, none of whom would necessarily know all of the data presented here. Much of this lore is based on the dream experiences of individual shamans, and differs in descriptive detail from informant to informant.

THE WARAO CONCEPT OF THE UNIVERSE

According to the Warao concept of the universe, the earth is saucer-shaped with a flat surface, and mankind—more specifically, the Warao themselves—lives at its center (Figs. 1, 2). The earth is surrounded by water that reaches to the horizon and to the very ends of the world. Submerged in the ocean and encircling the earth is the Snake of Being, a sea monster that adopts an *uroboros* position, with its featureless extreme ends approaching each other east of the earth. In a boxlike world below the earth and

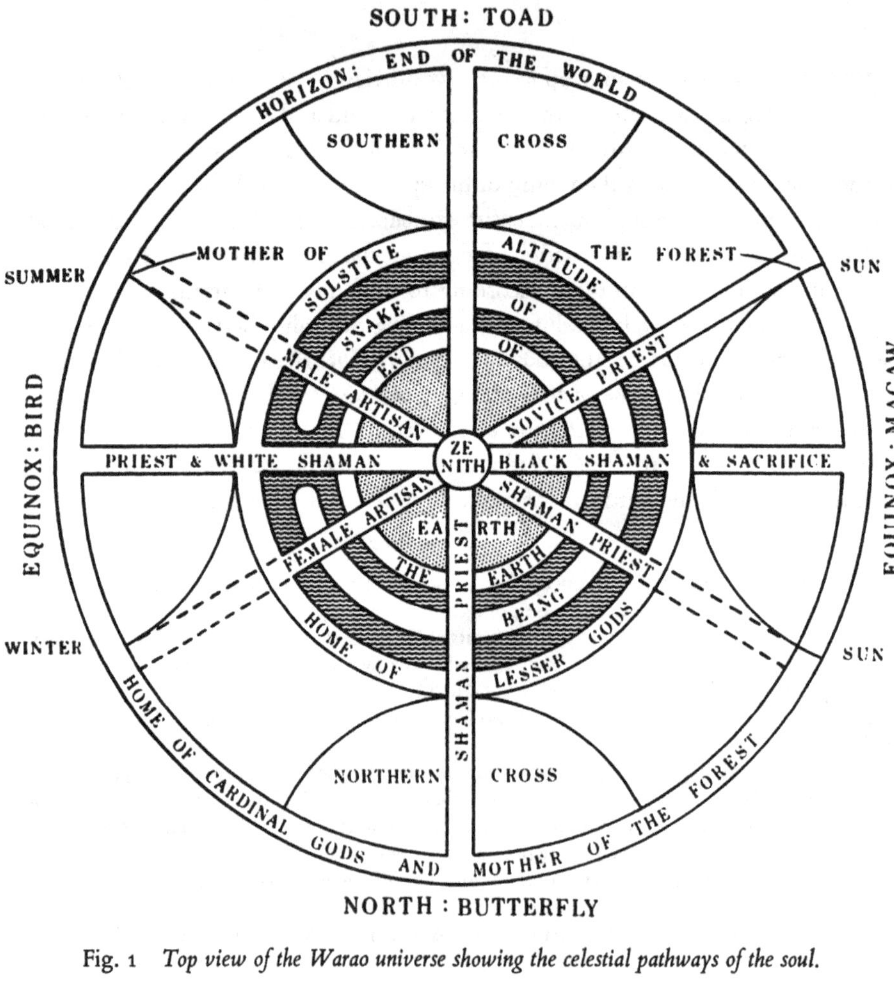

Fig. 1 *Top view of the Warao universe showing the celestial pathways of the soul.*

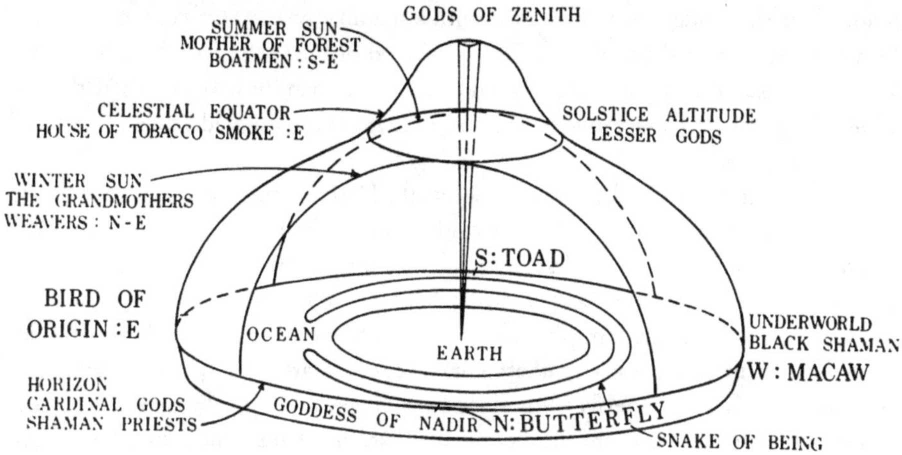

Fig. 2 *Profile of the Warao universe.*

the ocean, there exists the earth-monster, a four-headed serpent. According to some Warao, this *quadricornutus serpens* is a huge snake with deer horns on each of her four heads. There is supposedly no passage from this underworld to the surface of the earth, although others maintain that this Goddess of the Nadir can leave her world in the form of a woman, via a passage along the world axis, and manifest herself before human beings with her torso sticking out of the earth. She has also been encountered by wanderers in the forest who saw her from behind as she sat astride a fallen tree.

GODS OF THE CORNERS OF THE WORLD

At the cardinal and intercardinal points of the universe, there are world mountains that are believed to be gigantic petrified trees. These mountains are the abodes of certain deities whom the Warao refer to collectively as Kanobotuma = "Our Grandfathers." Included also are the gods of the zenith and nadir.

The cardinal god of the south is Uraro who lives at the end of the world (*aitona*). He has a companion by the name of Karoshimo who resides on a lesser mountain at the edge of the earth (*hobahi a kari*). Both gods resemble each other to such a degree that either can be invoked with the other's name. Nevertheless, Uraro is the senior of the two, and both gods of the south are the most powerful of the Warao pantheon. It is noteworthy that the left sides of the bodies of these gods resemble the skin of a toad. Their right sides are also covered with a toadlike, warty surface, but they look fiery red and shriveled as if seared. The Toad God of the south, like the other major gods, may assume a corpulent, light-complexioned human form. Together with their wives, the gods of the south dwell in enormous mansions, own golden horses, and lord it over many subjects.

Their counterparts are the gods of the north. Here on the highest of two world mountains, on the very edge of the world, resides Warowaro, the Butterfly God (*Calligo*, sp.). His companion lives on a smaller mountain, on the edge of the earth, and is known as Anabarima = "Father of the Waves." The gods of the north are surrounded by the same fine things as are the gods of the south, but the Warao consider them slightly inferior to their southern counterparts. Warowaro appears at times as a gigantic "owl-faced" butterfly with a huge eye on each wing. The mountain of the Father of the Waves has an enormous cave that harbors Haburi, the cultural hero, and his mothers.

Residing on the world mountain in the east is Ariawara, the God of Origin. He is described as valiant, vigorous, and very great. He is of avian form, like the Creator Bird of the Dawn, his companion who lives in a cave on a mountain in front of the God of Origin. Many things originated through the powers of this latter god, while the Creator Bird of the Dawn is particularly responsible for light-shamanism.

Finally, among the cardinal gods of the Warao universe, there is the Macaw God of the West. The Scarlet Macaw (*Ara chloroptera*) rules over the underworld, an abode of darkness, and is called Hoebo. The Macaw God is Hoebo's body, his soul residing at the zenith. While the supreme spirits of the south, north, and east are free to travel along the horizonal boundary of the world and down the world axis to earth, the Macaw God of the West cannot visit his fellow gods, nor does he descend to earth. Instead, ever since the connection between the underworld and the rest of the universe was severed in primordial times, he has remained confined to his part of the world, where he rules as the lord of dark-shamanism and death.

Although the sex of supernaturals is generally ambiguous, the gods of the cardinal directions are usually considered male. But there is also a goddess of the same rank, Dauarani = "Mother of the Forest." Like Hoebo, she is divided into a soul, which resides on the world mountain on the southeastern horizon, and a body, which lives on a mountain in the southwest. The locations of these intercardinal mountains seem to coincide with the observable points of midsummer sunrise and sunset, respectively. Body-Dauarani is the patron of male artisans, especially canoe-makers. Dauarani is the only female deity on the edge of the world. She is one of four supreme deities of the world of light, while only one cardinal god, the Scarlet Macaw, reigns over the world of darkness.

Opposite the Mother of the Forest, at the place of winter solstice, are the world mountains of sustenance and fertility deities, such as the Mother of Moriche Flour (Aruarani), at the rising point of the midwinter sun in the northeast, and the God of Dance (Oriwakarotu), at the point of midwinter sunset in the northwest. The winter solstice is also identified with the Natue, the Grandmothers, patronesses of the *moriche* palm, which in view of its great nutritional and material value has rightly been called the "tree of life" of the Warao Indians.

GODS OF THE MIDDLE WORLD

The zenith is inhabited by three lesser gods who direct the traveling spirits and souls to and from the earth via the *axis mundi*, as well as along the paths that connect the zenith with the various world stations described.

First, there is the god Yaukware who in ancient times ascended to the zenith by means of his sacred rattle. He is recognized as the God of the Center of the World. His companion spirit is his own son, whom he had taken along on his celestial journey. The two live in a beautiful adobe house, with a banner in front and such furniture as tables, chairs, and beds within. They also keep ritual paraphernalia in readiness, among them various kinds of rattles, trumpets, clarinets, necklaces, and, above all, tobacco. Everything up here—the god, his son, the instruments, the house, and its inventory—is white and bright with light. Yaukware is a contented god who, since his ascension, has never left the zenith. On the threshold of his house originates a network of paths that interconnect the cardinal and intercardinal points of the universe, excluding the underworld in the west and the House of Tobacco Smoke in the east.

The latter is related to a second supernatural denizen of the central dome, whose place is situated slightly to the east of the zenith. I use the vague term "place" because this spirit and his whereabouts are invisible. He is a psychopomp who guides the traveling spirits and souls across a white bridge with colorful flowers to the House of Tobacco Smoke in the east.

The third spirit in the center of the world is Soul-Hoebo (the Scarlet Macaw at the world mountain in the west being Hoebo's body). The black adobe house of Soul-Hoebo is a dark and dreadful place. Filled with the stench of rotting cadavers and filthy with a blood-soaked floor, it heralds doom for all souls passing through on their dread journey to the Lord of the Dead. Soul-Hoebo's house is furnished with chairs made of human bones and skin. There are also hammocks of coagulated human blood within. Hoebo's one-year-old son lies in one of them, and the child's mother rocks him so as to keep him from crying. From Soul-Hoebo's house there leads one solitary path, slippery with human blood, straight to the underworld.

Looking at the Warao universe in profile, one can picture the cosmic vault as bell-shaped rather than rounded like a dome (Fig. 2). The upper rim of the depression occurs roughly on the imaginary level marked by the maximum altitude of the summer and the winter suns. From here to more or less the lower third of the bell-shaped vault exist such gods and spirits as the minor companion gods of the south (Uraro) and the north (Anabarima), the House of Tobacco Smoke (Amawari) in the east, the food-related gods of the northeast (Aruarani) and the northwest (Oriwakaroto), the snake goddess of boat-builders and priest-shamans in the southeast and the southwest, as well as several others beyond the scope of the present discussion.

Thus we can distinguish five cosmic strata in the Warao universe: (*a*) the flat surface of the earth, (*b*) the cardinal and intercardinal gods on the world mountains at the horizonal ends of the world, (*c*) the gods residing on the imaginary belt mid-high around the bell-shaped cosmic vault, and (*d*) the gods and spirits of the center of the world at the zenith. Below the earth and the ocean is (*e*) the almost featureless and dark realm of the Goddess of the Nadir. This realm below is solid; it supports the earth, serves as the bottom of the ocean, and carries the world mountains. On the latter rests the cosmic vault which in its center is supported by the world axis.

ALIGNMENT OF MAN WITH THE SUPERNATURALS

A Warao Indian's alignment with the metaphysical world begins the moment he makes his appearance on earth. In fact, it commences with the baby's first cry, when it echoes across the earth and the sea to the world mountain of the God of Origin. Soon after the "new cry" has reached his distant abode, the deity can be heard acknowledging the baby's cry by crying himself.

There is another supernatural personage eager to confirm the arrival of a new human being—the Snake of Being. She is the womb of all life on earth. A Warao myth explains the nature of this *uroboros* snake:

> There were male voices to be heard, and many women were heard talking in Warao. Children were crying, and all kinds of animal voices reached the surprised Natue's ear. "What are all these voices in your body?" she asked Hahuba. "There seem to be many people and animals living inside of you." "You are right," answered Hahuba. "These are my grandchildren. I am the grandmother of them all."

The serpent's acknowledgment of a baby manifests itself on the third day after its arrival, when she embraces the entire village with a balmy breeze.

Finally, there is the mythical turkey-bird, Shiborori, whose permanent residence lies at the foot of the eastern world mountain, but who also has a resting place at the top of the world. He comes to the meridian at noon and midnight to chant for the boys and girls on earth whom he considers his brothers and sisters.

From this early age on, the individual Warao remains engaged in a relentless tug-of-war between himself and the supernaturals, a contest that may not be settled even by a man's physical death. He must weigh his every action to remain on good terms with the gods, and to be protected against attacks or defeat. There is no pardon in this struggle, mistakes are intolerable, and disengagement fatal; for the entelechial cause that forces upon life a proposition of mutuality and participation is governed by the very dictates of survival. The gods need man to provide them with food, and man needs the gods to protect his life and goods. The gods demand *moriche* flour, honey, and, above all, tobacco, which calls for major inputs of human energy and time. Worse still, the Lord of the Underworld requires human flesh, blood, hearts, and livers, and destroys a person body and soul.

Much of a Warao's life is, therefore, spent fulfilling his part of the bargain, and he avails himself of the services of three different religious practitioners who know their way through this maze of celestial stations and who are experts at arranging a *modus vivendi* among all parties concerned. These practitioners are the priest-shaman, who mediates between man and the *kanobo* gods, including those of the zenith and nadir; the light-shaman, who stands between his fellow men and the powers of the Land of Light; and finally, the dark-shaman, who communicates between this world and the Land of Death. The shamans serve as media in this dialogue between mortals and the supernaturals, anxious to negotiate a *quid pro quo* that makes life a little more livable for their fellow men. The Warao, however, do not engage in self-deception; they have no word in their language for living, only for dying. If one asks a Warao who is suffering from a generalized feeling of indisposition how he is doing, he answers, *wabaia subuka* = "somewhat dying." A sick person is *wabaia* = "dying." A corpse is *waba* = "dead," and buried in a *wa* = "a dugout canoe." Thus the various forms of sickness are but different stages of death, and both states are referred to by one and the same term, *waba*. The dugout canoe, as is explained later, is the vagina of Dauarani, Goddess of the Forest, so that life, according to Warao symbolism, can clearly be recognized as a process of dying by returning to the womb. Death occurs almost exclusively through the intervention of dark- and light-shamans, as well as of several supernatural powers. How and through what agent is of secondary importance. What matters to the Indian is the survival of his soul, *mehokohi*, the light in his breast. All Warao hope for a life after death and arrange their affairs teleologically toward an existence in the heaven of their predilection.

JOURNEYS OF THE SOUL: THE AFTERLIFE OF SHAMANS

Warao shamans die with the relative certainty of an afterlife in the company of their patron gods. During their lifetime the spirits of shamans travel routinely to their respective heavens in trance states and in dreams. They are familiar with the roads and are confident that they will survive their final journey as did all the others who came before.

The Priest-Shaman

The priest-shaman, for example, will listen to the falling night of his approaching death for the beating of the hoofs of the golden horse dispatched by his patron god to carry him to his eternal home. He sits on this winged spirit mount and rides upward to the zenith. Here, in the house of the God of the Center, the soul rests for four days. Yaukware queries his guest concerning his final destination. If a particular priest-shaman has served the God of the South, his soul will go to reside with him. If he has served the God of the North, or that of the East, he will proceed in the appropriate direction. On the fourth day, the God of the Center provides him with his final cigar. Again he mounts the winged horse and sets out on his ultimate journey. The souls of shamans travel like shooting stars, comets, or lightning bolts to the house of their patron deity. While traveling, they always face toward the end of the world, never backward toward the center. They arrive with a thundering noise that resounds throughout the world, and when they alight, hot and perspiring, the companion god hands them a fan with which to cool themselves. The priest-shaman also receives beautiful clothes, a hat, and shoes, and is taken to his own dwelling which is furnished in gold like the residence of the god himself and laid out in a garden of beautiful white flowers. He keeps looking at his god and begins a restful life in the company of the peers that preceded him. Theirs is a life of peace and contentment; no sickness reaches their beautiful city atop the mountain; their supply of delicious tobacco smoke, provided by their fellow shamans on earth, is always plentiful. The latter invite them periodically to feast in their temples and send smoke offerings up to keep them warm and contented. There is nothing to disturb the tranquility of this heaven so long as man provides ample supplies of tobacco smoke. Man, being in possession of fire, is the only source of this divine sustenance.

Among those who attempt to become priest-shamans are many who fail. Their fate is sealed when, on their initiatory ecstatic journey, they have the misfortune of succumbing to one of the twelve tests or ordeals along the road. The road of this maiden voyage into the otherworld must be traversed by all novice shamans during initiation. It leads from Yaukware's house, at the zenith, to the world mountain of the Mother of the Forest in the southwest. Multitudes of men have perished on this hazardous pilgrimage, their bodies having been devoured and their souls destroyed.

Once the novice priest in his tobacco trance has left Yaukware's house, he sets out on his journey accompanied by an invisible soul-guide who leads the way but leaves to the young traveler the decisions that must be made along the road. Dangling from a rope, he must propel himself across an abyss filled with hungry jaguars, snapping alligators, and frenzied sharks, all eager to devour him. He has to clear an extremely slippery section in his path, surrounded by demons brandishing spears with which to impale him should he lose his balance. The hungry traveler is tempted by people barbecuing meat that is taboo for priest-shamans, and by women making bark cloth for pubic covers. Next, the shaman's soul reaches a terrifying place where he meets the giant hawk stretched out before him on his back, snapping his razor-edged beak, flexing his sharp talons, and flapping his wings fiercely. The shaman must step over this rapacious bird and disregard the pile of bones of his less fortunate predecessors.

Finally, the soul of the novice priest-shaman reaches the abode of the Mother of the Forest. He beholds an enormous petrified tree trunk, its left side covered with thorns and its right with leaves. There is an entrance to a cave that leads into the mountain, but he has to step through a rapidly opening and shutting door. Jumping through, he finds himself inside a cavern and in the presence of an enormous anaconda with four multi-colored horns on its head. At their bases these horns are blue; the tips of the right pair are red and those of the left yellow. The horns are bent forward and threaten the soul of the young man, who beholds a fiery-red, luminous ball on the tip of the reptile's tongue that moves in and out of the mouth to the rhythm of the opening and shutting doors at the entrance to the cave.

Souls that fail to clear the gate are instantly devoured by the snake, who leaves only the bones of its victims. These are collected by the snake's companion spirit, whose upper body is that of a man and whose lower body is that of a snake. There is an enormous cavern at the foot of the mountain into which the servant dumps the bones of the snake's victims. (The giant hawk burns the bones of his prey and fans the ashes away.) Only those souls who return successfully from Dauarani's world mountain receive six tutelary spirits into their breast and become priest-shamans. And only their souls will eventually proceed to live with their patron god following their life on this earth.

The Light-Shaman

The accomplished light-shaman also dies confident of the immortality of his soul and of a blissful life in the company of his patron deity and fellow shamans. For the light-shaman, as for the priest-shaman, dying is only the last of the numerous occasions when he embarks on the celestial journey typical of his profession. The soul of the light-shaman ascends to the top of the sky to rendezvous with the invisible psychopomp who resides to the east of the zenith. After resting here for several days and being provided with a last cigar, he follows the soul-guide to a bridge, made of thick ropes of solidified tobacco smoke, which commences a short distance from the center of the world. Beautiful flowers border the bridge—a row of red and a row of yellow flowers on the left, and lines of blue and green flowers on the right.

At the end of the bridge is a white globular house, also made of tobacco smoke. This is the residence of Kanobo Amawari, the patron deity of light-shamans. In primordial times, this birthplace of light-shamanism originated through the will of the Creator Bird of the Dawn. It is inhabited by a hierarchy of four powerful spirits—Black Bee, Wasp, Termite, and Honey Bee—each of whom occupies a chamber along the eastern wall of the house and incessantly chants the song of light-shamanism.

Inside the house is a table draped in white and set with four dishes in a row; also on it are a bow and two arrows. Through the floor of this sacred mansion, there emerges from time to time the head of a serpent with four colored plumes on its head: white, yellow, blue and green. They chime a musical note like a bell. Rhythmically, the snake produces from within its mouth a glowing white ball on the tip of its forked tongue. A novice shaman who ventures into the presence of this snake during initiation instantly receives the entire wisdom of his profession.

Ever since the first light-shaman ascended to live in this sacred mansion, the souls of light-shamans have followed his example. Also, just as with the primordial light-shaman, the wives of light-shamans follow their husbands. The male light-shaman is the father of the tutelary spirits in his breast; his wife (through a ritualized sexual union) becomes the mother of these same spirits. Some women are known to have thereby received the power to cure seizures. Again, as in the case of the cardinal and intercardinal gods, the souls of light-shamans and those of their wives live exclusively on tobacco smoke supplied by their colleagues on earth.

Besides the souls of light-shamans and their wives, there is yet a third category of souls that comes to live on Amawari's mountain—the souls of basket-makers, of whom more will be said below.

The Dark-Shaman

Of the three different religious practitioners, we have finally to consider the fate of the dark-shaman, whose soul belongs to the Macaw God of the Underworld.

The Warao underworld, situated on a world mountain in the west, engulfs in its darkness the entire region between the setting points of the summer and winter suns. Ruled by the Scarlet Macaw, this Land of Death has existed since time immemorial, and was originally connected with the earth through an umbilicus-like artery that reached from the west along the curvature of the celestial vault to the zenith, whence it dangled down to the dancing platform of the Warao village. The end of this duct was provided with a brilliant ball of light which at night sought out and penetrated the heads of sleeping people in order to drain their hearts of blood. The blood flowed through the artery to the underworld, where the spirits drank it from an enormous canoe of bone or ironlike rock. In a violent act of jealousy, this blood duct was severed in the mythical past, the artery snapped back to the west, and thus the flow of nourishment for the spirits of the underworld was interrupted. Since then it has fallen to the dark-shaman to guarantee the survival of these spirits. By means of his magical arrows he kills fellow Warao, preferably those of neighboring villages, and carries them head down on his back to the Hoebo house at the zenith and beyond to the Land of Death. Besides two tutelary spirits in his breast, the dark-shaman also carries a sling below his sternum which assists him in sacrificing his victims by throttling them. The pathogenic bolt is carried by tobacco smoke he blows from his reversed cigar that, searching for the heart, enters the individual's rib cage to perform the sacrifice.

The Land of Darkness is the final destination of many souls—souls of dark-shamans and souls of the common man, but especially of children. Let us consider first the final journey of the souls of dark-shamans, who, the Warao believe, depart immediately after death for the Soul-Hoebo, west of the zenith. From the time of his initiatory journey, the dark-shaman has become thoroughly familiar with the road and its two major stations: the black house at the top of the world (with its Hoebo-Family, the crying child in the hammock of dried blood, and furniture of human skin and bones) and, of course, the underworld itself. Here on the western world mountain stands the house of the Macaw God, completely dark except for a faint white light and a yellow light. The house is surrounded by innumerable smaller houses inhabited by the souls of dark-shamans who have come to live near their master. The houses are built with posts and beams of iron, and stand on top of this bald mountain. The soil is a blood-soaked black morass, and the air is heavy with the stench of putrefaction that serves the approaching soul as a guide. Also, big black flies fill the air and thickly cover every surface of the land.

The supreme Hoebo spirit has the appearance of a man with long blood-clotted hair. But he is also the Scarlet Macaw with fiery-red plumage covering his entire body, a black beak, black feet, and black streaks on his cheeks. His voice is harsh and his beak sharp and strong. He uses it to attack his victims by the neck and to tear off their heads.

The approaching soul of the dark-shaman smokes a cigar which from earth looks like a falling star. He listens to the continuous hooting of the trumpet of the Macaw, which, in this case, is made not of a conch shell but of a human skull. The piercing sounds of a clarinet can also be heard. The instrument is made of long human bones and has a skull as its resonance chamber. Upon his arrival, the soul is greeted by his patron god who allows him to drink blood from the canoe and eat as much human flesh as he pleases—food that was denied him in life. He is given a necklace of human rib bones—similar to the one the master wears—and proceeds to occupy his personal dwelling in the joyful company of his fellow dark-shamans. Like them, he assumes a body that is half-parrot and half-human, with the tail of a monkey.

AFTERLIFE OF THE COMMON MAN

The Sacrifice for the Underworld

Not so joyful is the lot of victims sacrificed as food for the inhabitants of the underworld. Nothing awaits them but complete death of body and soul. Although the congregation of shaman souls is numerous, even larger is the number of souls that end up in this dark world without ever coming to enjoy the gift of immortality.

When an ordinary man succumbs to the magic arrow of a dark-shaman, he dies in the knowledge of having been singled out as a sacrifice for the Macaw God in the House of the Dying Sun. (The underworld is identified as the place where the sun sets, but it is not identified with the Macaw itself.) His flesh is to be eaten by the spirit-shamans, his blood will be their drink, the god himself will relish his heart and liver, and his bones and skin will serve as raw materials in this sinister world. No wonder that this is the most dreaded death a Warao Indian can imagine. The spirits of the underworld demand a steady supply of human flesh and blood, and no one is safe from the magic arrow of the dark-shaman.

"One cannot imagine what would happen if our dark-shamans were to stop providing nourishment for the spirits of the west," is a common reply to a field-worker's query. "The world would probably come to an end. All children would die and so would the gods."

Meanwhile the infant son of the Soul-Hoebo at the zenith continues to cry over the earth, and his crying is the chanting of dark-shamanism. A novice on his first ecstatic journey learns his chant by listening to the crying baby. It is hungry, and the novice shaman pledges to contribute his share.

The Artisan Boat-maker

Fortunately, not all people end up as sacrifices for the underworld, with only a select group of religious practitioners able to look forward to an afterlife. Instead, with some wit and luck—that is, by not offending the gods and the shamans—a person, man or woman, can succeed in living a full life, learning to perfection the skills of his or her sex, and dying to join his or her respective patron deity.

That is the lot, for instance, of the soul of an expert canoe-builder. Throughout his adult life, this artisan practices his trade with diligence and careful observation of the ethical code that governs it. He knows that only utmost dedication will please the Mother of the Forest in the southeast and guarantee him a place on the sacred mountain with this patroness of the boat-builder and his fellow artisans.

Accomplished canoe-makers die with the certainty of eternal life because, as apprentices, they have successfully completed their initiatory journey to the house of the Mother of the Forest, Dauarani. After a preparatory period of fasting and much smoking, and the completion of four trial dugout canoes, the spirit of such a neophyte ascends to the zenith where a black psychopomp leads him to the beginning of a celestial bridge that connects the zenith with the world mountain of the Mother of the Forest. The bridge is an enormous snake, the male companion spirit of the goddess. The huge reptilian head rests close to the zenith, and the tip of the tail reaches to the roots of the tree-mountain in the southeast. The snake never closes its mouth, and it hisses when a spirit or soul draws nigh. It has eight horns, four in front and four at the rear. The two pairs on the right side of the body are red and green; those on the left are yellow and blue. Flowers of the same color decorate each horn and chant the ceremonial songs peculiar to the profession of builders of dugout canoes.

The body of the snake is silver-colored and decorated with lines of red, green, white, blue, and yellow. Spaced out over the body at regular intervals are four perpendicular dotted lines of the same colors. The snake has no luminous ball on the tip of its tongue, but its whole body smells very agreeably of curucay (*Protium heptaphyllum*), the *caranna* of the Orinoco.[3] A peculiar characteristic of the snake is that it never coils but always remains perfectly straight. Nor does it ever turn but only crawls forward and a little backward, back and forth, in either direction.[4]

Although this sky snake fills the novice boat-builder with horror, he must step on its head, shake its horns, and then either pass through it to exit and return through its anus, or walk over its head and body. In any case, the young man is allowed to

3. Priest-shamans use the same resin for incense, burning it at the tip of their ritual cigars or in braziers in the temple. The fragrance of the incense is most pleasing to the spirit world they communicate with, and is, therefore, of great ritual significance in connection with the cult of the cardinal gods. I am indebted to Professor Richard Evans Schultes of the Botanical Museum of Harvard University for the botanical identification of the resin.

4. This may be in simulation of the moon risings in the course of a lunar month.

pass his hands along both sides of the serpent's body, and thereby receives the proper measurements of a perfect canoe. Should the snake swallow him while he passes through its body, the novice will die.

Thus begins a lifelong courtship between the man and the snake-goddess Dauarani. Both the goddess and her companion, the sky snake, watch carefully over their servant's conduct as he makes his boats in the likeness of the great goddess' vagina. He abstains from sexual intercourse throughout the time he is engaged in making a new canoe (30–60 days), especially to make certain that in the process of opening the hull with fire (exposing the vagina of the goddess), the heat will not crack the gunwales. He smokes abundantly but restricts his food, making offerings of *moriche* flour and cigars of black tobacco. Soul-Dauarani is a priest-shaman and appreciates only tobacco smoke as her proper food.

These are some of the rules the craftsman observes when engaged in making a canoe, especially a large one. But, if throughout life he obeys the rules, he will leave earth perfectly confident that his soul will pass the snake bridge again unharmed and that he will be received into the village of boat-makers. The souls of those who offend the Mother of the Forest by violating her ethical code are devoured by the sky snake and are lost.

The people on earth ponder the nature of this final decision five or six days after the craftsman passes away. A black soul-guide comes to take his soul to the zenith, where he lets him rest and where he furnishes him with his final cigar. Several days later the soul departs with lightning and thunder to his final destination in the southeast. "Rest now," the artisan's wife, or someone else close to the deceased, says. "You made many big boats." The soul can hear this and may become sentimental about it, but this he must avoid. Instead he must hasten on through the sky snake without ever looking back to earth. If he passes his final test and exits at the anus of the snake, he will find there the abode of the Master Spirit of Boat-making.

This rectangular windowless house has only one arched entrance toward the west. Notwithstanding this, however, its interior is bathed in light and never darkens. Therein is a bed and a table, and on the table a bowl of water perfumed with incense. The roof of the house is beautifully decorated with six pairs of flowers at the four corners and at the center of the long sides: blue and yellow flowers at each of the eastern corners, green and red flowers on each of the western corners, and yellow and red flowers on each of the lateral sides of the roof. The stalks of the flowers are hooked on top and are of the same colors as the leaves and petals. They chant the same song as do the eight horns on the sky snake, orchestrating with them. Their perfume of tobacco smoke and incense is most agreeable to the arriving soul, who is given a similar house for his own use. In it he finds a complete new wardrobe which he puts on after taking a bath in incensed water. He has reached his heaven in proximity to the patron deity he has served so diligently throughout his adult life.

The Weavers of Baskets and Hammocks

Basket-making is an occupation practiced by both sexes among the Warao, and some old men and women, on achieving a high degree of proficiency as weavers, become known as *uasi*. The hands of an expert weaver are identifiable by the permanently damaged nail on his left index finger. But the *uasi* himself sees a vastly more significant change occurring with his hands. He or she notes the gradual whitening of his palms and believes that a small hole will eventually appear in each of them. Through continuous handling of the reeds, the spirit of the plant converts the *uasi* into a light-shaman of the *sehoro* reed. The spirit appears in the artisan's dream, and hands him a cigar and a set of tutelary spirits. This gift makes the *uasi*, man or woman, equal to a light-shaman. It is believed that the maggot that can often be seen in the pithy core of the reed burrows a tunnel leading from the artisan's chest, where the nascent tutelary spirits reside, through each arm to the opening in each hand (cf. Wilbert 1972: 66–9, 71–2). In other words, the weaver is aware that the reed spirit is at work in his body, and one day, upon noticing the supernatural holes in his hands, he knows that the transformation from ordinary person to light-shaman has been accomplished. Henceforth he or she has to live by the same rules as the light-shamans who came to office through a long process of initiation. If the artisan complies, his or her soul will go to live after death with the Creator Bird of the Dawn in the east.[5]

Hammock-making is an exclusively female occupation. "The women belong to the Mother of Moriche," I was told. She lives on the winter solstice in the northeast. In primordial times, this goddess was transformed inside the body of Hahuba (the *uroborus* snake encircling the earth) from a woman into a palm, and all *moriche* palms on earth are her children. She makes them fertile each year, thus providing an abundance of fruit and *moriche* flour for the people.

A woman who becomes a *uasi* in making hammocks will find the Mother of Moriche waiting for her soul upon death. The same is true of the expert music master who is in charge of playing the sacred trumpet (clarinet) during the annual *moriche* harvest festival. His soul goes to a place right next to the Mother of Moriche, where the spirit of the sacred trumpet lives. This spirit is the Mother of the Sacred Trumpets on earth, and, when the Mother of Moriche hears the master tuning his instrument for the

5. Métraux (1948: 129) found that the Tupinamba call those who had achieved fame *karaï* or *pay-wasu* = "great medicine men," a possible terminological and conceptual parallel.

Fig. 3 *Ceremonial center of a Warao band. The dancing platform separates the temple (background) from the settlement* (after Barral 1964: 41).

festival, she releases her fertilizing energy and thereby guarantees food in abundance. To be the player of the sacred trumpet of a particular group is an exacting office, but he will reap the reward for this service when his soul finds eternal happiness on the mountain of these sustenance goddesses.

No Heaven for the Children

Since the turn of the century, and especially since 1925, when the Capuchins established their first permanent mission in Warao territory, the Indians have become increasingly more riparian, moving out of the *moriche*-palm forest to the banks of the large rivers. Before that time, local groups, consisting mainly of a matrilocal extended family, settled in a cluster of houses deep inside the *moriche* forest. Several such local groups congregated periodically for ritual purposes as a predominantly endogamous band. The gathering place was a ceremonial center in the *moriche* forest, with a simply constructed temple or shrine on the eastern side of the clearing and a single or double row of houses on the western side. Separating the two areas was a large dancing platform of juxtaposed poles or stripes of *moriche* bark that served as the plaza where most of the ceremonies were performed (Fig. 3).

For several months each year, the members of the band worked together to prepare the palm-flour festival in honor of the directional gods. The patron god of the community, either the Toad God or the Butterfly God or the Bird God, was represented in the temple in the form of a sacred rock, to whom the members of the band had pledged allegiance. Several, but not all, of the Warao bands possess such a sacred stone even today, and believe it to be the severed head of the son of either one of the mentioned supreme spirits. The highest-ranking priest-shaman is considered to be the father of the rock spirit. He addresses it as his son, whereas the congregation calls it "Grandfather." Whenever the band moves to a different location the rock is carried in a basket on the back of an apprentice shaman.

The size of a pre-contact local group averaged from 45 to 50 people, a figure that remained stable until very recently. Thus, the 1960 National Census of Venezuela registered 11,412 Warao, settled in 249 villages, which averages out to 46 persons per village.[6] The band was and continues to be the largest social grouping the individual Warao feels affiliated with, and the maximum band size probably never exceeded 250 persons. For example, in 1954, one band, the Winikina, comprised 195 individuals who lived in four local groups with an average of 49 people each (Table 1). Taking into consideration the four local groups, one can deduce from this table that a typical

6. This corresponds to the figure at which Goodenough arrived by examining "the relationship between the size and type of communities or local groups and subsistence activities" of forty different tribes throughout the world (1969: 291). The fishing tribes included in his sample had a mean population of 46 (*ibid.*: 298). The tribes practiced fishing as a primary or secondary subsistence activity coordinated "with some other source or sources of subsistence." Both the total Warao population and the average settlement size of the tribe have changed drastically since the 1960 census was taken. Dr. H. Dieter Heinen and I estimate that the tribe may number as many as 15,000 today. We have no recent data on the number of settlements in the Orinoco Delta.

local group of the Winikina band at that time consisted of 3 babies, 19 children, 5 teenagers, 9 men, 11 women, and 3 seniors; totaling 50 souls of 27 children and 23 adults.

TABLE 1. SEX AND AGE RATIOS OF LIVING WINIKINA—1954

*Age Category**	*Total No.*	*Percent*	*No. of Males*	*Percent*	*No. of Females*	*Percent*	*Ratio of Males to Females*
Baby	12	6	7	58	5	42	4:3
Child	75	38	34	45	41	55	4:5
Teenager	19	7	12	79	7	21	4:2
Adult	78	43	36	55	42	45	4:5
Senior	11	6	4	36	7	64	4:7
TOTAL	195	100	93	48	102	52	9:10

* Baby = offspring below one year of age; child = prepuberty offspring between 1 and 10 years; teenager = unmarried adolescent; adult = married individual of reproductive age between 18 and 49 years; senior = man or woman approximately 50 years or over.

As for the adults of the local group of my sample, of the nine men and one senior male, more than half were probably religious practitioners of one kind or another, with their final destinations well defined. A local group would not want to live without the protection of a priest-shaman, a light-shaman, and a dark-shaman. Judging from experience, I venture the guess that there was more than one shaman of a kind in any given local group, some senior and accomplished, others junior and beginners. Several of those men who had not embarked on a religious career were probably expert artisans, basket-makers, or boat-makers, aiming for the heaven that corresponded to their profession. The souls of the undistinguished rest are believed to roam perpetually through the neighborhood as invisible dwarflike spirits. Similarly, the eleven women and two senior women of the local group could aspire to some kind of life after death, either as artisans, basket- or hammock-makers, or as wives of the light-shamans. Of course, some adults would be accounted for as victims of dark magic, and again, some common women's souls would remain on earth as companions of the souls of the undistinguished men. But it is conceivable that all adult members of a local group believed that they had a future life as long as they succeeded in escaping the curse of magic.

Looking now at the children of the active generations, we find that in the entire band they had 172 children, of whom 87 were alive and 85 had died (Tables 2 and 3). Infant mortality amounted to 49 percent, and the living prepuberty offspring accounted for 45 percent of the total Winikina population (Table 2).

TABLE 2. INFANT MORTALITY AMONG WINIKINA—1954

Sex	*No. of Living*	*Percent*	*No. of Dead*	*Percent*	*Total No.*	*Percent*
Boy	41	43	54	57	95	55
Girl	46	60	31	40	77	45
TOTAL	87	51	85	49	172	100

TABLE 3. DEFUNCT PREPUBERTY OFFSPRING OF WINIKINA—1954

Age Category	*Total No.*	*Percent*	*No. of Boys*	*Percent*	*No. of Girls*	*Percent*	*Ratio of Males to Females*
Baby	69	81	41	59	28	41	4:3
Child	16	19	13	81	3	19	4:1
TOTAL	85	100	54	64	31	36	

In examining the genealogical statistics of children, there arises the interesting question of what parents thought had actually happened to their 85 deceased little ones. If these children were believed to have possessed a soul, there is certainly no obvious place within the Warao universe where they might have gone—except, of course, to the underworld. I asked the parents this question, and was told that, to the best of their recollection, twenty-two children had died of dysentery, twenty-one of *hoa* (the magic arrow of the dark-shaman), twelve of *hebu* (spirit sickness), five of measles, and the rest of bronchitis, vomiting, and several other specified and unspecified causes.

Interpreting these figures in eschatological terms, I believe they point to one very interesting fact, namely, that many of the twenty-two children who died of dysentery and the twenty-one who died of *hoa* were believed to have been claimed as food for the spirits of the underworld. (I include dysentery because, to the parents, the symptomatic loss of blood often associated with this disease is indicative of *hoa* sickness. We could probably also include some or most of the deaths that occurred by vomiting. Bloodless dysentery is *hebu* disease caused by directional gods other than *hoebo*.) The twelve children who died of *hebu* perished through the magic of the directional gods, and the five deaths from measles were specifically caused by the Toad God of the south (whose head, it will be recalled, is covered on one side with the warty skin called *borabora*, the Warao word for measles). Bronchitis, too, probably falls into this category of causes of death, interpreted by the people as such because of the fever frequently associated with the sickness. Some of the less well defined deaths can most certainly be ascribed to the magic of malevolent light-shamans.

What all this amounts to, I suppose, is that if these dead children had souls, as many as half of the eighty-five had theirs possibly destroyed in the underworld. I assume that the belief is that the directional gods also destroy the souls of their victims, just as the Goddess of the Nadir, for instance, is believed to kill the body and steal the souls of babies whose mothers are careless enough to spill their milk on the ground where the goddess can lap it up. The other half of the souls of diseased children continues their existence on earth like the invisible souls of the undistinguished men or women. Some Warao also believe that they may re-enter the womb of their mothers to become reborn. Others say that some of the children's souls can be sent by the priest-shaman to a spot in the cosmos where any one of their relatives abides. Finally, the figure of 49 percent infant mortality reflects the nature of the stakes involved in this tug-of-war between the Indians and the supernaturals, since more than half the population is believed to perish in the struggle.

RITUAL PROTECTION FOR THE CHILDREN

To the Warao of a local group, the rate of infant mortality does not present itself statistically through retrospective calculations spanning entire generations. They experience the total number of children at any given time, they carry their dead offspring in a seemingly unending procession to the cemetery, and, in some years, when the waters swamp their islands with foul debris, as many as two-thirds of the entire infant population of the band may die (Barral 1964: 69). Supernatural protection on a continuous and daily basis was, therefore, an absolute necessity for the children. This was accomplished through frequent *moriche*-flour festivals and through Shiborori, the Bird with the Beautiful Plumage.

The constellation of the Southern Cross is believed to be a mythical turkey-bird (*Pauxi pauxi*) with a green head and a green body and tail. It has a yellow tongue with a blue ball on the tip. Its crest, eyes, beak, right wing, and right leg are red. The left wing and left leg are blue. The red right wing (female) is polka-dotted with three rows of blue, green, and blue dots; the blue left wing (male) with three rows of green, yellow, and green dots. On its chest it has a bone-colored emblem in the shape of a coat of arms.

Every evening at nine o'clock, so goes the myth, this bird rises in the southeast to fly to the meridian. Here its blue (male) wing chants to protect the newly born girls on earth.[7] In return, an older woman of the settlement, upon hearing the turkey's call,

7. The issuance of a peculiar chantlike sound is characteristic of the *pauji* turkey, as Schomburgk (1922–3, I: 327) observed. The *Crax tomentoso*, identified by the Guayana Indians with the Southern Cross, begins to sing at the beginning of April, just before midnight, which is, supposedly, when the constellation reaches its highest point.

shouts back and encourages it to fly on and not to resign itself to the idea that the cardinal gods, who perennially pursue it, will eventually capture and rob it of its feathers. If a baby girl has been born to the group that night, the old people may also sing a special chant. Shiborori needs this encouragement by a Warao mother, because he knows that she understands the predicament of the hunted, which is similar to that of the children. The bird calls the Warao children his siblings and knows that the gods pursue them as tenaciously as they pursue it. Reinvigorated by the mother's compassion and encouragement, the bird continues on its journey to reach its home at 3 A.M. The bird rests here and then returns to the meridian where at twelve o'clock noon, it will chant with its red (female) wing for the protection of the boy children, especially the newly born. Thus women belong to the night hours and men to the day, and, again, if a boy baby has been born that day, the old men will also chant with Shiborori for his protection. This makes for a most powerful chorus when the people sing and the bird produces its song by shaking its wings and projecting it through the blue ball on the tip of its tongue.

Shiborori learned its chant from the flowers of the Creator Bird who originated *sui generis* as a pair of male and female birds in a cave at the foot of the world mountain in the east. Here the couple planted a square garden of four beds of flowers: the male bird grew one black and one green bed, the female one white and one red bed. Only the female flowers know how to chant; the male ones are mute. Each time the Bird of the Beautiful Plumage returns from the center of the world, it enters this flower garden to rest in the house. From here it has direct access to the house of the Creator Bird since it is situated in the middle of the bifurcation of pathways that lead from the house of the Creator Bird to the male (left) and female (right) flower beds.

Should Shiborori one day fail to return and be caught by the pursuing directional gods, he will lose his feathers, his song will never be heard again on earth, and the supernatural hunters will fall upon the village, spreading sickness and death among the children and the rest of the people. The Warao know about Shiborori because their priest-shamans can see the beautiful bird in dream and trance states. Neither the ordinary people nor the dark- and light-shamans ever see him. They may listen to his chanting only at noon and at midnight, when it never sounds quite as beautiful as it does when it comes straight from the blue ball on the bird's tongue in the priest-shaman's vision.

There is only one other bird that can match Shiborori's beauty of appearance and song, and that is his twin, the Northern Cross. The northern spirit bird, Akuehebu, flies to the meridian, just as the southern one does, and performs the same magic for the children as does his counterpart. But the two birds must never look at each other lest they lose their song and power.

Searching the sky at night for the beautiful birds that are so important for the survival of half the Warao, the Indians are quick to point out the constellation of the Southern Cross, which they call *yaromu* = "pauji," or simply *domu* = "bird." It dominates the southern sky from April to June, and the hunters pursuing it so relentlessly (α and β Centauri) are also clearly visible (Heinen and Lavandero 1973: 11). But in Warao country (at ±9° N.lat.), the Southern Cross never seems to make it quite to the meridian by midnight when it rises at 9 P.M., as it spends ten hours rather than six above the horizon.

For this phenomenon to occur according to the specifications of the myth, one has to instruct the machine of a modern planetarium to change latitude so that the Cross remains visible for only six hours. If in addition one follows the earth's motion of precession back in time until the Southern Cross appears at exactly 12 hrs. right ascension, this day of the year on which the Cross reaches the meridian at midnight will be precisely the first day of spring instead of about a week later as at present. As it turns out, at certain latitudes on earth the constellation can rise at 21 hrs., transit at midnight, and set at three in the morning on one day each year.

In conducting this experiment at the planetarium of the University of California, Los Angeles,[8] we had to go back in time about five hundred years and move northward from the Warao country to a latitude between 20° and 30° North. An ideal position from which to observe this phenomenon of stellar movement is somewhere between these latitudes, and one is persuaded to fix one's observation point at 23 ½° N. latitude, the Tropic of Cancer, where at noon on the first day of spring the sun stands vertically overhead at the zenith. But the Tropic of Cancer happens to cut through Mesoamerica, not the land of the Warao.

From this vantage point and on the day when the sun is at the vernal equinox, the first day of spring, one can also observe the Northern Cross rising in the northeastern quadrant at about 2 A.M., when the Southern Cross is about to set in the southwestern quadrant (Fig. 4). Both constellations appear as mirror images; in fact, there are scarcely any other two constellations that resemble each other to the same degree. The similarity is in the shape and size, and in the brightness of the five stars involved, as well as in the fact that they are mirror images. There are three bright and two fainter stars in each cross, and the fainter stars in both crosses are closer to the horizon at this

8. I gratefully acknowledge the assistance of Mr. T. Ericson, a student at the California Institute of Technology, and Mr. Stephen Lattanzio, a graduate student at UCLA, for having helped me with the astronomical interpretation of the data. Mr. Lattanzio operated the planetarium at UCLA, and I express my sincere thanks to the Department of Astronomy for permitting me to make use of their fine facilities.

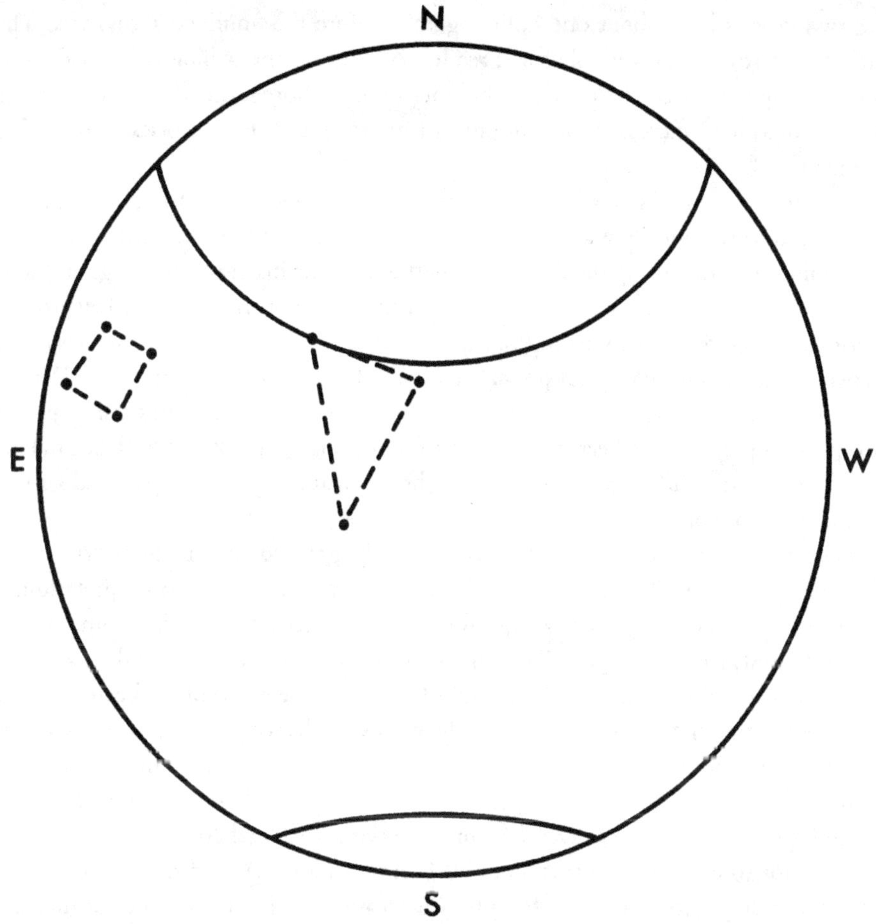

Fig. 4 *Reconstruction of stellar positions on March 21, 1500 A.D., at latitude ±23½° N. Path of the Southern Cross and of the Northern Cross: the Southern Cross rises at 2100 hours, transits at 0 hours, and sets at 0300 hours; the Northern Cross rises at 0200 hours and reaches 55° (Deneb) altitude before sunrise at 0600 hours. The Great Square of Pegasus becomes fully visible at 0600 hours. The Summer Triangle's position is also shown here as of 0600 hours.*

point in their trajectory. In addition, both constellations are situated in the Milky Way. The only dissimilarity is that the Northern Cross is tilted a little closer toward the horizon than is its southern counterpart.

Since the sun on that day is up exactly twelve hours and down exactly twelve hours, the two crosses have about one hour together before the Southern Cross sets. The Northern Cross remains visible for three hours longer, approaching the meridian to about 50° up the horizon before daylight blots it out. A more southerly latitude then or today would have increased the amount of time for which both crosses were visible simultaneously.

Thus at about A.D. 1500, at ±23 ½° N. latitude, the celestial bird could indeed be observed to carry out the mandate it had received from the Creator Bird, that is, to fly at midnight and during the day to the meridian, shake his beautiful wings and sing for the protection of the children on earth. At night Shiborori could soar toward the meridian as the Southern Cross (*Pauxi pauxi*) and, during the day, as the Northern Cross (*Nothocrax urumutum*). At present, because of the change in latitude, the Warao can no longer observe this phenomenon; the Southern Cross requires ten hours to complete its journey. So, because it follows a higher arc in the sky, at 9° N. latitude, it can never rise at 21 hrs. and transit at midnight. Even at 23 ½° N. latitude, it does not do this anymore on the spring equinox.

It also happens that on this day the last star of the great square of Pegasus rises synchronously or heliacally on the eastern horizon as, according to my interpretation, a brilliant square flower garden at the foot of the eastern world mountain, where Shiborori rests from his flight. The sun rises exactly to the east on this day, and the square appears a little to the north but right next to it. The house of the beautiful bird is situated within the triangle formed by the pathways that connect the flower patches with the house of the Creator Bird. This triangle of pathways, the summer triangle, is quite visible in the sky, with the apex star close to the zenith and the northern star, α Signi, popularly known as *Deneb*, connected with the Northern Cross.

So as not to extend this paper unduly, I leave a more detailed discussion of this astroarchaeological investigation for a future occasion. Suffice it to point out that the Warao, with a cosmological atlas of eschatological significance strongly reminiscent of Aztec and Mayan concepts, trust the well-being of their offspring to a stellar bird that cannot be observed in its full mythical context from where they live in our time, but which was observable in Mesoamerica and was recognized in a similar fashion by the Aztecs around A.D. 1500.

According to Durán (1971: 418–19), during the third month of the Aztec year, the Indians venerated "a beautiful bird with a bone piercing its body."[9] He "understood it to refer to a star formation that appears in the heavens like a bird." The main feast fell on the first day of the month, April 10, at the beginning of the rainy season, when

9. One is at once reminded of the white breast emblem of Shiborori in the form of a coat of arms.

the fields were planted. On the twentieth of April, "all children under twelve were bled, even breast-fed babies . . . in honor of the coming feast, which involved the general purification of the mothers." Soothsayers went from house to house to inquire about the children and to see whether their ears had been pierced and whether they were fasting on bread and water as prescribed. If so, the soothsayers decorated them by fastening red, green, blue, black, or yellow threads to their necks, strung with snake bones, beads, or small figurines. Obviously, then, the month of the beautiful bird was taken by the Aztecs as an occasion to petition the supernaturals for the gift of abundant crops and healthy children, and for their protection from evil and dark magic.

In addition to these characteristics, clearly reminiscent of similar concepts related to the Warao protector bird of children, the Aztecs "also made bouquets with flower buds in order to revel in them on that day. . . . This ceremony constituted the offering of the first flowers to the gods,"[10] and there were great masters skilled in the craft of flower arrangements (*ibid.*: 419).

Turkeys are important during the New Year ceremony of the Chortí-Maya at the beginning of the rainy season (Girard 1969: 106–7, 111–12). Following a ritual banquet, they sacrifice a pair of turkeys, a male one on the northern side of the altar and a female one on the southern side. Four priests take their places at the corners of the altar according to their positions in the cosmic quadrant. The blood of the decapitated birds runs into a hole in the ground, and the carcasses are opened to extract the hearts and intestines, which are thrown into the holes and stamped underfoot. The birds are then plucked and their feathers sacrificed as well. The sacrifice takes place under the supervision of a high priest, who starts the ceremony at twelve o'clock midnight and ends it at 3 A.M.; the actual sacrifice takes place at about 2:30 A.M.

Of the various parallels that present themselves in comparing this Maya ritual with Shiborori of the Warao, we notice its connection with fertility, the northern (male) and the southern (female) birds, the directionally positioned priests (probably representing the equivalent gods of the world quarters who sacrifice the feathers of the bird), and the timing of the ceremony, which begins at a time when, in A.D. 1500, the Southern Cross appeared at the meridian and which ends shortly before it set.

Before concluding, I might add that Shiborori's real prototype is probably the oscillated turkey (*Agriocharis oscellata*). The coloring of this rare bird of beautiful plumage corresponds largely to the specifications of the mythical Shiborori. What is of far greater significance in our context, however, is the fact that the oscillated turkey with

10. The *pauji* (*Crax alector*) eats flower buds.

the polka dots, or "eyes," on its tail- and wing-feathers occurs only on the Yucatán peninsula, where it is endemic to the tropical forest of southern Mexico, the Petén of Guatemala, and the adjacent areas of Honduras (Thomas R. Howell, personal communication).

These striking analogies, together with the startling astroarchaeological data, seem to be persuasive indications for contact between Mesoamerica and northern South America. Furthermore, as noted in an earlier paper (Wilbert 1972: 74), the analogies cited here are not the only ones that relate Warao mythology to Mesoamerica. However, for lack of space, I have to leave the discussion of the ethnohistorical questions raised by this evidence for a later occasion. Did these Mesoamerican influences reach the Warao via the Antilles through Cariban tribes, i.e., along the east and north sides of the Caribbean Sea? Or are these parallels between Mesoamerica and South America best accounted for within Lathrop's model of a Colombian hearth for proto-Mayan culture, i.e., along the western and southern sides of the Caribbean? Of course, there is also good evidence that the Caribbean functioned for two thousand years, at least, as "a wide open avenue of trade and intercommunication among all points on its shore" and that "the bulk of the trade was in the hands of peoples of Arawakan speech" (Lathrop, personal communication).

These and still other lines of diffusion deserve careful ethnographic and ethnohistorical examination. Not only are they of interest from a purely historical point of view but they also promise, as Peter T. Furst correctly observed, insights into the importance of non-physical, supernatural manifestations for a society's ecological adaptation and survival.

BIBLIOGRAPHY

BARRAL, BASILIO MARÍA DE
1964 Los indios guaraúnos y su cancionero: Historia, religión y alma lírica. *Biblioteca "Missionalia Hispánica,"* vol. XV. Consejo Superior de Investigaciones Científicas, Departamento de Misionología Española, Madrid.

DURÁN, FRAY DIEGO
1971 Book of the Gods and Rites and the Ancient Calendar. (Trans. by Fernando Horcasitas and Doris Heyden.) University of Oklahoma Press, Norman.

GIRARD, RAFAEL
1969 Die ewigen Mayas: Zivilisation und Geschichte. Rhein-Verlag, Zürich.

GOODENOUGH, WARD H.
1969 Basic Economy and Community. *Behavior Science Notes, HRAF Quarterly Bulletin*, vol. 4, no. 4, pp. 291–298. Human Relations Area Files, Inc., New Haven.

HEINEN, HEINZ D., and J. LAVANDERO
1973 Computación del tiempo en dos subtribus Warao. *Antropológica*, no. 35, pp. 3–24. Instituto Caribe de Antropología y Sociología, Sociedad de Ciencias Naturales "La Salle," Caracas.

HELITZER, FLORENCE
1973 The Princeton Galaxy. *Intellectual Digest*, vol. III, no. 10, pp. 25–32. New York.

LÉVI-STRAUSS, CLAUDE
1969 The Raw and the Cooked. Introduction to a Science of Mythology: I. (Trans. by John and Doreen Weightman.) Harper & Row, Publishers, New York and Evanston.

MÉTRAUX, ALFRED
1948 The Tupinamba. *In* Handbook of South American Indians (Julian H. Steward, ed.). *Smithsonian Institution, Bureau of American Ethnology, Bulletin 143*, vol. 3, pp. 95–133. U. S. Government Printing Office, Washington.

SCHOMBURGK, RICHARD
1922–23 Travels in British Guiana, 1840–1844. (Trans. and ed. by Walter E. Roth.) 2 vols. "Daily Chronicle" Office, Georgetown, B.G. (First published 1848: J. J. Weber, Leipzig.)

WILBERT, JOHANNES
1972 Tobacco and Shamanistic Ecstasy among the Warao Indians of Venezuela. *In* Flesh of the Gods: The Ritual Use of Hallucinogens (Peter T. Furst, ed.), pp. 55–83. Praeger Publishers, New York and Washington.

Death and the Afterlife in Pre-Columbian America: Closing Remarks

MICHAEL D. COE

In many ways this has been one of the most interesting conferences that I have ever attended. It has been a remarkable meeting of art historians, people interested in iconography, social anthropologists, dirt archaeologists, and economic determinists. We have all met here to talk about one theme, and I think that it has proved to be extremely stimulating.

First of all, I think that it should be pointed out that the ethnographic and ethnohistoric analogies—and perhaps in some cases even homologies—that have been raised here vary from area to area. For instance, for the Huichol of western Mexico, discussed in Peter Furst's talk, and for the Hopi of the southwestern United States, we have extremely rich data, which seem to be capable of successful application to the interpretations of West Mexican tomb art. For the cultures of the eastern or southeastern United States, especially the Spiro site which James Brown was talking about, I think that the ethnohistoric sources are very poor, as he would probably admit, for the interpretations of this material from a religious or iconographic point of view. For Mesoamerica, on the other hand, they are embarrassingly rich, especially for the Central Mexicans. For North Coast Peru they are practically non-existent. For the South Coast of Peru I gather that the sources are not too bad, but on the other hand they are not too good. They certainly do not compare with what the Spaniards gave us for Central Mexico on the eve of the Conquest. And, of course, we have incredibly rich data from unacculturated modern peoples, such as the Warao from Venezuela, of whom Johannes Wilbert spoke. I think that the success with which we are going to be able to interpret what we are looking at is going to depend, at least in part, upon exactly how rich these data really are.

A second point I would like to make is that there has obviously been a tremendous amount of reinterpretation of archaeological material. Most of the art that we actually see in museums from American Indian cultures (that is, the Pre-Columbian cultures), to the south of the Rio Grande and to a certain extent to the north of it, comes from tombs. In other words, it has mortuary associations. It comes as somewhat of a surprise to learn that these associations have generally been ignored by people dealing with this material in the past. I think that there is now a great interest in looking at the reasons *why* this material was actually put into tombs. Why was it made in the first place? Apparently mundane material, such as the so-called "realistic" tomb art of West Mexico, which was supposed to have been completely profane, or the "realistic" art of the Maya and the Mochica, which has long been said to represent the real world, has turned out to have very disturbing elements in it. Let us take, for example, the Mochica material discussed by Elizabeth Benson, specifically the plates and jars that one finds painted upon pottery vessels—these have a disconcerting habit of walking! Let us take the vegetation in deer-hunt scenes on these same vessels. These, as Peter Furst points out, are probably hallucinogens. In other words, these scenes, which were supposed to have been taken from the real world, have other possible interpretations that have to do with worlds beyond the grave and *not* worlds with which we are familiar. Consider the Maya palace scenes that I have pointed out on Maya pottery. These may *look* as though they are taking place in the here and now, but there are sinister elements of death and the afterlife that suggest that this is not the case. I think that there are very disturbing elements in these art styles that may lead us to question whether the mundane world that has been proposed by archaeologists, using economic and technical models, is really what is being represented. I suggest that what the ancient peoples were concerned with in these mortuary vessels and other tomb materials was *not* everyday life, but was aimed at another end.

Thirdly, I would like to touch upon some of the interpretations that have come up in this conference. I am thinking particularly of James Brown's social, political, and economic model to interpret Spiro art. He has pretty much avoided trying to attach a meaning to this material that has any implications beyond the social and political and economic determinants. I think it is interesting that he talks, for instance, of people impersonating birds, but does not suggest that these birds might have been gods. He is probably wisely avoiding the problem at this time, but I am wondering if some of his interpretations couldn't be followed up in the more ideological sphere. Brown is following a very old and honored tradition in social anthropology, that is, explaining mortuary customs by their social utility.

Perhaps the most convincing exponent of this point of view was the French social anthropologist Robert Hertz, a follower of Émile Durkheim. In his great essay on death, Hertz was also following the ideas of another member of the Durkheimian school, van Gennep, in looking at death as one of several kinds of rites of passage, a rite of passage being defined as the dangerous transition or journey of an individual from one social status to another, whether birth, puberty, marriage, or death. In this case we are dealing with the journey of the dead, the voyage of the soul to the underworld, and the reconstituting of society after the ultimate dissolution of the body has taken place. As the body decomposes, as it turns into incorruptible bone—or perhaps is converted by cremation into equally incorruptible ash—so does the social group, which has been so tremendously broken up and disturbed by this mysterious event, slowly reconstitute itself. This voyage of the soul has been considered by many of the world's peoples, whether "primitive" or "civilized," as a tremendously dangerous journey, fraught with perils, which can only be avoided—or at least mitigated—by the constant vigilance of the priests and survivors in performing the appropriate rituals at set times. Assuming this social interpretation, it quite naturally follows that the more stratified the society and the more important the individual in it, the more elaborate the death cult and rites that surround it.

In the aboriginal New World there is obviously a great emphasis upon the dead, and the elaborate emphasis upon this cult is most characteristic of the stratified societies within our hemisphere; compare, for instance, the great proliferation of Maya tombs and funerary pyramids with the treatment of the dead among the egalitarian Sioux of our western plains, where the body was simply exposed upon a platform left open to the elements. The Warao of Venezuela seem to constitute some sort of an exception to this rule of social stratification, and for this reason I follow Johannes Wilbert in his feeling that perhaps we are dealing here with a diffusion and migration from the more stratified and elaborated societies to the north, particularly from Mesoamerica. Now this social and political and economic model is, of course, what most of the new and newer and even newest archaeologists have been following today, and they have fairly rigorously eschewed—or, let us say, not been interested in—those esoteric or occult matters which to the Indians themselves were probably far more important than economic and social considerations. From the point of view of these investigators, the tomb, the grave, the mortuary house, and even the symbols which they contained, regardless of what they are, reflect little more than the concept of rank and stratification. Exotic materials, which were deposited in great quantities in such places as Spiro, with clear indications of far-flung procurement systems and large-scale social and economic interaction, are characteristic of what social anthropologists call "chiefdoms" and "early states." It seems to be a characteristic of the funerary cult that the amazing amount of goods that came from enormous distances, representing not only economic, political, and social power, but also tremendous amounts of work, is taken out of circulation before the values start to decrease through inflation. Those of us who have worked with the Olmec civilization in southern Mexico have seen the same sort of thing in the burial of vast quantities of jade and serpentine in ceremonial sites. As Brown points out, this is particularly true in wet climates with things which are durable, and of course this applies to the Olmec civilization.

The tremendous labor involved in this cult is, I think, well exemplified by what the Dwyers tell us about the number of persons involved in weaving a typical Paracas funerary bundle. It is interesting that on the South Coast of Peru—in contrast to, say, Spiro—*everything* is durable because of extraordinary conditions of preservation. Thus it may be that the emphasis upon textiles as opposed to pottery or stone in that area was because textiles took a lot more work and a lot more time and represented a lot more of the prestige involved, and, therefore, were more likely to be put out of circulation than were pottery or stone objects.

In the cult of the dead in Pre-Columbian America there is a tremendous difference between ordinary artifacts and funerary material. I have asked the Peruvian experts Clifford Evans and Gordon Willey if the Mochica pottery that we are so familiar with and think of as being typically Mochica does or does not occur in the ordinary household debris. They replied in the negative. I think the same might be said about Maya funerary ceramics. These are very rarely found among the millions of potsherds which one gets in a typically Maya site, and I think that when sherds from pictorial ceramics *do* occur, then it is purely an accident. I would, therefore, conclude from this that most of what one finds in art museums is not the stuff of ordinary life but, rather, is another form of scarce goods which have been taken out of circulation for this cult of the dead.

A somewhat different way of approaching the entire problem of the cult of the dead in ancient America has to do with the mental systems of these people. What has produced and generated this funerary material? Is it merely the social and political status of the individual in his society, or is it something more? What has produced the art of Spiro? What was generating what we actually see in Maya pictorial ceramics? To understand this we have to know the myths behind the motifs. And I might say, except for a few cases, we do not know what these are. Because of the total cataclysm of the Spanish and European conquest of the New World, we are left with very little data indeed. But this does not mean that we are faced with an impossible task. For the Aztec it is quite clear that we have incredibly rich material. Aztec practice relating to the dead is obviously so specific and explicit that we know, if not everything, at least a good deal about this because of the extraordinarily detailed ethnohistoric documentation. For instance, we have the pictorial manuscripts from Central Mexico which are glossed in either Spanish or Italian or perhaps even in the native languages written down with Spanish letters after the Conquest. And we are lucky to have the Popol Vuh of the Highland Maya, which is probably the most complete description and explanation of the ideology behind the funerary cult that we have or ever *will* have from anywhere in the New World. We have the wonderful material from the Huichol and the Warao and other contemporary Indian groups, and this shows us, when we do have it, another world that is totally different from ours. The problem is that we are so culture-bound! We are so likely to argue from *our* point of view (and not that of the Indian) and forget even that we are dealing with American Indians. For this reason, I think that a lot has been written about this material that is totally and utterly misleading. As an archaeologist friend of mine has so often told me, we have to think like the Indian. How can death, for instance, be related to such widely different concepts as water, fecundity, childbirth, and the completion of space-time cycles? One has to immerse oneself, as Cecelia Klein has done, in native thought—a native American Indian thought system in Central Mexico—to understand these concepts.

A corollary to this, which Johannes Wilbert raises in his Warao material, concerns the relationship of astronomy to these ancient beliefs. We know very little about native ideas of what went on in the night sky, the tie between the underworld and the night, and that between the underworld and specific constellations, stars, and planetary bodies. It is quite clear that shamanism has played a tremendous role in this, and I think that an exploration of the shamanistic side of ancient American art, as Johannes Wilbert and Peter Furst have suggested, is going to be tremendously important. Those pipes, for instance, which have come to us from the Hopewell and Mississippian cultures of the southeastern and eastern United States, are usually explained away in the following terms: well, these Indians had access to some rare stones, and they grew some tobacco, and they stuffed it in these pipes, and this was part of their leisure time, especially if they were high up in a well-stratified society, and they must have been so since they had such and such an economy. I think that other explanations are possible for the presence of these pipes, because of the rich lore and mythology of tobacco use among the shamans of the New World. All knowledge of this sort was obviously in the hands of occult specialists with a very high degree of knowledge, and also obviously in the hands of the elite; these two may have been the same people. Almost everything we have seen on the art objects that have survived from these ancient funerary cults belongs to an elite, aristocratic culture. I know that this is true of the Maya and certainly true of the Central Mexicans (these two are the ones I know best), but I think that this is probably true even for some of these supposedly egalitarian societies. I would imagine the great Huichol specialists to correspond to an elite, even though they might not be *economically* more advanced than their fellow man. Certainly, among the stratified societies of the New World, this material was a form of wealth, and I mean not just the artifacts themselves, but mythological material. These ancient myths were another form of scarce goods to which they had gained access. By means of such myths they were able to convert the act of death, which by its very inevitability they tried to avoid, just as we do. But they did something else with death; they tried to manipulate it. And I think that the glorious creations which we have seen this day have shown how everybody benefited by this view of death.

Finally, I do not wish to suggest that any one of the interpretations of these ancient materials that I have reviewed here is *the* correct one. All are obviously correct. Whether we view a Maya vase from a purely utilitarian point of view as a vessel or dish to hold food and liquids; whether we view it as a scarce item on which a great deal of work was expended to glorify a particular individual in his social and political role; or whether we view it as an object imbued with esoteric and spiritual wisdom related to the cult of the dead—all of these interpretations can be brought to bear on the mortuary furniture which has been brought to light by archaeology. The role of the archaeologist and of the art historian is to discover what these objects meant to the ancient peoples who made them. I think that this conference has gone a long way toward suggesting how some of these meanings might be discovered.